OLD-TIME HERBS
FOR NORTHERN GARDENS

OLD–TIME

HERBS

for

NORTHERN GARDENS

MINNIE WATSON KAMM

WITH ILLUSTRATIONS

DOVER PUBLICATIONS, INC.
NEW YORK

Published in Canada by General Publishing
Company, Ltd., 30 Lesmill Road, Don Mills,
Toronto, Ontario.
Published in the United Kingdom by Constable
and Company, Ltd., 10 Orange Street, London WC 2.

This Dover edition, first published in 1971, is an
unabridged republication of the work originally
published by Little, Brown and Company in 1938.

International Standard Book Number: 0-486-22695-6
Library of Congress Catalog Card Number: 79-143677

Manufactured in the United States of America
Dover Publications, Inc.
180 Varick Street
New York, N. Y. 10014

"It is not sight or sound
   That, when a heart forgets,
   Most makes it to remember:
   It's some old fragrant scent refound."
         — NANCY BYRD TURNER, *Years Afterward.*

CONTENTS

CONTENTS

CONTENTS

CONTENTS

CONTENTS

ILLUSTRATIONS

1. GARDEN SORREL
(Rumex acetosa L.)

2. DOUBLE ROW OF SALAD BURNET
(*Poterium sanguisorba* L.)

Courtesy of Parke, Davis and Company

3. PISTILLATE AND STAMINATE FLOWERS OF *CANNABIS SATIVA*

THIS IS NOT A TROPICAL SCENE BUT
CUTTING HEMP IN A FIELD IN MICHIGAN

DRYING HEMP IN SHEDS ON THE PARKE, DAVIS AND COMPANY FARM AT
ROCHESTER, MICHIGAN

4. RUE
(*Ruta graveolens* L.)

5. DILL
(*Anethum graveolens* L.)

Courtesy of J. Horace McFarland Comp

6. BORAGE
(*Borago officinalis* L.)

7. *Nepeta mussini* L.

8. CLARY
(*Salvia sclarea* L.)

9. BALM
(*Melissa officinalis* L.)

10. WINTER SAVORY
(*Satureia montana* L.)

11. HYSSOP
(Hyssopus officinalis L.)

12. DITTANY-OF-CRETE
(*Origanum dictamnus* L.)

Venus bringing the herb dittany to the priest-physician, who applies it
to the arrow wound of her son, Aeneas. A wall painting in Pompeii.

Courtesy of J. Horace McFarland Company

13. PEPPERMINT
(*Mentha piperita* L.)

14. SPEARMINT
(*Mentha spicata* L.)

15. PENNYROYAL
(*Mentha pulegium* L.)

16. SPIKE LAVENDER
(*Lavandula spica* L.)

17. ROSEMARY
(Rosmarinus officinalis L.)

18. SWEET BASIL
(*Ocimum basilicum* L.)

19. BENE
(*Sesamum orientale* L.)

A commercial planting of Digitalis near
Rochester, Michigan

1955 3

20. FOXGLOVE

(*Digitalis purpurea* L.)

21. CULVER'S ROOT

(*Veronica virginica* L.)

22. RED VALERIAN
(*Centranthus ruber* D. C.)

23. CAMOMILE
(*Anthemis nobilis* L.)

24.   FEVERFEW
(*Matricaria parthenium* L.)

25. LAVENDER COTTON
(*Santolina chamaecyparissus* L.)

26. SWEET MARY
(*Chrysanthemum balsamita tanacetoides* L.) Boiss.

27. TANSY
(Tanacetum vulgare L.)*

A two-year-old specimen
Wormwood

28. WORMWOOD
(*Artemisia absinthium* L.)

29. *ARTEMISIA*
"SILVER KING"
(*Artemisia albidum* var.)

A garden specimen of the
lovely "Silver King,"
Artemisia

30. ROMAN WORMWOOD
(*Artemisia pontica* L.)

31. "OLD WOMAN"
(*Artemisia stelleriana* Bess.)

32. THE SACRIFICE OF IPHIGENIA, ON THE WALL OF THE
HOUSE OF THE TRAGIC POET, POMPEII

OLD-TIME HERBS
FOR NORTHERN GARDENS

INTRODUCTION

As the interest in rock-gardening wanes, the growing of herbs finds increasing and widespread favor. The present popularity of these old-fashioned plants is well-deserved, for they have much to offer the home gardener. Some of them are attractive in the flower garden, with gay bloom or gray foliage or pleasing aromatic odor; indeed, many of our valuable garden plants, such as the rose, Madonna lily, lily-of-the-valley, poppy, lavender, garden heliotrope, marigold, monkshood, foxglove, hen-and-chickens, the Sedums, the Thymes, flax, rose mallow and germander, are old-time herbs.

However, by no means all the herbs with distinguished history are suitable for the flower garden; some of them belong in the kitchen plot for use as condiments. Sage as a seasoning for pork is prescribed as rigorously to-day as it was four hundred years ago; spearmint is still lamb-mint; fennel should accompany mackerel, the savories be used with poultry, dill with cucumber pickles, and tarragon with vinegar. Other condiments just as pleasing but little known include fresh chopped chervil, coriander, anise and basil, and the dried herbage of sweet marjoram, thyme, winter savory and so on.

Another group is grown for sentiment. An herb-garden would not be complete without rosemary although this lovely herb is not hardy in the north and has little practical use to-day; rue is hardy and just as essential for sentiment's sake, but of little other value; balm, camomile, woodruff, sweet mary, tansy, lavender cotton, all had their places in our grandmothers' gardens and we like to keep them for loving memory.

A group which offers little by way of decoration or utility, including woad, weld, cummin, lovage, borage, clary and burnet, may be grown once, for the sake of curiosity.

Practically all of our native woodland plants have been used as medicinal herbs by the Indians and our early physicians, spikenard, golden seal, gold-thread, bloodroot, wild ginger, celandine, cohosh, agrimony, culver's root, comfrey, coltsfoot, nettle, mandrake and others, and most of them adapt themselves admirably to the wild garden, multiplying apace in woodland soil, moisture and shade.

A last group of old herbs is frankly banned else they soon usurp a whole estate. These include plantain, purslane, the mustards, ground-ivy, cobbler's bench, viper's bugloss and horehound.

All herbaceous plants are not "herbs," neither are all so-called herbs herbaceous; some of them are shrubs, some even trees. However, most herbs are truly herbaceous, dying down to the ground in winter even if perennials, although a few which are hardy in our climate are semishrubs, having woody basal stems, such as lavender, germander, hyssop, thyme and winter savory. None of those hardy in this climate, however, are trees, all such being Oriental herbs.

There is no standard definition of an herb; some botanists say that any useful plant is an herb; others regard as herbs only those plants which have been or are utilized by the housewife. The present writer would class as herbs condiments and medicinals which have been grown in the home garden and stored by the grower for the benefit of the immediate family.

4

FOR NORTHERN GARDENS

Throughout the ages herbs have been grown for many purposes — for use as condiments to enhance the flavor of prosaic foods, as family medicines, as perfumes to lay away with sheets and winter woollens, as dyes to color home-woven textiles, as garlands and wreaths for victors in the games, as strewing material for floors of homes and churches, and even as amulets, love philters and witches' charms. Many herbs have served for several of these purposes, most of them for two or three. Rosemary, for instance, was used for low hedge material, incense, and garlands, as a condiment, as a medicinal, for strewing floors, as a perfume, as a symbol of remembrance at weddings and funerals and even in witchcraft. Saffron has equally as many uses, and lavender, marjoram, thyme and others have only a few less.

All parts of the plant were sometimes used, as in the case of the mustards, smallage (celery) and angelica; in a few instances the flower was regarded as the herb, as with spike lavender, camomile and carthamus; and true saffron comes only from the minute anthers of the crocus flower. Horseradish and madder roots were utilized, while the seed of most of the carrot family, such as coriander, dill, anise and cummin, found use as condiments, but in general it is the aromatic foliage and tender flowering tops of the plant which are used, as with most of the mints.

Most of the herbs possess very long histories and have been interwoven with human activities to an astonishing degree; a history of herbs is, indeed, a history of mankind itself. When a dozen of the very commonest herbs is listed in the Ebers Papyrus, which contains prescriptions older than the Book of Exodus, one may be sure they were only listed because they had been found efficacious long ages before. These herbs can be traced step by step from that time, 1500 b.c., down to the present and include

5

peppermint, caraway, fennel, saffron, opium poppy, coriander and wormwood. The Children of Israel used garlic and onions and leeks and mustard as foods and condiments in Egypt; an aspergillum of hyssop dipped in blood was used to save the homes of the elect at the Passover; Solomon sang to his beloved in similes of saffron, rose and lily; and the mints and anise and rue were named by our Lord in His sermon on the six woes.

Homer in the tenth century B.C. speaks of the saffron-hued dawn; Hippocrates used some four hundred simples in his practice of medicine; and the Greek poets are lavish in their praise of herbs. Pliny the Elder knew about as many herbs as we do to-day and many more uses for them, and Horace and Virgil and Martial often refer to them as condiments for humble fare.

When the Romans went to Britain they took with them some of their condiments and vegetables but few outside leeks and onions and lettuce survived the centuries of neglect and warfare. However, the plants were taken eastward, to Asia Minor, to Arabia, Persia, and India, and some of the commonest reached China and Japan by the first century A.D.

Elaborate compounds of Rome and the Near East, such as the Mithradates Antidote, the Drink of Antioch and Gratia Dei, were handed down by word of mouth for nearly two thousand years, some of these secret formulae containing as many as a hundred ingredients from herbs, the ash of vipers and horns of cattle, to human skin, and they were so precious that only the wealthy sick could purchase.

A knowledge of herbs was taken to Spain and Portugal by the Moors and from thence the plants worked their way north through France, Switzerland, Germany, Britain, to Scandinavia, even to Iceland. A few were used in Saxon kitchens as early as the sixth century and the Saxons devised a leechcraft of ointments and internal remedies made from the juices of herbs which was published in the year 1000.

Before the ninth century the monasteries of France and Switzerland began to collect all the available condiments and medicinals of the ancients and to cultivate them in plots for the treatment of the ailing who came to their doors and in order to enhance the vegetarian food which made up their plain fare. The religious houses, particularly of the Benedictine and Cistercian orders, became sanctuaries of plants during long periods of warfare and neglect, and to their kindly nurture we owe the preservation of many of the old herbs and a knowledge of their usages.

The Normans in France appreciated highly seasoned food and took many condiments with them to England along with medicinal herbs. Chaucer speaks of the travelling quack doctors or herbalists, women as well as men. In Plantagenet days, the chatelaine of every large manor was trained in the art of herb medicine and often an herb-woman was hired to grow and preserve the large assortment of herbs which her mistress administered for all the ailments of the household from those of the master down to the humblest serf.

By the latter half of the fourteenth century, wars ceased in England and trade with the Continent sprang up rapidly. The people were eager for new foods and condiments and the great trading companies like the Easterlings, the Hanseatic League and the Staple of Calais brought in precious new flavorings, perfumes and drugs. The breaking up of the monasteries, begun in 1534, helped to distribute the herbs which the brothers had brought together hundreds of years before to a wider and appreciative public, and the Huguenots, coming from the Continent around 1545 with a wide knowledge of horticulture, gave a new impetus to gardening.

Physic-gardens were established in various countries, the earliest at Padua in 1545, and others at Pisa, Leyden, Oxford and London during the next hundred years. Private gardeners took up the growing of herbs and William Harrison says by 1587 over three hundred medicinal herbs were grown in a single nobleman's garden in England, over half of them so new that a score of years before not even their names would have been recognized. Most of the great herbalists who published elaborate volumes during the century were head gardeners to the nobility and were given carte blanche to search out new garden material from the whole known world.

After the dissolution of the monasteries, the voluntary task of treating the sick was taken over to a lesser extent by curates of the established church, and their wives grew and often administered the old-time herbs to the members of their parishes who came to them in distress.

Drugs were always expensive even though the word, from the Dutch *droogen,* means "dried roots." As soon as plant material was available, cottage gardeners grew their own remedies and through the seventeenth and eighteenth centuries herb-gardens for the treatment of the immediate family were a concomitant of every cottage garden in England. These herbs were brought to America by our first settlers, but a knowledge of their use is now nearly extinct in America as well as in Western Europe.

The present interest in these old-time plants may be only a transitory one, for very few will be revived as medicinals in this age of highly complex biological remedies; none will be revived as dyes for commercial use because all are fugitive; few will be revived as perfumes for modern tastes incline rather to sophisticated synthetic odors than to the simple wholesome vigorous leaf aromatics.

8

However, the current popularity of herbs may lead to a wider use of condiments to vary the sage-parsley complex with which modern cooks — even the best — seem to be obsessed.

The herbs mentioned in the following pages include only those which can be grown with ease in our northernmost states, and, for lack of space, by no means all of these. Some are annuals, a few biennials, but for the most part all are perennials easily grown from seed and withstanding an aridity and sterility of soil which would discourage most flowering plants. Indeed, the old herbs would not have survived the ages and a variety of climate if they had not been sturdy and weedlike in constitution. Seed and plants of most are readily available and many may be found along back-country roadsides.

LILIACEAE

Garlic, *Allium sativum* L.

No plant has a longer or more distinguished history than the humble herb, garlic. It is supposed to have originated in Tartary but has been cultivated in Egypt from earliest historical times, coming at that period from Syria. While used as a condiment, it also served as the main article of diet for the slaves who built the Pyramid of Cheops for its abundant use served as a palliative from the burning rays of the tropical sun. Herodotus says garlic was the daily food of Egyptian laborers for a thousand years.

The Israelites depended on it for a part of their sustenance, and when starvation faced them on the long march homeward they looked back with longing upon their Egyptian food: "We remember," they complained to Moses, "the cucumbers and the melons and the leeks and the onions and the garlic" * which they ate in Egypt (Numbers 11:5).

Homer refers to garlic as a god, and the bulb was eaten on Greek festival days, and Aristophanes mentions it many times in his comedies. "Now bolt down these cloves of garlic. Well primed with garlic you will have greater mettle for the fight" he says in *The Knights*. In *Peace* he speaks of the "excellent commodities which flow to our markets, fine heads of garlic, early cucumbers, apples."

* Standard Edition of the Bible, 1901.

Garlic likewise was the food of Roman laborers and sailors. Pliny gives two pages of his *Natural History* to its culture, for the plant took three years to attain its maturity. Pliny as well as Hippocrates (400 B.C.) knew its value in medicine, although the latter says that too much of the plant causes flatulence and headache.

Garlic was known in China at least as early as 2000 B.C. and was used there as a condiment and as a mask for meats and fish which, to put it mildly, were not entirely fresh.

The whole onion tribe — garlic, leeks, shallots, chives, and onions — are listed among the eighteen herbs grown in the kitchen-garden of the monastery of Saint Gall near the shores of Lake Constance, during the ninth century, and Charlemagne grew them all in his great gardens at Aix-la-Chapelle, both for demonstration and for revenue, for this emperor imposed no direct taxes upon his subjects.

"Garleac" was widely used in England before the Norman Conquest, an early English recipe states that fish should be cooked in a sauce of parsley, costmary, dittany, thyme and garlic. All the onion tribe were grown in France by the thirteenth century and no doubt long before.

Chaucer says of the Summoner in the *Canterbury Tales* "garlic he loved, and onions too, and leeks." Dante mentions it and Shakespeare cites it several times. "The duke . . . would mouth with a beggar, though she smelt brown bread and garlic," he says in *Measure for Measure* (Act III, Sc. 2). "And, most dear actors," says Bottom just before putting on the play, "eat no onions nor garlic, for we are to utter sweet breath" (*A Midsummer Night's Dream*, Act IV, Sc. 2).

Sir Francis Bacon says "when kine feed on garlicke their milke tasteth of the garlicke." Izaak Walton uses it in dressing a pike.

This herb is just as indispensable to the cook to-day as it has been in the past, entering into the composition of many soups and sauces, for forcemeats, especially for goose, but also for mutton, and no salad is complete unless the mixing bowl has been rubbed with a clove of it.

Throughout the Middle Ages, garlic was the poor man's treacle, an inexpensive remedy for many aches and pains. An author of 1608 says, "You are still sending to the apothecaries and still crying out to fetch Master Doctor to me; but our apothecary's shop is our garden and our doctor a good clove of garlic." * A syrup was made of shredded garlic in honey and used for colds, coughs, asthma, and bronchitis, and to-day this herb and onions are sliced and incorporated into honey or stewed gently for household application for these affections.

The plant is not listed in the United States Pharmacopoeia but the extract is still widely prescribed by physicians for pulmonary afflictions.

There are some three hundred species in the genus *Allium,* this one being the rankest in odor. It is a tall plant with broad flat soft gray-green foliage and large round heads of white flowers. Several closely allied species obviously lacking in odor, with blue, pink, and yellow flowers, are recommended for the garden.

Several species occur wild in this country including the field garlic of Europe, *A. vineale* L., which is often a troublesome weed in pastures as cattle eat it greedily in spring.

* H. N. Ellacombe, *The Plant-lore and Garden-craft of Shakespeare,* London, 1884.

Onion, *Allium cepa* L.

The native home of the onion is not known for the plant has been cultivated at least since the Eighteenth Dynasty of Egypt (1580 B.C.). It is now found wild on the shores of the Dead Sea, in Syria, Persia, Egypt and India and is supposed to thrive in hot, dry, desert conditions although cultivation is now carried on upon irrigated muck soils.

Homer speaks of onions with high regard, for they were considered more of a delicacy than garlic or leeks. In *The Acharnians* by Aristophanes, a Megarian sells his children on the market place disguised as pigs. The purchaser asks, "What shall I give you for them?" to which the father replies, "I must have a gross of onions for this one here and the other you may take for a peck of salt."

Roman literature abounds with references to this bulb. Martial, Persius, Lucilius, and Juvenal all mention it and Pliny tells us there were no wild onions in Italy but many cultivated varieties. He says they were used for colds, quinsy, dropsy, piles, dysentery and other ailments.

They continued in use through the Dark Ages, called yn-leac in Saxon literature and oingnum, unyoun and onyoun in tenth-century leechbooks. Sliced onions with mustard and honey were used for incipient colds in the fourteenth century and they are still used to-day as a household remedy for bronchial affections, as a chest poultice and taken internally.

Shakespeare says onions are a convenience for actors:

> "And if the boy have not a woman's gift
> To rain a shower of commanded tears,
> An onion will do well for such a shift,

Which in a napkin being close convey'd
Shall in despite enforce a watery eye."
— *The Taming of the Shrew* (Induction, Sc. 1).

Sydney Smith (1771–1845), in a recipe for making a salad, says:

"Let onion atoms lurk within the bowl
And, half suspected, animate the whole."

C. D. Warner says in his delightful *My Summer in a Garden:* "If all men will eat onions at all times, they will come into an universal sympathy. Look at Italy. I hope I am not mistaken as to the cause of her unity. . . . All the social atmosphere of that delicious land is laden with it. In churches, all are alike; there is one faith, one smell."

Leeks, *Allium porrum* L.

There are four lesser members of the onion tribe with long history of use as condiments, leeks, chives, shallots and scallions, all having a milder flavor than garlic or onions. The native home of leeks cannot now be determined although a wild leek, *A. amelophrasum,* is found in many parts of Europe and the cultivated form may have been derived from it. Another, *A. tricoccum,* is found in large beds in woodlands from New Brunswick to Iowa.

Leeks were used by the ancient Egyptians and Chinese and Homer mentions them as laborers' diet. The Romans favored them and Nero is said to have eaten them in oil to improve his voice. Horace says in his satires, "And then I return to my dish of leeks, chick-peas, and pancake." Martial pictures a Roman meal thus: "You will dine nicely, Julius, at my house. First you will be given

OLD–TIME HERBS

lettuce and shoots cut from their parent leeks. Then tunny salted . . . and eggs garnished in leaves of rue" (Epigram XI).

Leeks were also used in medicine and Pliny lists no less than seventy diseases for which they were used. In Saxon times they were used for food, condiments and medicine and fourteenth-century recipes include them minced fine and added to meat and fish sauces.

Wild leeks occur in Britain and are the badge of the Welsh. The origin of their use in Wales is obscure but may have arisen from the neighborly practice of farmers meeting to till the land of one who had no team, each bringing his own leeks for the common pottage. However, in a battle with the Saxons in 640 A.D., the Welsh wore leeks in their caps for identification, and, again the bulb is said to have been the symbol of Ceres in the Druidic priestcraft. David, the patron saint of Wales, is said to have fasted upon leeks which he gathered in the fields and Shakespeare has the knight address the King thus in *King Henry V* (Act IV, Sc. 7): "Your grandfather . . . and your great-uncle Edward the Plack Prince of Wales . . . fought a most prave pattle here in France. . . . The Welshmen did good service in a garden where leeks did grow, wearing leeks in their . . . caps; which . . . to this hour is an honourable badge of the service; and I do believe your majesty takes no scorn to wear the leek upon Saint Tavy's day." To which the king replies:

"I wear it for a memorable honour;
For I am Welsh, you know, good countryman."

And leeks, real or artificial, are still worn by all good Welshmen on the Saint's day.

By mediaeval times leeks were so highly regarded in the British Isles that kitchen-gardens were called leek-gardens and their

16

growers leek keepers. Sixteenth-century herbalists list many uses for the plant in medicine and one old rhyme reads:

"Eat Leeks in Lide and Ramsons in May,
And all the year after physicians may play."

"Lide" was March, and "Ramsons" related to leeks.

Unlike onions or garlic, the leek has very broad flat leaves and long stout white stalks. Seedlings are grown in six-inch trenches which are gradually filled and hilled so that the stalk becomes tender and mild, when it is favored in salads, soups and stews.

Chives, *Allium schoenoprasum* L.

Chives, often called rush onions, have cylindrical foliage but are small and grow in compact masses. They are hardy perennials and occur in rocky pastures in northern Asia and Europe. They are cultivated for the foliage, used in salads and soups. Clumps are often grown in pots in kitchen windows and the foliage clipped back to make it tender, ever ready for use.

This plant was used by 300 B.C. in China and very early in Europe.

Shallots, *Allium ascalonicum* L.

Shallots are little grown in this country although much used in Europe in early summer dishes. They are probably a form of onion, and not a true species, for wild species have not been discovered. Like the rest of the genus, they reach far back into antiquity, the earliest records coming from Syria. They appeared in England in the sixteenth-century as "Spanish garlic."

Ciboles, *Allium fitulosum* L.

Ciboles or scallions are lesser onions from Siberia and known in Europe at least since the fourteenth century, called variously Welsh onion, stone leek, rock leek, chebottes and so on. In China they are called the poor man's meat, eaten with rice or millet. To-day they are largely superseded by the larger members of the family.

Ramsons, *Allium ursinum* L.

Ramsons, still less known than scallions, are broad-leaved, rank-smelling plants related to garlic. They go back at least to Saxon times and are remembered chiefly for the jingle already quoted.

Madonna Lily, *Lilium candidum* L.

One may be surprised to learn that our beautiful white lily is an herb of long antiquity and that its petals and bulb were used in poultices and ointments and even the powdered seeds used in medicine. However it has escaped the ignominy of being eaten as a pot-herb.

The Madonna lily is native to southern Europe, the Caucasus and Persia. It is probably the white lily mentioned in the Bible and was well known in Greece. In the Theocritan Idyl *The Lover* (XXIII) are these beautiful lines:

"The rose is lovely; and time withers it. And the violet is beautiful in spring, yet quickly it grows old. White is the lily; when it falls, it

withers: the snow too is white, and it melts after it has become frozen. And the beauty of childhood is fair, yet it lives but a short space."
— Banks translation.

Virgil mentions the flower as the symbol of death thus:

"Full canisters of fragrant lilies bring,
Mix'd with the purple roses of spring;
Let me with fun'ral flow'rs his body strow."
— *Aeneid,* Book VI, Dryden translation.

And the Madonna lily has ever since been used at funerals. It was used by the Romans in medicine, the macerated root steeped in wine and drunk to alleviate stings of insects and reptiles and applied externally to leprous sores and scurfy skin. The petals in vinegar were used as a plaster for wounds and the powdered seed in ale used for erysipelas.

This lovely lily was grown in England as early as the eighth century, both for its stately beauty and for use in medicine. The Benedictine monks had a bed of it among their sixteen plots at Saint Gall, Switzerland, by 812 A.D. for the bulb contains considerable mucilage and is slightly astringent and was a component of electuaries so popular during the Middle Ages. The snowy petals were used, according to the Doctrine of Signatures, to induce a lily-white complexion. "To make thy face whyte," reads a fourteenth-century prescription, "wash when thou gost to slepe with lyly petals and that wilt make it whyte and do away with the spottings." Even as late as the last century, Richard Jefferies says in *Wild Life in a Southern County,* "The English do not make many medicinal portions at home, but lily petals are still used to allay inflammations of the skin."

The Madonna or Annunciation lily is the emblem of purity and sweetness and no flower save the rose has been more often cited by the poets from ancient times to the present.

Lily-of-the-Valley, *Convallaria majalis* L.

Our familiar lily-of-the-valley is also an old-time herb with an economic history by no means obsolete at present, for the powdered root is used in medicine to slow the pulse beat and is more effective in certain heart affections than the official drug, digitalis.

The flowers are emetic in action and an extract of the whole plant was formerly used in epilepsy. At present it is used as a diuretic in cases of dropsy.

Lily-of-the-valley grows wild in woodlands over much of Europe and western Asia and occurs in the high Alleghenies from Virginia to South Carolina.

LILY-OF-THE-VALLEY

URTICACEAE

Stinging Nettle, *Urtica dioica* L.

Certain of the mints of the genus *Lamium* are often called nettles but they are quite different from the true nettles, which are also old-time herbs with a long history belonging to the family Urticaceae, from the Latin *uro,* to burn.

Stinging nettle is familiar to every country-bred child and is one of the plants he early learns to avoid.

> "Tender-handed stroke a nettle,
> And it stings you for your pains;
> Grasp it like a man of mettle,
> And it soft as silk remains."
> — AARON HILL, *Verses Written on a Window.*

It is a tall perennial, up to four feet in height, with long, heart-shaped, deeply-incised, rugose, opposite leaves which are beset on both petiole and blade with long, hollow, exceedingly sharp hairs charged with free formic acid, which is also the basis of the bee's sting. Cream-colored florets occur in short spikes clustered in the axils of the leaves.

The prophet Job bewailed the wretchedness of his old age saying (Job 30): "Men in whom ripe age is perished . . . are gaunt with want and famine; . . . they are driven forth from the midst of men . . . so that they dwell . . . in frightful valleys . . . under the nettles they are gathered together," and a goatherd in one of the Idyls of Theocritus (VII) scourges the image of the god Pan thus: "Mayest thou be scratched all over thy flesh by nails and mayest thou sleep among nettles."

The plant was taken to Britain by the Romans who used it to chafe their skins against the bitter northern blasts and for long periods thereafter it was only to be found on the sites of their en-

campments. It is mentioned in old English texts as early as 725 A.D., again in the Saxon Leechdoms of 1000, and during the fourteenth century was used as a poultice for stanching the flow of blood from open wounds, being said to stop bleeding when other things failed.

It is surprising to note that such a plant was ever used as food, but from Roman times to the present the tender young shoots have been used

STINGING NETTLE as greens with pork and in soups. Horace mentions nettle broth and Persius, the satirist, inquires, "Am I to have a nettle or a smoky pig's cheek cooked for me on a festival day that that spendthrift grandson of yours may stuff himself with goose giblets?" In Scotland a soup is still made called "nettle kail."

The word "nettle" is said to have come from the German "nessel" and to mean "that which one sews." The Scottish poet Thomas Campbell once wrote, "I have slept in nettle sheets and dined off a nettle tablecloth and I have heard my mother say that she thought nettle cloth more durable than any other linen." Paper and rope have also been made from the plant and the root gives a beautiful yellow dye.

ARISTOLOCHIACEAE

Wild Ginger, *Asarum canadense* L.

Not many plants from the woodlands adapt themselves to a city dooryard, but wild ginger makes an admirable base planting for the north side of a house between the foundation and a driveway or as a ground cover under trees if planted in good soil and kept reasonably moist. The plant is a prostrate perennial with

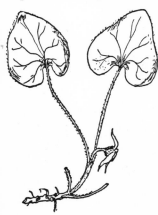

WILD GINGER

large light-green heart-shaped leaves which lie rather flat and form a conspicuous mosaic pattern on the forest floor in most of our Northern states. The rope-like rootstocks lie just above the ground and are pungent and aromatic, smelling like ginger. The flower is a large fuzzy purple-brown bell on a very short stalk between the two leaves and bent downward so as to lie hidden in old vegetation.

Our American plant has acquired a long list of colloquial names. It was used by the Indians for indigestion and an extract of the plant is still used as a substitute for true ginger (*Zingiber officinale*) in the treatment of dyspepsia. An European species very similar to it, *Asarum europaeum,* has been known from ancient times as asarabacca and used for the same medicinal purpose.

The plant is a member of the Aristolochiaceae, the family name coming from the Greek and meaning "childbirth" for some members of the family have been used by the Greeks and Romans in promoting childbirth. The Arabs and Hindus and the American Indians have used other species for the same purpose, but the American species, *Aristolochia serpentaria,* found in the Alleghenies, while still a collectable plant, is now only used as a simple tonic.

POLYGONACEAE

Garden Sorrel, *Rumex acetosa* L.

"Sorrel" includes several plants with sour herbage, as garden sorrel (see Picture 1 at end of book), wood sorrel, sour dock, mostly of minor importance to-day either in the kitchen or as medicinals, but all of them popular in times past for their refreshing sour taste and antiscorbutic qualities. Garden sorrel is not the common red sorrel, *Rumex acetosella* L., which infests

sterile fields but is a larger plant much less acid, two feet tall, with greenish flower heads. It is a perennial easily raised from seed and one planting will last for years if the plants are kept from seeding.

The plant is native to pastures over much of Europe and has been improved by cultivation and the amount of acid decreased. It is found locally in a few places in our Eastern states, escaped from cultivation.

GARDEN SORREL

The plant was used in Egypt as far back as 3000 B.C. as a culinary herb, and the Greeks and Romans both knew it. Because of their heavy diet, the Romans preceded their main meal with a course of emetics such as rue, lettuce, or sorrel. In one of his satires (Book 2), Horace advises for a regulatory diet after feasting "the low-growing herb of sorrel with a cup of Coan wine."

It first appears in an English plant list among the twenty-one culinary herbs grown by the Abbot of Cirencester in 1217 A.D. Apparently it preceded mint as a sauce for mutton, for a recipe of 1420 reads: "Wyth gynger the pygge eaten shall be, and sorrel with the moton." In a recipe of 1589 "sorrel soppes" were used with roast mutton and poultry. Another recipe of this century includes "sorrelle" as used for sauce, and as late as 1771 another reads: "Lay the mutton in a dish with some sorrel sauce." Sorrel jelly and jam have long been used to accompany various meats and the foliage chopped fine, for salads. The juice was used in "sorrel water" and it was added to give body to ale.

The plant was in high favor when our first colonists left England for it was one of the first herbs planted around Salem and Boston where it was used both as spring greens and as a mild laxative. It was also used as a dye, "an excellent black color being given to woollen stuffs," and it contains sufficient oxalic acid to be useful as an ink-stain remover.

Sour Dock, *Rumex crispus* L.

Yellow Dock, Curled Dock, Narrow Dock, Sour Dock, are all names which characterize this weed with long, narrow, sour-tasting foliage curled on the edges. The stout bifurcate root is familiar to all gardeners who try to extract it from the soil.

It goes back in recorded literature to 500 B.C., when root, juice and seeds were used in Greece in medicine as a mild astringent and tonic. It is still listed in the National Formulary and used in proprietary medicines, similar in action to rhubarb and sarsaparilla.

The plant has been regarded as a desirable potherb for hundreds of years and is still used in this country in early spring before garden supplies are available and before the foliage becomes rank and bitter.

Wood Sorrel, *Oxalis acetosella* L.

Another sorrel with long history as a potherb is the dainty little wood sorrel, belonging to the Oxalidaceae. This small plant with cloverlike leaf and delicate white pink-pencilled flowers is found in cold damp forests in our Northern states but not easily transferred to the garden. It possesses antiscorbutic qualities and was formerly much used as greens.

Goldsmith tells us that it is boiled with milk in Lapland and the coagulated mass kept underground in casks to be eaten in winter when food is scarce. It had a wide vogue in medicine in the past but is now obsolete.

WOOD SORREL

Burdock, *Arctium lappa* L.

Still another "dock" regarded as an herb is bitter dock or burdock, far removed from those already mentioned for it belongs to the composite family. Its medicinal virtues were commended by the ancients and it was used by the Lake Dwellers of Switzerland. The large fleshy root is a noted "blood-purifier," "bitters," and spring medicine, and until recently was much used in country districts in this country.

It possesses antiscorbutic qualities and in northern Europe the tender shoots are still eaten as a potherb while the stems, stripped of the fuzzy outer coat before the flowering season makes them bitter, are eaten raw with vinegar or oil, or boiled as a substitute for asparagus.

Rhubarb, *Rhum rhaponticum* L.

Garden rhubarb is a native of southern Siberia and the Tartary states and was known in medicine as early as 200 B.C. by the Greeks and Arabs. However, this is not the famous rhubarb of the pharmacopoeia. That plant, *R. officinale* L., is a native of China and has been used there for thousands of years as a safe purge. It was one of the plants brought out of the Far East by Marco Polo (1298 A.D.?) and it at once sprang into prominence in Europe. However, its transport offered such difficulties and its keeping qualities were so poor that it was an extremely expensive drug. In 1542, Chinese rhubarb was twice as costly as opium, four times more valuable than saffron, and sixteen times the worth of fine myrrh.

The Chinese plant was introduced into England through St. Petersburg but it could not be cured successfully and a substitute was sought which would thrive in Europe. The garden species was brought to England by Sir Matthew Lister, physician to Charles I, the plant being of Siberian origin, and the root used like that of the Oriental plant which it soon replaced, although less potent. Both species are still among the most important of vegetable drugs.

Rhubarb was not recognized as a garden vegetable until 1807 when a Mr. Myatt, market gardener, sent his sons into London with a few bunches. Myatt's rhubarb became known the world over and the plot south of Lambeth which he leased grew excellent rhubarb from 1818 until 1869. This plot is now known as Myatt's Park, being presented to the nation by the owner of the plot in whose family it had been held since 1870.

Rhubarb is largely grown in this country under glass for early spring use and the largest acreage of the forced plant is said to be that of a group of Belgian gardeners just north of Detroit.

CHENOPODIACEAE

The goosefoot family is a large one consisting for the most part of weedy often mealy-leaved annuals of wide distribution. Few

GOOD KING HENRY

have any economic importance to-day, spinach (*Spinacia oleracea*), the beet (*Beta vulgaris* L.), and worm-seed (*Chenopodium ambrosioides anthelminticum* (L.) Gray), a specific for the removal of ascarids and hookworms, being exceptions. Good King Henry (*Chenopodium Bonus-Henricus* L.) was a potherb in good repute in Europe during the Renaissance, and orache (*Atriplex hortensis* L.) is another often encountered in old herbals and used as greens.

PORTULACACEAE

Purslane, *Portulaca oleracea* L.

David Harum advises a young man to go west and take up land and then he will get along "like pussley in a flower garden," and Charles Dudley Warner has a delightful passage on the plant in *My Summer in a Garden:* "The sort of weed which I most hate is the 'pussley,' a fat ground-clinging spreading greasy thing and the most propagatious plant I know, but I saw a Chinaman once boil a lot of it in a pot and stir in eggs and mix and eat it with relish."

PURSLANE

One evening when a group sat around a blazing Adirondack campfire telling tall yarns, says Warner, the guide finally spoke up and all expected a thriller. "Well, there's one thing that beats me!" he drawled. "What's that?" they gasped in unison. "That's pussley," he sighed in the tone of a man who has come to one door in life which is hopelessly shut. "Everything seems to have its special enemy but nothing ever troubles pussley."

Purslane originally came from India and Africa and was introduced into Europe as a salad plant about the fifteenth century. It is a fleshy wide-spreading prostrate annual branching

31

freely and with tiny green to red leaves, reddish stems and minute yellow flowers. Both stem and foliage are oily and meaty in flavor; and in the past were used as greens and the stem cut into six-inch strips was pickled in stale beer or vinegar.

The plant was early introduced into American gardens for food. Manasseh Cutler says as late as 1785 it was eaten as a pot-herb "and esteemed by some as little inferior to asparagus."

Our gay garden portulaca is a near relative from South America, much improved and doubled by selection.

RANUNCULACEAE

A number of plants of the crowfoot family have been regarded as culinary herbs in the past and some are still of inestimable value in medicine. Some are acid-loving bog plants, others are found in rich woodlands and easily transferable to the wild garden, while still others are among the finest of our rockery and perennial-border specimens.

Monkshood, *Aconitum napellus* L.

Several species and varieties of aconite are popular garden subjects, most nurserymen offering two or three, from dwarfs to plants growing five feet tall, with flowers from porcelain blue through pink to yellow, and blooming from midsummer to frost. Several species are native to this country.

The aconites are popular because of their beautiful blues, which are rather rare in the garden, and for the lateness of their bloom, after most perennials are past. They are easily grown, even under trees, although seeds need the action of frost to germinate.

It is dangerous to grow these plants where children are likely to taste the pungent rootstocks or even the foliage, for aconite is one of the most deadly of poisons, depressing the heart action and slowing the respiration. However, in well-regulated amounts it is used as a circulatory sedative and externally to relieve neuralgia and sciatica. The blackish root, two or three inches long, contains aconitine, an alkaloid which dulls the nerve endings.

This poison was employed as early as 1000 B.C., the Greeks, Romans, and even the Chinese employing it widely for sinister purposes. It was used to poison arrows by the people of ancient Gaul, and is mentioned in *Romeo and Juliet* and in *King Henry IV,* and again as

> "That poisonous stalk
> Of aconite, whose ripened fruit hath ravish't
> All health, all comfort of a happy life."
> — JOHN FORD, *The Broken Heart,* 1633.

Black Hellebore, *Helleborus niger* L.

The Christmas rose is often grown in northern gardens for its very early bloom, even before the snowdrops and crocuses, and it is often forced for Christmas bloom. The plant is fairly expensive for it is slow to propagate.

Hellebore is a dwarf evergreen plant with five large white or pale-rose sepals, the petals being minute and mixed with the numerous yellow stamens. It is found on meadows in central Europe and many other species are grown abroad, not reliably hardy in our Northern states.

The plant has been employed in medicine since the time of the ancient Greeks in the treatment of gout, epilepsy, paralysis, and insanity. Horace says in one of his satires (II: 3, 82), that the world is like a great asylum with four classes of madmen. "By far the largest quantity of hellebore should be administered to misers" for the avaricious are the most numerous class of the insane. Hippocrates used it as an ointment and Virgil (3rd Georgic) says:

"They mix a med'cine to foment their limbs, . . .
Fat pitch and black bitumen, . . .
And hellebore, and squills deep-rooted in the seas."

— DRYDEN translation.

In the *Faerie Queene,* Spenser leads Mammon into a garden "direfull deadly black both leaf and bloom, fit to adorn the dead," in which grew mournful cypress, dead sleeping poppy and black hellebore.

The plant was widely used in the Middle Ages as a purge and anthelmintic, also for dropsy and jaundice, and much later by cottagers in domestic medicine although highly toxic, overdoses often proving fatal.

White Hellebore, *Veratrum album* L.

White hellebore is not related to the black species except in similarity of the common name, being a member of the lily family. Since the time of Hippocrates, however, the two species have been confused, for the white species was also widely used in medicine to reduce the pulse rate and in respiratory affections. It is a powerful irritant.

While white hellebore does not occur in this country, green hellebore, *V. viride* Ait., is found in swamps and wet meadows from Newfoundland to Alaska and south to Georgia, appearing in spring even before skunk cabbage. It is a rank, luxurious plant attaining a height up to eight feet with broad light-green corrugated foliage topped with a cluster of foamy greenish-yellow bloom.

The Indians scattered the powdered root of this plant over fresh wounds, and it is still used as a purge and vermifuge and

35

as an anti-spasmodic for epilepsy. It is still a collectable herb, the bitter acrid rhizome being dug after the foliage has died down.

Our early settlers soaked their corn in hellebore to prevent its being eaten by crows.

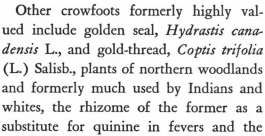

Other crowfoots formerly highly valued include golden seal, *Hydrastis canadensis* L., and gold-thread, *Coptis trifolia* (L.) Salisb., plants of northern woodlands and formerly much used by Indians and whites, the rhizome of the former as a substitute for quinine in fevers and the fine golden threadlike rootlets of the latter as a household remedy for cankers. Both are still collectable herbs. The former is a desirable plant for the wild garden, but the latter is a bog plant.

GOLD-THREAD

The rootstock of black cohosh, *Cimicifuga racemosa* (L.) Nutt., has for long been used in the treatment of rheumatism, dropsy, bronchitis, and even tuberculosis. It was a favored tonic of the Indians for many afflictions. It is toxic but valued as a sedative and often prescribed in place of digitalis.

Cohosh is a native perennial

LIVERWORT

easily transferred to the garden, although its large size proscribes its use.

FOR NORTHERN GARDENS

One of the loveliest plants for the shady, moist wild garden is liverwort, *Hepatica triloba* (L.) Karst, and one is certain spring has arrived when the fuzzy-stemmed little hepatica is in bloom. The old-time Doctrine of Signatures prescribed various leaves and roots as cures for organs of the body which they resembled in form, and it is obvious that the trilobed hepatica would be a sure-cure for liver complaints and the dried foliage was long given innocent patients before it was learned that the plant was wholly inert.

Another very choice early blossom is pasque flower, *Pulsatilla patens* (L.) Mill., with fuzzy-bracted violet bloom before the foliage begins to show, and the plant continues in bloom in the rockery long after many other things have passed. The bulb is highly toxic but was used in medicine even in

PASQUE FLOWER

China and Japan before the Christian Era, for dropsy, rheumatism and paralysis. It is still used sparingly but has been largely supplanted because of its toxic effects.

The plant is native to calcareous soils of the prairies from Illinois westward as well as to plains and meadows of northern Europe and western Asia.

PAPAVERACEAE

Opium Poppy, *Papaver somniferum* L.

"The poppy flaunts a petticoat
Of airy films that fly and float;
Of fairy gauzes, fairy-fine,
Lucent and crystalline."
— KATHERINE TYNAN, *Poppy.*

The poppy family is represented in herb lore by several plants

OPIUM POPPY

of minor importance and by one which ranks high in economic importance. Gayly colored improved varieties of the opium poppy are widely cultivated in our gardens, but the original wild plant from southern Europe and Asia is a stout annual with lacinate-margined gray-blue foliage with a whitened bloom and large single bluish-white flowers with a large purple blotch at the base.

The plant was grown by the Egyptians as early as 1500 B.C., for its copious milky juice which exudes from the half-ripe pod when scarred and hardens to a blackish gum. The Egyptians used it for headaches, without realizing its chief value. The poppy was a love

charm in ancient Greece, being a familiar plant in the meadows;
Theophrastus wrote of it in his *Enquiry into Plants,* Theocritus
sings of it in his *Idyls,* Aristophanes mentions it in *The Birds,* and
Hippocrates used it in his medical practice, how, we do not know.

However, the Romans knew of the somniferous quality of the
sap and Virgil says in the *Aeneid* (Book IV):

> "The poppy seeds in honey taught to steep,
> Reclaimed his rage, and sooth'd him into sleep."
> — Dryden translation.

Every early monastery grew poppy for use in its hospital and
the sap was used freely throughout the Middle Ages during crude
internal operations and after serious battlefield injuries. "For to
make a man sleep three dayes so his woundes will heal" a drink
was given consisting of henbane, lettuce seeds and opium, but
the careless use of such a powerful combination led to many
tragedies and in the fifteenth century the drastic potion was dis-
continued, although the poppy-head water continued in use to alleviate coughs and catarrh and as a sedative. The macerated green
tops were also used as a plaster on wounds and for erysipelas.

The introduction and cultivation of the opium poppy into the
Orient is a long and sinister story, the greed of civilized peoples
debasing whole populations, entering into politics, causing wars,
and dethroning dynasties. The history of this single plant in the
Far East is one of the most sordid pages on record.

However, many passages in literature use poppy as the symbol
of sleep.

> "Not poppy, nor mandragora,
> Nor all the drowsy syrups of the world,
> Shall ever medicine thee to that sweet sleep,
> Which thou ow'dst yesterday,"

says Iago in *Othello* (Act III, Sc. 3), and in *Urn Burial,* which is "one of the noblest examples of eloquence in the English language," Sir Thomas Browne (1682) writes on individual mortality thus:

"There is no antidote against the opium of time; our fathers find their graves in our short memories, and sadly tell us how we may be buried in our survivors. Gravestones tell truth scarce forty years. Generations pass while some trees stand, and old families last not three oaks . . . But the iniquity of oblivion blindly scattereth her poppy, and deals with the memory of men without distinction to merit of perpetuity."

"Nature wherever she maims her creature," says Emerson in *Representative Men,* "lays her poppies plentifully on the bruise" in the form of gentle sleep. And Horace Smith (1779–1849) in his poem *Poppies and Sleep* says:

> "Gentle sleep!
> Scatter thy drowsiest poppies from above;
> And in new dreams not soon to vanish, bless
> My senses with the sight of her I love."

Thomas Warton wrote these beautiful lines:

> "On this my pensive Pillow, gentle sleep!
> Descend and place thy crown of poppies on my breast!"
>
> — *Ode to Sleep,* 1790.

Celandine, *Chelidonium majus* L.

The dainty celandine is a plant worthy of a place in the flower-garden for its lovely gray-green whitened foliage although the four-petalled sulphur-yellow flowers are rather insignificant. It blooms over most of the summer, however, although the long slender seed capsules make the plant appear a little weedy.

The plant is still grown in English gardens and was one of the first simples introduced into this country. To-day it is found in fence corners and other forgotten spots in our Eastern states and the writer recently saw a colony at the back door of the Daniel Webster homestead at Whitefield, New Hampshire. Plants are readily obtainable from dealers in native material.

CELANDINE

Celandine was used in medicine at least by 300 B.C., and called in Greece "swallowwort." Pliny says the flower bloomed when the swallow arrived and the petals dropped when it left. He also tells of a Greek who long before had punctured the eyes of young swallows and then restored their sight by poulticing with the juice of this herb. Although this story obviously was distorted in translation somewhere in the distant past, still it persisted through the ages and swallow-wort was used for fading sight. A prescription of 1310 advised that a fomentation of "celydoyne and sauge" be used over the eyes; one of 1430 commences, "Take the ius of salendyne," and in 1562 the great herbalist Turner says, "The iuice of Selendin maketh the eyesight clere." As late as 1787, the British botanist Withering says the plant "consumes the white opaque spots upon the eyes." Thus it is seen that the tradition persisted, was copied and elaborated upon by physicians and herbalists for over two thousand years, even though probably only a mild sedative. As a medicinal, it is now totally obsolete.

Another plant goes by the name of celandine, *Ranunculus*

ficaria L., a crowfoot, often confused in old literature. The lesser celandine or pilewort, still used in home medicine for piles, occurs locally in meadows in our Eastern states. Wordsworth's two poems on the celandine refers to this plant.

Bloodroot, *Sanguinaria canadensis* L.

Our beautiful little native bloodroot has enjoyed considerable reputation in early medicine with both the Indians and the

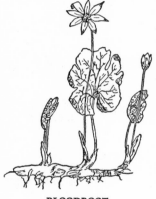

BLOODROOT

whites for, according to the Doctrine of Signatures, its copious orange-red milky juice was indicated for jaundice, for which, by the way, it is totally inert. It is highly astringent, however, and was used successfully on open sores, for ringworm and ulcers.

Bloodroot is a most satisfactory wild-garden plant, spreading and seeding itself readily on rich, moist ground. The flower is most attractive when the leaves are half grown and the large foliage makes a delightful ground cover later in the season.

CRUCIFERAE

The Cruciferae include many of our most valuable vegetables as well as several plants used widely as condiments and in medicine.

Black Mustard, *Brassica nigra* (L.) Koch
White Mustard, *B. alba* (L.) Boiss

The mustards, black and white, are so well known as pernicious weeds throughout our country that they need no description. They were introduced by our first settlers as potherbs, salad ingredients and home medicinals, but their numerous seeds, long tap-root and ability to survive on dry and sterile soils have caused their familiarity to breed contempt. They are found wild throughout most of the civilized world and have been known for so long that the specific locality of their origin cannot be determined.

BLACK MUSTARD

The parable of the mustard seed is stated in almost identical words in Matthew (13:31) and in Mark (4:31), and man's faith is compared to a mustard seed in Matthew (17:20) and Luke (17:6), but the particular species which grew into a tree so the birds could lodge in its branches (Matthew 13:32) cannot be identified.

Both species were well known to the Greeks as food and Hippocrates, the celebrated Greek physician (b. 400 B.C.) who emancipated medicine from the superstition and priestcraft which had previously enslaved it and substituted proper diet and wholesome living instead, used the powdered seed among his four hundred plant remedies.

Pliny enumerates some forty-odd uses for the plant and seed in medicine; he says it "burns like fire though at the same time it is remarkably wholesome for the body." He says further that it

was used on roast meats, losing much of its pungency in cooking and that the foliage was cooked as a potherb. It is interesting to note that he says also that "mustard is extremely difficult to get rid of once it is planted."

Black mustard was used as food and medicine in India as early as 75 A.D., and Charlemagne grew it (sinape) in his

WHITE MUSTARD   large gardens at Aix-la-Chapelle in the ninth century. Saxon leechbooks mention both species for medicinal use, and the white species seems to have been grown first at Cirencester, England, 1217 A.D., by Alexander Neckam, the abbot horticulturist, under the name carlock.

During the Middle Ages, winter fodder was scarce and domestic animals had to be killed and salted or dried for winter use and mustard was used as the chief condiment to render the meat more palatable. Its chief constituent, allyl isothiocyanate, is rapidly absorbed into the system, stimulating the salivary secretions and increasing the peristaltic action of the stomach.

"What say you to a piece of beef and mustard?" asks the servant of Katherine (*The Taming of the Shrew,* Act IV, Sc. 3).

"A dish that I do love to feed upon," replies the Shrew.

"Ay, but the mustard is too hot a little," remarks Grumio.

"Why, then the beef, and let the mustard rest."

"Nay, then, I will not; you shall have the mustard,
Or else you get no beef of Grumio."

"Then both, or one, or anything thou wilt," replies the Shrew in exasperation, to which the witty servant counters,

"Why, then the mustard without the beef."

Shakespeare mentions the plant again in *As You Like It* (Act I, Sc. 2) as a condiment for pancakes; and in the best-known drama of Beaumont and Fletcher (*The Knight of the Burning Pestle,* Act IV, Sc. 2), the Princess of Moldavia tells Ralph of the dish of salted beef with mustard which her father had enjoyed in England:

> "My father oft will tell of a wild fowl
> Which powder'd red-beef-and-mustard called is."

But the plant was not grown widely in England until relatively late and tons of the seed were imported yearly from Russia and India until the excessive price and tariff necessitated the beginnings of wider home culture. By the sixteenth century seed was ground and pressed into little balls called from the place of origin "Tewkesbury Mustard, the best the world affords." To tell a man that he looked as though he lived on Tewkesbury mustard was equivalent to telling him he was peevish and ill-tempered, says an old chronicler, although it also signified stupidity when Falstaff said of Poins, "He a good wit? . . . his wit's as thick as Tewkesbury mustard." (*King Henry IV,* Part II, Act Ii, Sc. 4.)

However, "some think their conceits, like mustard, not good

except they bite," said Fuller in 1642, and one of the fairies in Titania's train was Mustardseed, probably because of his sprightliness and pungency of wit. John Gay, the brilliant Devonshire poet of manners (1685–1732), has "A New Song of New Similes" which begins thus: "My Passion is as mustard strong."

In 1720, a Mrs. Clements conceived the idea of grinding black mustard seed to a fine powder and sifting out the hulls. This farina pleased the palate of King George I and speedily attained popularity. Later on, the pungent flavor was diluted with the seed of white mustard and still later wheat flour, starch and cayenne pepper were added to cheapen the product and aid in its keeping quality. By the nineteenth century the center of cultivation and preparation was transferred from Durham to York, where as late as 1834 it formed one of the principal products of export.

The use of mustard in medicine kept pace with its growing popularity as a condiment and potherb. An oily extract was being imported into England by the thirteenth century, and its use in the household has now become well-nigh universal as an emergency emetic, as a poultice for chest affections, for a foot bath in incipient colds and so on. It is irritating to the skin and causes burns which are slow to heal, but being rapidly absorbed is a valuable counterirritant. The fresh herbage also is used externally to relieve local pains.

Mustard is cultivated to-day as a seed crop in California, the seed pods being gathered when nearly ripe, and it is a collectable herb in the wild state. Carloads of the greens are sent to New York and elsewhere in the winter, chiefly for the delectation of our foreign populations who knew it abroad.

Water-cress, *Sisymbrium Nasturtium-aquaticum* L.

> "Lord, I confess too, when I dine,
>   The Pulse is Thine,
> And all those other Bits, that bee
>   There plac'd by Thee;
> The Worts, the Purslain, and the Messe
>   Of Water-cresse,
> Which of Thy kindnesse Thou hast sent."
> — ROBERT HERRICK, *Noble Numbers,* 1647.

Water-cress occurs in brooks and running streams throughout much of the temperate world. It was introduced into Abyssinia some seventy-five years ago by the noted German botanist, Professor A. F. W. Schimper, who spent a lifetime there collecting the countless unnamed plants to the enrichment of European herbaria, and in the streams about Aduwa it is known simply as "Schimper." Thus how lasting but how casual is fame!

WATER-CRESS

It was known to the ancient Greeks as "kardamon" or headsubduer, and Pliny says in Rome it was used as a brain stimulant as well as a favorite salad ingredient. It was grown in the monastery garden at Saint-Gall (812 A.D.) and in Stockholm in the twelfth century, being established in England two centuries later.

Eaten at breakfast it was regarded as a gentle stimulant after the old Roman custom of preceding the main meal with a course of lettuce or rue or sorrel. One of the old "Cries of London" reads:

> "Young cresses fresh at breakfast taken
> A relish will give to eggs and bacon;
> My profits small, for I put many
> In bunches sold at three a penny."

The painter Whistler is said to have favored a breakfast consisting only of bread and butter and water-cress.

Many a poet mentions the little plant in running brooks. Southey says:

> "There were water-cresses growing,
> And pleasant was the water's flowing."
>
> — *Crossroads,* 1799.

and Longfellow in *Tales of a Wayside Inn* speaks of the man who

> "Loves his brook with its water-cresses."

Lodge has another sentiment:

> "My Love shall grow up as the Water-Cresses
> Slowly, but with a deep roote."
>
> — *Euphues,* 1590.

Water-cress was introduced very early into this country as a spring salad plant and to-day is of considerable commercial importance. It may be grown in a flowerpot in the kitchen window if kept wet.

Horseradish, *Radicula armoracia* (L.) Robins

Horseradish is a luxuriant dark-green perennial native to the plains at the foot of the Ural Mountains and was taken to Greece as early as 1000 B.C. The Romans also were familiar with its culinary and medicinal virtues and it was introduced into

HORSERADISH

Britain even before Caesar's invasion. It spread widely and now grows wild from Turkey to Iceland.

Like the other mustards, horseradish stimulates the flow of the digestive juices and aids in the breaking down of meat fibers. It is widely used to-day freshly ground in vinegar or in cream sauces with beef and ham and no doubt many can remember as children digging up the long stout white roots in early spring and grating them, along with the fingers, on a lemon grater and enjoying the pungent but extremely hot paste spread over after-school sandwiches. A few hundred years ago when home-cured meats were liable to be tough and dry, horseradish was put into the stew pot with the meat, and the greens were used as a potherb, ready long before spring-planted cress or mustard.

Izaak Walton used the root in dressing some of his famous catches, even for trout "which of all fish is the most delicate in flavour and must be eaten within four or five hours of its taking," and Samuel Pepys tells us in his Diary that his host at a certain party "must needs have me drink a cup of horse-radish ale," for this strong herb along with wormwood and tansy were ingredients of strong drink before hops were known.

The physicians of old did not disdain the pungent root to induce sweating in cases of dropsy and rheumatism and the Greeks used the foliage as a rubefacient for sciatica and paralysis and it was an excellent antiscorbutic. The wilted leaves are still used in this country as a poultice to relieve toothache and facial neuralgia and are placed in the soles of the shoes to relieve hot, tired feet.

Garden Cress, *Lepidium sativum* L.

The cultivation of garden cress has never attained the degree of popularity in America that it has abroad; however, it affords refreshing early salad material, ready for use in six weeks' time, being pulled before seed forms, after which it becomes too hot for use.

It is native to Persia and Macedonia and was cultivated by the Greeks and Romans as well as by the people farther east. It was used for toothache, as a plaster for leprous sores and for scabs caused by the itch. Under the name "nasturtium," it was grown by the Saxons and by the Emperor Charlemagne, and for several hundred years cottage gardeners grew it for spring salads and as an antiscorbutic.

Scurvy Grass, *Cochlearia officinalis* L.

True scurvy grass is found only in Arctic America, Europe, and Asia, along seacoasts and rivers, and it was a very important plant for hundreds of years, collected in bales and placed aboard ships commencing long voyages as the only plant available to combat the scourge of seafaring men. James Cook took it on his voyage around the world and Byron, another world-voyager, in 1767, says "the ship's company carried a great quantity of coconuts, scurvy grass, and other vegetables for the use of the sick." Obviously, it plays no part in present-day shipping.

SCURVY GRASS

Woad, *Isatis orientalis* L.

When Caesar landed on the shores of Britain, it is said that he found naked people stained a ghastly dark blue in order to

WOAD

frighten his legions and that the plant they used was woad. A sixteenth-century translation (Golding's, 1565) of Caesar's *Gallic War* states that "all Britons doe dye themselves wythe woade which setteth a blewish colour upon them." However, the Britons had been using a native woad to stain their skins and hair during certain religious rites long before Caesar's arrival, a rhyme by Garth (1715) facetiously referring to the time

> "When dress was monstrous and fig-leaves the mode
> And Quality put on no paint but Woade."

51

Martial, the Spanish-born Roman epigrammatist, says: "Though Claudia has sprung from the woad-stained Britons, how she possessed the feeling of the Latin race!" Pliny calls the stain *glastrum* while Caesar uses *vitrum*, and there has been considerable discussion as to the proper translation of the words. Caesar says the plant used was rank in growth and looked like plantain, both of which characteristics apply to woad, while Pliny does not designate the stain, saying it is bluish like the tints of Roman glass.

Isatis is a genus of the mustard family and a close relative of the radish, a coarse weedy annual up to three feet tall, with large sessile hairy foliage of a soft gray-green color and four-petaled yellow flower in small racemes. The species *orientalis* is native to the eastern Mediterranean area and was the woad generally used by the ancients although *I. tinctoria* was native to Greece and Italy and was also used. It is the latter species which became established throughout Europe, even in Sweden, and which is available in this country.

Pliny says woolens were dyed with woad and that the bruised foliage was used as a plaster to reduce swellings. The species *tinctoria* was cultivated in the north very early and, with madder, comprised practically the whole dye range. By Charlemagne's time it was widely cultivated and the early Irish grew only two plants extensively, woad and flax. Saxon manuscripts mention it and Chaucer says in the Canterbury Tales:

> "No dyer with his weld or woad was there,
> But every fleece was of its natural hue."
> — HILL translation.

By 1495, woad was being imported into Britain by the ton, coming from France and the Azores and it was the chief export

FOR NORTHERN GARDENS

from the Islands. In a manuscript of 1548, there is a statement that the "Merchaunt Strangers daily brought in oade (woad), oyle, sylke, and other merchaundyse" and so lucrative was the traffic that finally it was decreed that it could be imported only in British-owned ships.

A writer of the seventeenth century speaks of "the deep woad of intense displeasure" as we say that a man "has the blues" or has "a dark blue feeling."

Broad-scale cultivation was begun in England in the sixteenth century and the plant was brought to America very early and has escaped, but not as widely as most mustards.

The plant is still used commercially in the dyeing industry because of the fairly lasting color and the simplicity of operation. Indigo is the blue dye longest associated with the human race in spite of the complexity of its use but woad could be grown where indigo could not and did not require the skill of manipulation of the older plant. Both woad and madder were relatively sunfast and did not fade when soaped and for hundreds of years have been used in Oriental rugs and peasant fabrics and are not entirely supplanted in this day of brilliant synthetic dyes.

CRASSULACEAE

Houseleek, *Sempervivum tectorum* L.

It may be surprising for one to learn that hen-and-chickens, a plant found in almost every rock-garden, is a medicinal herb with an interesting history. The common houseleek is native to mountainous parts of Europe, and one species, *S. arboreum,* was known to Hippocrates who boiled the thick leaves and used them as a poultice for ulcers, a minor ailment common to ancient

HOUSELEEK

Greece. Theophrastus also mentions the plant in his treatise on plants.

The species *S. tectorum,* a native of the Alps, was used as an ointment in France in the time of Charlemagne, this emperor growing it under the name "Jupiter's Beard," from the fancied resemblance of the red stamens to the traditional rufous beard of that god. In a tenth-century manuscript it is called *semper ius,* or ever-living, from its tenacity of life when uprooted, and this name was corrupted later to "sengrene," by which the plant was known for hundreds of years. Other old names are aigrene, live-forever, thunder plant, healing blade and poor man's leaf.

A writer in 1562 says "houseleke groweth in mountaynes and hylly places and some vse to set it upon theyr houses" believing that a house would never be struck by lightning if houseleeks grew on the roof, and there is no doubt a roof damp enough to support a growing plant is not an easy prey to fire. Bulwer-Lytton speaks of "roofs green with mosses and houseleeks," and even yet one sees in Devonshire and in Germany rambling old stone and stucco farmhouses and outbuildings topped with a thatch vividly green with mosses and great ancient tufts of houseleeks.

These rosettes, however, served the cottager in another respect, for the succulent leaves contain a fairly strong astringent, valuable for stanching the flow of blood, and were an ever-ready household remedy in cases of cuts and mowing accidents. They were also used for burns when crushed and clamped on the abrasion, acting as a cooling antiseptic and keeping out the air. An ointment was made of the juice incorporated into some fatty substance and the expressed juice was also used as a refrigerant for fevers.

The British botanist, William Withering, said as late as 1787, "There is no doubt a medicine of such activity as houseleeks will one day be converted into more important purposes," little realizing that the era of herb medicines would in less than a hundred years be supplanted with biological and chemical remedies and that many of the old-time plants would be cultivated only for their sentimental and historical associations.

Houseleeks were brought to America before 1672, when Josselyn mentions them growing at Salem. Some forty species are known, many of them in our rock-gardens for the pretty and hardy rosettes which adapt themselves admirably to crannies between the rocks. Seeds are almost microscopic and germinate poorly and the plants are generally propagated from the runners.

Live-forever, *Sedum telephium* L.

The Sedums are closely related to the Sempervivums and this, the type species, is native to cool mountainous regions of Europe.

The word *Sedum* is from the Latin meaning "to sit," i.e. to squat upon the rocks, and the species *telephium* was named for Telephus, a son of Hercules.

Pliny and Plutarch both mention its tenacity of life and the Chinese have for long grown it on their housetops as protection from lightning as Europeans planted the houseleek. It was grown in English gardens by 1387, when we find references to it as "Anglice orpine" and "Crassula major." It was also called midsummer men, from the custom of setting a plant of it in the window on Midsummer's Eve; as the stalk turned next morning, the maiden of the house knew from which direction her lover would come.

LIVE-FOREVER

The plant had some virtue as a vulnerary, like hen-and-chickens, and the dried plant is still sold in Sicily for use in dysentery and diarrhea. It was brought to this country very early for medicinal use and occurs to-day sparingly throughout our Eastern and Middle states, generally on the sites of abandoned homesteads although one can sometimes find it along unimproved roadways. It is listed in catalogs under the name *S. purpureum,* for there is some dissension among systematists as to its correct appellation.

Wall Pepper, *Sedum acre* L.

Most rock-gardeners possess this little stonecrop, its compact mossy foliage an excellent carpet for rocks. The plant is covered with yellow star-flowers in June. It also goes by the common names biting stonecrop, pepper grass and poor man's pepper, and was formerly widely used as a seasoning.

It is also a mild astringent, and Culpeper
(1665) says it was used on "canker sores, ulcers,
and for the King's Evil (scrofula) and other
knots and kernels in the flesh." Hill (1756)
says a decoction was used for sore mouth and
scurvy. The fresh foliage applied to the skin
will raise a blister, hence it had to be used
sparingly and was rarely taken internally.

The plant is native to much of Europe and
has escaped from cultivation in various parts
of this country, notably along our Canadian

WALL PEPPER

border where it often covers rocky outcrops and sandy banks.

ROSACEAE

The great rose family includes very few herbs and those only of minor importance; the rose itself is classed as an herb, having been used both as food and medicine in the past but it possesses so many other virtues that it can well afford to leave to humbler plants those of practical use. The rose is said to have sprung from the blood of Adonis, and *Rosa centifolia,* native of western Asia, was well known in ancient Greece. In Roman times it was used in plasters and eye salves, but practically disappeared from Europe until the Crusaders brought it back from Asia Minor in the eleventh century when it again was grown for use in eye salves, ointments and vinegars. Attar of roses, rose oil, rose vinegar, and rose water all played a part in mediaeval medicine, and love philters consisting of dried rose petals and violets, saffron and myrrh, lavender and rosemary, mixed with the dried flesh of vipers and incorporated into honey were given love-sick youths and maidens.

Rosa gallica was grown in Plantagenet times along with Madonna lilies, clove pinks, honeysuckle, peonies, iris, lavender and violets, and rose petals and violets were candied for use in salads and desserts. Many of the old roses are rapidly coming back into American gardens and a comprehensive booklet on the hundreds of species and varieties with the dates of their origin was published in 1932 by Bobbink and Atkins, *Old-Fashioned Roses.*

Salad Burnet, *Poterium sanguisorba* L.

There are three burnets or herb bennets, two belonging to the rose family and one, saxifrage burnet, to the carrots. They are all similar in appearance (see Picture 2 at end of book) with pinnate foliage eight inches or so in length, with seven or more deeply-cut leaflets, and all occur spar-ingly on waste ground in our East-ern states, adventive from Europe. The two rose burnets flower in small globular or ellipsoidal greenish heads of minute florets, while the saxi-frage burnet has the characteristic carrotlike flat umbel of minute white flowers.

"Burnet" is a modification of the French "brunette" or brown, from the brown color of the long stamens and flower head, and the genus name *Poterium* is from the Greek for goblet or beaker, hinting at the use

SALAD BURNET

of the plant in drinks. However, the most important use of the rose burnets is their ability to contract small blood vessels and retard the flow of blood, indicated in the species name *sanguisorba*. Being a common meadow plant of southern Eu-rope, there is little doubt that this virtue was known in ancient times and that the foliage was crushed on the field of battle. In this country we have a plant used for similar purpose, New Jersey tea, *Ceanothus americanus,* an infusion of which was drunk by the Revolutionary soldiers on the eve of battle; this internal use of a vulnerary is unusual but is said to have been effective.

Burnet was sold in drug shops during the Middle Ages for this purpose and was used by the ancient Chinese as a styptic and plaster on wounds. A tea is still made of the plant as a cooling agent in fevers, the crushed foliage having the odor of cucumbers.

Having a mild flavor, the plant was widely used in salads in the spring although many plants must have been available which were superior. Seed is available and the plant desirable as edging for the front of the perennial border. It is a perennial, neat in habit and ferny in appearance, and while the flower heads are not attractive, the plant will bloom again if kept from seeding.

Great Burnet, *Sanguisorba officinalis* L.

The two rose burnets are confused in old records for they are similar in herbage and flower; both are meadow plants throughout most of Europe and western Asia and both have for long been considered efficient astringent agents and excellent fodder plants for cattle although at present superseded by fodder of leguminous types.

While the foliage of both burnets has very little odor or flavor, young shoots of both were valued as what Evelyn calls "sallet furniture" during the Middle Ages and one of them, which one we do not know, was brought to this country among the very first consignments of seeds for use in home medicine and for salads.

The vulnerary usage of the burnets which was known to the ancients was later lost but rediscovered in the thirteenth century. It was an ingredient in the "save" which Chaucer mentions often in the *Canterbury Tales*. Frequent wars, jousts, and accidents gave the chatelaine of every large manor abundant opportunity to exercise her medical skill in saving the lives of her menfolk and servants; arrow, spear, and knife wounds formed a large part of medieval medical practice and the "ius" of the numerous astringent herbs was valued for stopping hemorrhages. These juices were also incorporated into ointments and salves with various sorts of animal fats and used as dressings for ulcers and wounds.

Great burnet seems not to be available to American gardeners.

Agrimony, *Agrimonia eupatoria* L.

Another astringent of the rose family long used in medicine is agrimony, mentioned by Strabo (b. 63 B.C.) along with wormwood and betony. However, like many other plants, its usages were lost sight of in literature for a thousand years, to be mentioned again in the Saxon Leechdoms of 1000 A.D., when it appears as *agremoman*. Chaucer calls it "egrimoyne" in *The Yeoman's Prologue,* and in the fourteenth century it was used for liver troubles, to clarify fading vision, and to cleanse wounds.

The plant was brought to America very early and has for long been used in domestic medicine as a mild astringent, from the presence of a small amount of tannic acid, the dried plant being steeped to form a tea. This tea was also used widely in home dyeing for woolens, giving a good yellow.

Agrimony is a pretty woodland perennial familiar to most country people east of the Mississippi, with five-parted palmate foliage and a tall wandlike spike sparsely set with tiny yellow florets, several species being very similar in appearance.

Tormentil, *Potentilla procumbens* Sibth.

The unusual word "tormentil" is often met in old herb literature and arouses curiosity as to its origin. The earliest English citation of the little plant appears to be that of 1387, "because the powder or decoction of the root doth appease the rage and torment of the teeth." Through the years, it came to be used for piles,

fevers, canker sores, and so on, and Richard Jefferies, the nature-essayist who preceded W. H. Hudson by several decades, says in *Field and Hedgerow,* 1890, that cottage folk in England still made a tea of tormentil to relieve pain.

Tormentil is a fragile prostrate little plant with the characteristic five-palmate foliage of the genus, but with a small four-petalled yellow flower instead of the regulation five. It occurs on heaths and pastures in Great Britain and on the Continent, and its roots are a fairly strong astringent, used since the time of Hippocrates for skin affections. The

TORMENTIL

plant was introduced into this country very early but has gone wild only in Labrador and Nova Scotia.

LEGUMINOSAE

Like the rose family, the pea family while of great economic importance has never entered into herb lore to more than a minor extent; a few species are regarded still of medicinal value, including the native senna, *Cassia marilandica* L., which is used as a substitute for the African drug *C. acutifolia* with similar but less potent results. There are no salad plants or condiments among the peas adapted to northern gardens but several species are well known as home dyes.

Broom, *Cytisus scoparius* (L.) Link.

Broom is native to dry rocky hills and barrens in southern Europe and western Asia and is mentioned in the Bible as food sufficient for old men gaunt with hunger: "They pluck salt-wort by the bushes, and the roots of the broom are their food" (Job 30:4). It was used in Greece and Rome, not as food, but as a green dye, for which purpose it is still in use.

In Saxon England it was cited for use in medicine and the nameless Welsh physician of Middvai (d. 1233) who compiled a list of medicinal plants still extant mentions broom. Chaucer calls the plant by name in his *Canterbury Tales,* and it was used as a vulnerary like many another mild astringent. It was also used fresh or dry as a diuretic and purgative, and the ash of the foliage was drunk in wine for liver troubles. Unlike most old herbs,

63

broom still appears in the United States Pharmacopoeia, prescribed for dropsy, and affects the heart and blood vessels similarly to digitalis.

Broom is a shrubby perennial difficult to keep alive through the first winter in Northern states, but subsequently hardy although the fall shoots will die back. It spreads widely from the base and covers several square feet in a short time. Seeds are available but slow to germinate. The island of Vancouver, British Columbia, is overrun with broom, introduced from England and thriving in the mild moist climate; it also occurs on sandy barrens from Novia Scotia to Virginia, introduced by early settlers as a dye.

Broom is the symbol of humility and was adopted as the badge of the Norman line of kings descended from Geoffrey of Anjou, 1150 A.D., and who were subsequently known as the "planta genista," or Plantagenets; however, the species name *genista* meaning in Celtic "bush" was later applied to a closely related plant, *Genista tinctoria*.

Dyer's Greenweed, *Genista tinctoria* L.

Dyer's greenweed is a low shrubby plant similar to broom, but not thorny; it branches from the base and sends up striated green branches with undivided foliage, while broom has three-foliate leaves. Small yellow flowers occur in loose racemes half the size of those of broom.

This plant also is native to southern Europe, and is mentioned by Pliny and Virgil. During the Middle Ages it was a standard green dye plant called variously woodwax, woadwaxen, dyer's greenweed, dyer's broom, whin, and base broom. Used alone the shoots give a good yellow dye and when used with woad an excellent green. Alum is required to fix the stain.

It "was not well received in medicine," according to an old-time herbalist, but was an ingredient in a gout remedy and one for broken bones. Our early colonists planted seed at Salem for dyeing purposes and the plant escaped to Salem pasture lots, and came to be called "Salem woodwax." It spread very slowly and by 1814 "hardly extended more than a mile from town." By 1872 it extended scarcely three miles, but monopolized barren hillsides and colored them golden in June. Now the plant may be found around Lynn, Beverly and Swampscott and even in eastern New York State, possibly by transplantation. Would that most of the other herbs introduced at Salem had been as conservative!

DYER'S
GREENWEED

Weld, *Reseda luteola* L.

WELD

Weld, woad, and woodwax are similar names but represent very different plants, all three having been dyes of considerable importance in the past. Dyer's rocket, Dyer's mignonette, Dyer's weed, yellow rocket and Dutch pink are other names for weld, which gives a yellow dye used widely for cotton, silk, wool, and even for paper. With mordants, it also gives a good green.

Weld belongs to the Resedaceae, the mignonette family, and resembles garden mignonette, with a slender spike of minute greenish-yellow flowers and a small horned

65

capsule for a seed pod. The word *resedo* means "to calm" and this plant was formerly used as a sedative. It occurs sparingly in waste places in our Eastern states.

LINACEAE

※⊱⊰※⊱⊰※⊱⊰※⊱⊰※⊱⊰※⊱⊰※⊱⊰※⊱⊰※⊱⊰※

Flax, *Linum usitatissimum* L.

Linen is the oldest known fabric and flax is supposed to be a native of the Mediterranean countries from Greece to the Pyrenees, although it was cultivated in Mesopotamia in prehistoric times. It was widely grown in ancient Egypt and used for the finest clothing. When Herodotus visited Egypt around 455 B.C. he found the priests by law garbed in snowy linen, and Joseph was clothed by Pharaoh in "vestments of fine linen."

Hundreds of yards of the finest linen cloth were often wrapped around the mummy of an important Egyptian, linen of quality so fine and smooth that it can scarce be equalled to-day. The process of transforming the flax of the fields into fine raiment is depicted on the walls of Egyptian tombs and differs but little from the process in use to-day. Coarse strands of hemp with flax for strength were woven into the rope without which the massive blocks of stone could not have been transformed into the Pyramids.

The Jews cultivated flax and the Romans used mostly the product imported from Egypt but made into textiles at home. The Lake Dwellers of Switzerland (2000 B.C.–500 A.D.) used flax for fish nets, ropes and clothing, and flaxseed to flavor their bread, for the seed and rope have been found on lake bottoms in a remarkable state of preservation.

The crop is an exacting one although it rapidly impoverishes the soil upon which it is grown. It requires a moist subsoil, and early came to be a chief crop in Ireland. In our Northwest and California, it is grown widely, chiefly for the seed.

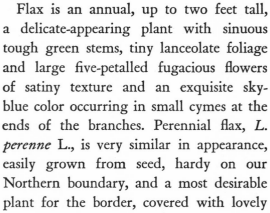

PERENNIAL FLAX

Flax is an annual, up to two feet tall, a delicate-appearing plant with sinuous tough green stems, tiny lanceolate foliage and large five-petalled fugacious flowers of satiny texture and an exquisite sky-blue color occurring in small cymes at the ends of the branches. Perennial flax, *L. perenne* L., is very similar in appearance, easily grown from seed, hardy on our Northern boundary, and a most desirable plant for the border, covered with lovely blue flowers up to noon of every day from midsummer to late fall if kept from setting seed. Several other species are offered for garden use.

Flaxseed or linseed has been used in medicine since ancient times, being valued for poultices for pleurisy, for ripening boils, for softening tumors, for drawing out thorns and splinters, in cough medicines and as a liniment for burns, and is still listed in the United States Pharmacopoeia and widely used in household medicine.

Hemp, *Cannabis sativa* L.

Hemp (see Picture 3 at end of book) belongs to the nettle family but finer grades are often mixed with flax in the same fabric. It is a coarse weedy annual growing up to ten feet tall, the inner tough fibrous bark forming the article of commerce. Mature plants are pulled and retted like flax and the separated strands used for making rope, sacks, sailcloth, carpets and so on, and as far back as ancient Greece finer grades were used for clothing and sheeting.

Hemp is a native of most of temperate Asia and due to its early and widespread cultivation now grows over much of Europe as well. It occurs wild in many parts of this country, having been brought in for cultivation. Much improved strains give a finer or a tougher fiber, as desired.

A resin develops on the foliage and flowering heads which finds appreciable use in medicine to relieve pain, allay spasms, and produce sleep, often substituting for opium. Formerly it was thought that only cannabis from India was potent in medicine but now plants grown even in Michigan are equally of value.

The plant is widely used in the Orient for smoking and chewing, being highly intoxicating in its effects. The seed is used in soap making and as bird seed, while the residue after extraction of the oil makes splendid fertilizer and cattle food. It is the marihuana now widely grown surreptitiously in this country and recently proscribed by law because of its baneful habit-forming effects.

RUTACEAE

Rue, *Ruta graveolens* L.

None of the old-time herbs has a more varied history than lead-colored rue (see Picture 4 at end of book) which has been

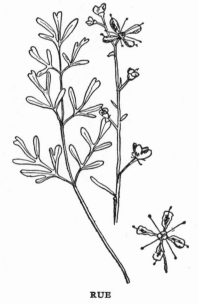

used in food, as a medicament, for strewing floors, as a symbol of remembrance, and in witchcraft.

The thick, smooth foliage of rue can scarcely be matched in color in all nature, a dull leaden blue-green with a whitened bloom, and the feather-veined leaf is divided into many leaflets which instead of tapering at the tips are broader there than elsewhere giving the leaflet the appearance of a tree toad's foot. The plant is a hardy perennial two feet tall, somewhat woody near the base, and all the young stems will die back over winter. It may be cut back to the root in early spring without damage to the plant. Seed is easily available and seedlings easy to handle. In fact, like most of the hardy herbs, the plant all too readily reseeds itself.

RUE

The flower appears in July on second-year plants and older, a dull golden four-petalled crumpled star nestling deep in a green calyx, several flowers appearing in a flat corymb. The seed pod is a several-loculated capsule.

The foliage is bitter but not poisonous and the chief value of the plant lies in the strong indescribable odor, at once highly disagreeable and fascinating, the species name of the plant, *graveolens,* meaning "having a strong or offensive odor."

Rue is a native of eastern Mediterranean countries and is mentioned in Luke 11:42 in Christ's denunciation of the Pharisees who "tithe mint and rue and every herb and pass over justice and love of God."

The plant is now found wild over much of Europe. It was used by the Greeks as a potherb and in medicine. In large doses it was a rank poison, but in small quantities was soothing and somewhat narcotic and was used in ointments for erysipelas, skin ulcers and the like, and the juice drunk for sore eyes. By Aristotle's time it was used as a disinfectant hung in fresh bunches from ceilings or scattered about floors to dispel insects, scorpions and serpents from dwellings. A sprig of the plant was hung round the neck as protection from disease, and this ancient custom continued down to the mid-nineteenth century.

By Roman times rue was even more popular and Pliny cites no less than eighty-four remedies in which it was an ingredient, saying "it is one of the most active of all medical plants." He also gives directions for its cultivation in the garden. It was believed to grow best if the plant was stolen, and was also said to thrive only on a place where the mistress was master.

Although in itself a poison, rue was used as an antidote for such things as aconite, mistletoe, fungi, serpent stings, bees, salamanders, and dog bites. The juice was used for leprous sores, ulcers, scrofula, erysipelas, the itch and other skin diseases.

The plant was used as food by the Romans and was so valuable that it came to have a place in every Roman household, "a few crops of rue" or rue tea preceding every main meal, and it is still used in Italy as a body regulator. Many Roman writers mention this use.

Mithradates, tyrant ruler of the province of Pontus in Asia Minor, having murdered most of his relatives who were close to the throne, anticipated similar extinction himself, and so compounded a potion consisting of all the poisons with which he might be dispatched, aconite, hellebore, fungi, opium, rue and so on, and drank minute doses of it daily, increasing the amount gradually until his body became relatively immune to them. This draught, the recipe of which was found on his body after he had been murdered with a knife, came to be very popular. With the passage of time the contents varied and the application modified, but it always contained rue leaves and was in steady demand until the middle of the nineteenth century. It gave rise in early Christian times to a host of lesser compounds, such as the "Drink of the Apostles," the "Drink of Antioch," and "Gratia Dei," some containing as many as a hundred plant and animal ingredients and used for all sorts of ailments. These secret formulae were the only medicinals available to the sick who had to pay exorbitant prices for them.

Rue is mentioned in the Talmud as a valuable medicine and went tithe-free. In the sixth century A.D. Alexander of Tralles in Lydia used it in the treatment of gout. In Saxon times it was imported in the dried state by apothecaries, and as soon as plants could be obtained and its hardihood established cultivation was begun in England and northern Europe. Charlemagne grew it, as did the monastery of Saint-Gall, and Alexander Neckham at

FOR NORTHERN GARDENS

Cirencester, England, in 1217 A.D. The Swedes cultivated it in 1400 — "a bitter but worthy grass."

> "Plant your sage and rue together,
> The sage will grow in any weather,"

reads an old rhyme.

The plant is mentioned in no less than thirty-five prescriptions in a single fourteenth century manuscript and used for almost every known disease from the itch, boils, ulcers, and snake bite to tuberculosis and the plague. Many directions commence: "Take twelve leaves of rue," adding numerous other herbs all pounded in a mortar fresh, and the resulting minute quantity of juice mixed with stale ale or wine or honey or even water, and eaten with a spoon or drunk for a definite number of days. Tuberculosis was rampant in this dark age — dark from a lack of windows and sunlight — and cough medicines were many, one reading: "Who-so haue the perlus cohu (perilous cough), take sauge, rue, comyn (cummin), and papyr and sethe hym to-geder with hony, eat a spoonful morning and eve and thou chalt be delyvered." Another "For spitting of blood" reads: "Take ache (smallage, wild celery), mynte, and rewe and betony. Boil with goat's milk and drink for three days."

An amusing ointment for gout uses juices of catnip, rue, comfrey, plantain, smallage, mayweed, and the fungus morel incorporated into the fat from all these animals — dog, sow, capon, deer, sheep, rabbit, cat, and badger. "Hit ys the best oyntment for the gout that ys."

From ancient times to the Renaissance sore eyes was one of the commonest of afflictions, often leading to blindness, and many herbs were used to alleviate the dimming sight. "For to have good syght and clere, take rue ilka day a pourcion and it shal wel clere thy syght," reads a fourteenth-century direction. Edmund Spenser knew of this use when he said in *Muiopotmos,* "Rank-smelling Rue and Cummin good for eyes," and Milton recognized the use of fomentations of rue and eyebright (*Euphrasia* sp. in *Paradise Lost,* Book XI) although it failed to brighten his own fast-fading vision.

Rue was also the strewing herb par excellence; most of those scattered about the floors of manors and churches were sweet-smelling, intended solely to impart their fragrance to the air about, but rue was used because of its reputation as a disinfectant, and if there had not been a germ of truth in this conception it is doubtful if so disagreeable a plant would have held its place for two thousand years, in spite of the fixity of ideas once implanted and once published.

Several outbreaks of the Black Death occurred during the reign of Edward III, from 1357 to 1368; superstition came to be rife and the people caught at a straw. The ancients had used rue, and so it was hung in rooms and carried in the hand to ward off the dread disease. Other outbreaks occurred in 1592, 1599, and 1603, 380,000 people dying in England in the last outbreak, and over a million in Egypt. Again in 1625, 35,000 died in England, and in 1665, in the worst attack of all, 68,000 in London alone. It is said that 33,000 plague victims were buried in a single churchyard, St. Johns, Regent Park. Much of our knowledge of these horrors comes from Samuel Pepys, who so graphically describes the great fire which at last put an end to them. He speaks of the quantities of rue strewn on floors and even streets.

Alessandro Manzoni gives an account of the plague which swept through Milan in 1630 in his novel *I Promessi Sposi,* when distracted people carried sprigs of mint and rosemary and rue and a vial of vinegar, not speaking to each other without holding the little twig before the mouth to prevent others' exhalations from entering, little recking that it was water and milk and the insects harbored in their clothing and not air which carried the germ.

Holinshed in his *Chronicle of Elizabethan England* (1577) says rue was sprinkled over the floors of the law and criminal courts just before prisoners were brought to the bar so that the justices would not catch jail fever. Dickens refers to such a scene at Newgate in 1775 in *A Tale of Two Cities* and the custom was in use in 1810, when the British botanist, William Thornton, says, "Our benches of judges have their noses regaled with the most fetid plant; this arose from the ancients' belief that mithridate, in which rue has a principal role, repels all poisons." A. E. Newton in his delightful *End Papers* (1933) says Sir Henry Dickens took him to Old Bailey where the desk and carpet in front of the judges' bench was scattered with herbs, "a custom introduced centuries ago to sweeten the air and reduce the chance of gaol fever."

Rue very early in history became symbolic of repentance and took its English name from this association — Old English *hreow,* "to be sorry for." In early Catholic churches, stems of rue were used for sprinkling holy water which symbolized the washing away of sins. This custom originated in the Roman purification of weapons and standards directly after a military victory, an aspergillum of laurel cleansing from blood-guiltiness. During the Middle Ages the Church generally used hyssop but rue was substituted often because of its supposed disinfectant quality.

It came to be called the "herb of grace," and even yet in rural England often goes by the name "herbygrass." Rosemary, the herb of remembrance, is often associated with rue in the language of flowers:

> "Reverend sirs,
> For you there's rosemary and rue; . . .
> Grace and remembrance be to you both,"

says Perdita in *A Winter's Tale* (Act IV, Sc. 4) and the gardener in *King Richard II* (Act III, Sc. 4) soliloquizes thus:

> "Poor queen! . . .
> Here did she fall a tear; here, in this place,
> I'll set a bank of rue, sour herb of grace:
> Rue . . . here shortly shall be seen,
> In the remembrance of a weeping queen."

Ophelia (*Hamlet,* Act IV, Sc. 5) says:

> "There's rue for you; and here's some for me:
> we may call it herb of grace o' Sundays."

It is also the symbol of sorrow, as expressed by Scott in the song in *Rokeby,* as the soldier takes leave of his lady love:

> "A weary lot is thine, fair maid,
> A weary lot is thine!
> To pull the thorn thy brow to braid,
> And press the rue for wine!"

Whittier has these beautiful lines on it:

> "I wait and watch: . . .
> And see across the twilight glance,
> Troop after troop, in swift advance, . . .
> For one shall grasp and one resign,
> One drink life's rue, and one its wine,
> And God shall make the balance good."
>
> — *The Waiting.*

Like rosemary, rue came to be widely used at funerals, probably from the reputation of both as disinfectants. Sir Walter Scott refers to this usage in *Rokeby:*

> "When villagers my shroud bestrew
> With pansies, rosemary, and rue."

Besides surrounding the corpse, sprigs of the plants were given the mourners to hold and then throw into the open grave. The new mound was often planted to both plants or either.

Rue played still another role in herb lore for in old Arabian tales it was said to be potent against the jinn and in English fairy tales it is often mentioned. A man who was captured by the pixies and kept imprisoned underground, only allowed above by night, observed that the little folk always avoided a certain lead-leaved plant. Thereupon he plucked a double handful and gave it to his captors, whereupon the charm was broken and they had to let him go. To preserve a household against the baneful influence of a house brownie, the kitchen maids kept a bunch of rue hanging from the rafters. If they did not do so, the naughty elf would steal things by night and drink up their cream.

It was also an ingredient in witches' charms, worn to ward off evil influences. It is said witches in France would take to the air on a broomstick, crying:

> "By yarrow and rue,
> And my red cap, too,
> Hie over to England."

When our first colonists left Europe, the plant was at its height of popularity and Governor Winthrop had it in his Boston Common garden but Josselyn, English gentleman-traveller to the colonies in 1669 and 1672, says "rewe will hardly grow at all" around Salem, not realizing perhaps that the tops often die back to the root in winter.

Like many other herbs of considerable importance in the past, rue is used very little to-day; it is sold in limited quantity by druggists as an emmenagogue, but has strong competition and its chief use seems to be for roup in fowls.

MALVACEAE

One member of the mallow family is of great economic importance, viz. cotton (*Gossypium herbaceum* L.), and a few others enjoy some reputation as food and medicine, but as a whole the family is of little importance as "herbs."

The plants are coarse and save for the hollyhock, of rather secondary importance in the flower-garden. One species, however, the large shrubby marsh mallow (*Althaea officinalis* L.), was used in medicine by 200 B.C., the Greek name, *althaea,* meaning "to cure." The long thick root abounds in mucilage differing little from gum arabic and has been used in cough medicines from ancient Egyptian times to the present. The large percentage of starch in the root, twenty-five per cent., has made it popular for use in pastry and confectionery.

Marsh mallow is a salt-marsh plant naturalized from Europe and not adapted to garden culture. However, a close relative, rose mallow (*Hibiscus Moscheutos* L.) named for the ancient Greek poet Moschus, makes a beautiful if coarse garden plant, with its lovely rose flowers six inches across. It occurs in brackish marshes along our eastern seaboard and also inland where salt is found, as around Port Clinton and Sandusky, Ohio.

UMBELLIFERAE

The large aromatic and for the most part pleasantly scented carrot family contains many plants regarded as herbs. Foliage, seed, and root are all employed as condiments in cookery and the oils to mask unpleasant flavors and odors in medicines rather than for positive curative properties in themselves.

Caraway, *Carum carvi* L.

Caraway seed is one of the best known of all old-time herb products and is just as widely used to-day as it was in the Eighteenth Dynasty of ancient Egypt; it was prescribed by Egyptian priest-physicians before the Book of Exodus was written.

The plant is a native of southeastern Europe and western Asia and was taken to Egypt by traders. It supposedly takes its name from the ancient state of Caria, in Asia Minor, where it was cultivated in early times although it does not occur there to-day. The Arabians called the plant *Karauya* from this state, which was the seat of the ruler Mausolus.

Recognizable seeds have been recovered from ancient Swiss lake dwellings and the plant was grown by the Romans as a condiment. Galen, the Roman physician of the first century A.D., used it as a medicinal. We next hear of it as grown in the gardens of Charlemagne (812 A.D.). It was probably first used in medicine by the European apothecary shops to mask odors and flavors,

79

brought by the great trading companies who procured it in the East, and when found hardy introduced for cheaper use, and from thence spread to culinary use.

Many of the refinements of cooking reached England only after the Norman Conquest and in a cookbook of 1387 used by royal cooks for Richard II the seed seems first to appear under the name "careum." It was still being imported, however, and used along with coriander, anise, garlic and pepper, a condiment for kings and the nobility.

In the fifteenth century it was being grown in France for use in soups but its long delay in reaching the kitchens of the common people lay in the fact that its cultivation was not understood. The plant demands diligent care, coming into seed often only in the second year, then dying out. It requires clay soil and seed ripening at various times must be harvested periodically by hand before it darkens in color. By the Renaissance the plant was cultivated widely, large tracts in the south of England being devoted to its culture.

Turner (1551) is one of the first British herbalists to mention it, calling the seeds "caruwayes, which the pothecaries call carui." A few years later a physician found that "caraway breaketh wind," and the delightful custom rose of placing a little dish of the seed beside a baked apple. Cogan in *The Haven of Health* (1594) says: "Careway seeds are used to be eaten with apples and surely good for that purpose, for all such things as breed wind should be eaten with other things that breake wind."

Shallow says to Sir John Falstaff in *King Henry IV,* Part II (Act V, Sc. 3):

"You shall see my orchard, where, in an arbour, we will eat a last year's pippin of my own graffing, with a dish of caraways . . . and then to bed."

It is said the custom is still kept of serving roasted apples with a saucer of the seed at Trinity College, Cambridge, as well as at London Livery Dinners.

The seed was used in ground meats and sausage very early, for a reference of 1620 reads: "In meates I prefer the careways before fennel seeds." It was also used in biscuits, cookies, cakes and cheese, for once introduced and inexpensive the flavor immediately became popular.

Like many an herb, caraway was used in the treatment of various diseases during ancient times. Dioscorides, Greek herbalist who travelled extensively with the Roman legions and left an account of his findings, says the seed was soothing to the stomach and that it was given pale-faced Greek girls. Withering in 1787 says it was still being used in England for this purpose.

The plant is missing from the physic-gardens of all the early monasteries although it appears in a list of medical plants compiled in Wales in 1233 and again in Germany in the thirteenth century. However, it came to be used widely during the Renaissance especially in comfits, little titbits used in churches during long diatribes and often mentioned in literature.

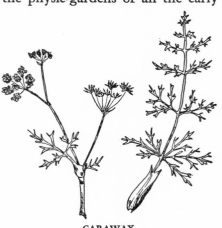

CARAWAY

By 1694 the essential oil was being extracted from the seeds and used as flavoring for foods and liquors — gin, wines, and light drinks — and it is still used in the German kümmel and in French cordials.

While the foliage and root played a minor part in the importance of the plant, still Parkinson, the sixteenth-century English herbalist said: "The roots of caraway are better eating than parsnips and the tender leaves are boiled as a potherb." The root is still used, especially in Germany.

The plant is a biennial or an annual in long seasons, up to two feet tall, with large finely dissected foliage and minute white flowers in large flat cymes. Seed is spindle-shaped, slightly crescentic, with conspicuous ribs bearing oil tubes. The plant is grown commercially in Europe as far north as Russia and Norway, in Morocco, in Japan and in this country. Northern-grown seed is said to be richer in oil and better in flavor than that grown elsewhere.

Parsley, *Petroselinum hortense* Hoffm.

Parsley is the universal garnish to-day, adorning alike the hotel chef's prize dishes and the housewife's mashed potatoes.

"Parsley, parsley, everywhere
On my daily bill of fare.

See that kippered herring staring
At the silly sprig he's wearing.

Be it steak or creamed potatoes,
Oyster plant or grilled tomatoes,

Squash or scrambled eggs or scrod —
Each must wear its little wad;

Each must huddle underneath
Its accursed parsley wreath.

Parsley, parsley, everywhere.
D —— ! I want my victuals bare."
— Margaret Fishback, *Out of My Head,* 1933.*

* Courtesy of E. P. Dutton and Company.

And, indeed, it is high time some of the other herbs are given a chance to show what they can do. Fennel, chervil, caraway, dill, anise, basil, balm, the two savories, sweet marjoram, thyme, and many of the mints are all superior to what George Rector calls the "queer, half-acid, half-musty flavor" of parsley, and if out of season they can be grown somewhere and shipped on ice like water-cress and the decorative ferns in meat markets.

Parsley is a biennial, or, if kept from seeding itself, a perennial, a foot or more high with much divided foliage and tiny yellow-gold flowers in flat terminal umbels. "Seeds," which are really fruits, are ovoidal with the characteristic oil tubes of the family. The plant has escaped sparingly from cultivation in our Eastern states but would scarcely be recognized except by a botanist, for it reverts to straight foliage. The plant has undergone radical changes under cultivation and many mossy curled varieties as well as plain may be purchased. Seed germinates slowly and there is an old saying in England that it goes three times to the Devil before it comes up. The Romans trampled on it and bruised the outer coat to hasten germination. It may require four weeks to appear above ground.

The plant is thought to have originated in Sardinia but was cultivated in ancient Egypt as a condiment. Both wild and garden forms were known to the Greeks. Homer speaks of it in the *Odyssey,* when Hermes goes to the cave of the nymph of the braided tresses, where all around her cave "soft meadows bloomed with violets and parsley." Theocritus favors the plant, mentioning it many times in his Idyls, and Moschus, his Sicilian follower, mentions "the green parsley and blooming crisp dill."

Pliny says the word parsley is from the Greek *petroselinon* "rock-breaker." The Romans held the little herb in great esteem for seasoning sauces — Horace refers to it as a garnish — and seeds are found on the sites of Swiss lake dwellings. It was one of the kitchen herbs grown at the monastery of Saint-Gall. It enjoyed favor in England long before the Norman Conquest, when very few condiments were known — garlic, onions, leeks, cummin, sage and thyme, with parsley about completing the list. Chopping tables were an essential part of the kitchen equipment of manors in this age, where herbs were minced for use in sauces to accompany meats and fish as well as for stuffings.

Miss Keeler relates (*Our Garden Flowers*) that the Emperor Charlemagne while dining at a bishop's palace was given cheese flavored with parsley seeds and liked it so well that ever after he had two cases of this cheese sent yearly to his capital and grew the plant for the edification of his countrymen.

Numerous recipes from the fourteenth century to the present attest the long-time favor of this herb, and poets from that time on sing its praises. Shakespeare, Robert Herrick, John Gay, Jean Ingelow and Keats all have interesting verses concerning the plant.

Parsley was brought to America before 1620, when John Mason, British sea captain, planted it on Newfoundland with a few other sturdy herbs. The Mayflower contingent grew it by 1629 at Salem.

The herb has enjoyed favor as a medicinal since ancient Greek times, the Roman physician Galen copying and thus perpetuating a Greek inscription on the Temple of Asclepius, on the island of Cos, a remedy containing parsley, thyme, fennel, anise and other herbs, powdered and mixed with wine and taken as a cure for most ailments of the time. This formula is the basis of the thousands of similar thericae which were so popular during the Middle Ages.

Pliny names seventeen remedies containing the plant but a

commentator says in a footnote to one edition in English: "What Pliny says respecting it (parsley) is a tissue of fables," and likewise what he says in respect to many another herb, for his vivid imagination and facile pen have perpetuated countless usages of herbs for which they are totally unfit.

The plant was an ingredient in the Mithradates antidote and most of the other secret formulae. Its chief virtue was said to be its effect on the bladder and stomach, for which reason, and not because its roots could force rocks apart, the Greeks gave it the name "petersilie" or stone-breaker. Several other herbs have been called stone-breakers, chiefly among them saxifrage. So potent was parsley considered for bladder and stomach ailments that root, seed and foliage all were used in one compound.

Parsley entered into folklore in the late Middle Ages and little children were told in England that their mothers found them in a parsley bed which was probably adjacent to every cottage. John Gay in a delightful "Recipe for Stewing Veal" flavors the knuckle with

> "Some sprigs of that bed
> Where children are bred."

The story persisted well into the eighteen hundreds and may still be heard in out-of-the-way places.

From earliest times, the ancient Greeks crowned some of their athletic heroes with this plant. Winners in the Olympic Games were crowned with olive, those of the Pythian Games with laurel, but the heroes of the Nemean and Isthmian Games for five hundred years (500 B.C.–67 A.D.) were wreathed with wild parsley.

Anacreon (b. 560 B.C.) sings to the cup in the November of man's life, when all victories are past and

OLD-TIME HERBS

"our wreaths of parsley spread
Their fadeless foliage round our head."

Parsley wreaths were also worn on lesser occasions in Greece, maidens and youths being thus crowned at public and domestic festivals. In a Theocritan Idyl (III) a lover crowns his beloved with it in token of his affection.

The foliage was strewn about floors and on beds on special occasions in Greece, as for instance at the annual harvest festival in honor of Demeter (Theocritus, Idyl VII).

The Romans also prized parsley very highly and used it for garlands. Horace sings:

"I have a cask of Alban wine,
Phyllis, that counts its years at nine,
And parsley in my garden-grounds
For garlands. Ivy too abounds . . .
To deck thy shining tresses."
— *Odes*, Book 4.

And again:

Fill tankards bright, thy toils to drown
In Massic: who shall quickest twine
The parsley or the myrtle crown?"
— *Odes*, Book 2.

Saint Paul refers to the parsley wreaths of the Roman athletes as "corruptible crowns" and Keats in *Endymion* includes the plant with others used as incense in Druidic rites.

There is one more use to which parsley was put in ancient times. It was used as funeral wreaths and the new mound covered with its fresh and lasting greenery. Later the grave was planted to the herb as a hardy evergreen covering.

Plutarch relates the story of a Greek force, on its way to meet an enemy, which became panic-stricken when it was met by a column of mules laden with parsley going to a city market; soldiers took the parsley for an ill omen of their fate in the ensuing battle.

Fennel, *Foeniculum vulgare* Hill

"Little things catch light winds, and fancie is a worm that feedeth upon fennel," says Lyly, in *Sappho,* 1584, for this tall feathery plant was regarded during the Middle Ages as hot and exciting, and the emblem of flatterers.

"Say, oh, how this smells of fennel!" says Ben Johnson sarcastically (*The Case Altered,* 1601), and a modern writer calls it "that crazy plant which looks something like celery and tastes far too much like licorice."

But fennel goes much farther back in history than the Middle Ages for it was mentioned in the Ebers Papyrus (1500 B.C.), although it is thought the plant was not a native of Egypt but taken there from lands to the east of the Mediterranean and cultivated like many another exotic.

The Battle of Marathon was fought on a field covered with a weed "marathron" which is none other than fennel, the battle-name having lost an "r" somewhere through the ages just as the word marjoram has gained one through an error of an amanuensis. The noted runner Pheilippides (the preferred spelling of the word) who in 490 B.C. hurried to Sparta to spread the alarm that the Persians were landing on the shores of Greece was presented with a sprig of meadow fennel upon his return, and ever after the hero is shown in statues with a sprig of meadow fennel in his hand.

OLD–TIME HERBS

"Let this, foreshowing the place, be the pledge!
(Gay, the liberal hand held out this herbage I bear
— Fennel — I grasped it a-tremble with dew — whatever it bode.")
           — *Pheidippides,* ROBERT BROWNING.

and later in the poem these words appear:

"The space 'twixt the fennel-field
And Athens was stubble again."

Because the herb had brought victory to the Greek warriors, it came to be symbolic of success and one of the garland plants with which athletes were crowned and was woven into garlands and chaplets worn by Greek youths and maidens at private as well as public festivals.

The annual fete to Adonis, favorite of Aphrodite, symbolizes the return of spring and is far older than the Christian Easter; small pots of seedling plants which faded rapidly, called Adonis' gardens, were carried through city streets to denote transitory pleasures, fennel and lettuce being the chief offerings.

In Aristophanes' drama *The Knights* the sausage seller celebrates the news of an offer of peace from Lacedaemon thus:

"I dashed down to the market-place headlong;
And bought up all the fennel, and bestowed it
As donative, for garnish to their pilchards."

The Romans also used the plant for garlands but they ate it as well, boiled as a green vegetable and chopped fine for salads served with vinegar and oil. It is still popular with Italians wherever they are; the whole plant is used or only the white thickened basal stalks.

The genus name *Foeniculum,* diminutive of *foenum,* refers to the pleasant haylike odor of the plant which occurs on the Campagna so abundantly that until the recent drainage project it appeared to be a cultivated plant. The plant was taken to Arabia and India very early as a potherb and it is grown to-day on the slopes of the Himalayas as a cool-weather vegetable. It is also used by the Japanese as a vegetable.

We know very little of gardening in Europe in Saxon times, when almost constant warfare destroyed possible sites of a fixed abode and the people had to depend on the fruits of the hunt rather than on the products of established orchards and gardens. The monasteries were the only permanent habitations and were it not for the records of their gardens our knowledge of herbs — indeed of history itself — during the first thousand years of the Christian Era would be meager indeed. Most of the herbs known to-day were grown in these secluded gardens, but most of them as curative agents rather than as culinary condiments.

In northern Europe fennel appeared first as imported seed for medicinal use. Only in the fourteenth century was the seed used in the household, and it was still expensive. A woman in *Piers Ploughman* says:

> "I have a pound of garlicke
> A ferthyngsworth of fenel seed, for fastyng days,"

and it is said that eight pounds of seed was required by a king's household during a single month.

It was probably cultivated in France a century earlier, as indicated in Chaucer's translation of *The Romaunt of the Rose* from the French of de Lorris of 1237 A.D.:

> "Then went I forth on my right hand
> Downe by a litel path I fond
> Of mintes full and fennel green."

However, by the fifteenth century the herb was grown widely in the north, for it was found to mature and set seed in England and came to be popular as a potherb. Shakespeare mentions it as an accompaniment to a dish of conger eels (*King Henry IV,* Part II, Act II, Sc. 4) and chopped fine it was used with mackerel, a usage which has continued to this day.

When it became abundant, the fresh aromatic foliage was strewn upon floors of monasteries and manors and even of

FENNEL

churches to mask unpleasant smells beneath. Fennel must have been ideal for this purpose, with its strong licorice aroma. It has also long been used to flavor gin and the seed is used in Germany to flavor cookies and bread, like caraway and anise. It was also used like the former to accompany baked apples. In Italy pork liver is rolled in fennel seed and roasted.

Fennel had still another use in the past; it enjoyed considerable medical reputation very early in history. The Greeks used it for failing sight, and Pliny relates that serpents look around for fennel while casting their skins, the herb clearing their temporary defective vision. The tenth-century Leechdoms copied the old usage, saying fennel was good "for mistiness of the eyes." In a fourteenth-century manuscript it is listed "for fading eyesight."

The gentle hint of Ophelia to her brother Laertes, "There's fennel for you" (*Hamlet,* Act IV, Sc. 5), refers to the belief that "the plant hath a wonderful propertie to take away the film or web that overcasteth and dimmest the eyes," the sister hoping by its use figuratively to quicken his consciousness to the evil which surrounded him.

FOR NORTHERN GARDENS

Longfellow sums up the virtues of fennel thus:

> "Above the lowly plants it towers,
> The fennel with its yellow flowers,
> And in an earlier age than ours
> Was gifted with the wondrous powers—
> Lost vision to restore.
> It gave men strength and fearless mood,
> And gladiators fierce and rude
> Mingled it with their daily food:
> And he who battled and subdued
> A wreath of fennel wore."
>
> — *The Goblet of Life.*

It had other medicinal uses than for renewing fading sight, and was a dyspeptic and sudorific remedy in Rome, Arabia, and China; was grown by early European monasteries and in Spain for these uses and even yet appears in the United States Pharmacopoeia as an ingredient in laxative syrups. Fractions are separated out and used also in the present-day perfume industry.

To a lesser degree than rue or dill, fennel was hung in bunches over doorways to ward off evil spirits.

Goldsmith speaks of

> "The hearth, except when winter chilled the day,
> With aspen boughs and flowers and fennel gay."
>
> — *The Deserted Village.*

Fennel is a biennial, or, if kept from fruiting, a perennial, up to four feet tall, much branched, with large leaves finely dissected and almost capillary. Flowers occur in large flat cymes of minute golden-yellow florets. Roman or sweet fennel is a variety of common fennel, smaller in size with darker foliage and thicker basal leaf stalks. Several other species and varieties occur in southern Europe, differing little in appearance.

Giant fennel (*Ferula asafoetida* L.) is a closely related plant which exudes a resin from the scarified root called in medicine asafoetida which finds wide use as a carminative and antispasmodic in croup, colic, asthma, whooping cough, and bronchitis and may be the lost *silphium* of the ancients so highly valued for these same purposes. The plant is native to Persia.

Prometheus is said to have brought fire from Mount Olympus to the earth in the hollow stem of *Ferula communis,* which has a stem so stout that it is used for canes. Prized manuscripts have been secreted in the hollow stems, and the pith taken from the cane is a valued slow-burning tinder. This species is hardy in our North and makes a desirable plant for the back of the perennial border.

Sea Fennel or Samphire, *Chrithmum maritimum* L.

Samphire, a plant known by name only in this country, is a small fleshy-stemmed and much branched umbellifer which clings to sea cliffs from the Mediterranean to England and was highly prized by the ancients as a salad and pickle.

"It is terrible to see how people gather it," says Sydney Smith in his *History of Waterford* (1774), "hanging by a rope several fathoms from the top of the impending rocks, as it were in the air." In Shakespeare's time the herb was a favorite relish with meat, and the Earl of Gloucester

SAMPHIRE

is led by his son Edgar to imagine such a gatherer on the cliffs
below (*King Lear* Act IV, Sc. 6):

> "How fearful
> And dizzy 'tis, to cast one's eyes so low! . . .
> . . . Half way down
> Hangs one that gathers samphire, dreadful trade!"

The pretty name samphire is a corruption of "Saint Peter," in
French "Saint Pierre."

Fennelflower (*Nigella sativa* L.) bears no relation to fennel
save in name. It resembles the garden Love-in-a-Mist (*N. damascena*) and is a member of the Ranunculaceae. It is identified as
the "fitches" of Isaiah 28:25–27, the black seeds sprinkled over
bread like sesame and cummin, all pleasantly aromatic when
roasted. It is also called gith, black cummin and small fennel.
The Romans used it as a spread for bread and also in medicine.

Fenugreek or Greek hay (*Trigonella foenumgraecum* L.), with
the pleasing odor of coumarin or vanilla, was a potherb of Roman
times in India, Egypt and China, and a medicinal from ancient
times through the Dark Ages almost up to the present. The
plant, a member of the pea family, seems unavailable to American gardeners although still cultivated in France and Germany.

Anise, *Pimpinella anisum* L.

Anise was rare and highly prized in England during the Middle Ages. An old manuscript informs us that the London Bridge
was repaired by a fund obtained from the imposition of a special
tax on imported condiments including the seed of anise. The
royal linen of Edward IV (1480 A.D.) was perfumed with "lytill
bagges of fustian stuffed with anneys" and as late as the reign

of Charles I (1630) the seed was still being imported only after the payment of heavy duty.

However, anise is an herb of great antiquity, the name appearing in the Ebers Papyrus, a manuscript containing names of medicinal plants found on a mummy of 1500 B.C. In a scathing denunciation to the multitude assembled at the temple for their laxity in paying their taxes, Christ says, "Ye tithe mint and anise and cummin and have left undone the weightier things of the law" (Matthew 23:23), but to-day we think the "anise" is really dill, for anise was not a native of Palestine, while dill grew there.

The plant is indigenous to Greece, Crete, and Egypt and Hippocrates lists it with his simples. Pythagorus says held in the left hand a prescribed time it was a sure cure for epilepsy, and Theophrastus lists it in his great work *Enquiry into Plants.* In Roman times, if not long before, the seed was used to flavor foods; Pliny says, "Be it green or dry it serveth well for seasoning all viands and the kitchen cannot get along without it." He says the seed was used for some sixty ailments, as a carminative in flatulence and indigestion, to promote sleep, for hiccough, for lung troubles and for affections of "the diaphragm where the body is tightly laced." One is perhaps surprised to learn that tight-lacing was a fashion in Roman times! The seed was also chewed to sweeten the breath, as it still is in the Orient. Galen says the seed was used in epidemics of cholera, and, although this may not be the cholera of modern times, it indicates that even in Roman times devastating diseases were known.

Alexander of Tralles, sixth century A.D., used anise in his famous gout remedy, and it is mentioned by early classicists in India. "Water of anise" has for long been a popular perfume in India. The plant was grown by Charlemagne under the name *anesum,* and while it was grown in some early monasteries it was omitted from others. The Abbot of Cirencester grew it in England around 1217 A.D. and it appears in a French list of the fifteenth century in a "garden for herbes of good smell," which included as well camomile, lavender, balm, sweet mary and pennyroyal.

It seems to have been established in England when the *Mayflower* left for America, for it was one of the first herbs planted around Boston. Josselyn (*New England Rarities,* 1672) says: "Coriander and dill and annis thrive exceedingly but annisseed and also the seed of fennel, seldom come to maturity, the seed of annis is commonly eaten by a fly."

ANISE

In Josselyn's comment probably lies the secret of the limited culture in northern Europe in previous times, for although an annual the plant does not ripen seed in northern climates except in very warm summers and seed must be imported annually. Anise foliage, unlike that of many umbellifers, is not finely dissected or capillary, but entire, deeply notched or divided into three leaflets sharply serrate on the margins. The plant is delicate and sprawling with a heavy cyme of white florets. Seeds are spindle-shaped with numerous corrugations which contain oil tubes. Much of the seed used in this country comes from Syria and retails in herb shops at around fifteen cents a pound.

Anise still enjoys much of its ancient reputation and is a home remedy for stomach ailments, especially of children, a few drops of the oil in a teaspoon of sugar being not at all difficult to take. The oil in hot water gives relief in difficult breathing and is used in remedies for asthma and bronchitis. It is also a constituent of cough medicines and holds a place in the United States Pharmacopoeia. It is also widely used in alcoholic and non-intoxicating beverages, and the seed is used whole in cakes, on bread, and in prepared meats.

Chopped anise foliage is a pleasant garnish for white sauces and a round-rinded cheese from the Netherlands is liberally sprinkled with the seed.

Star anise (*Illicium anisatum*) is a tree of the magnolia family native to southwestern China and supplies much of the commercial anise oil possessing the main constituent of the seed, anethole.

Pimpinella saxifraga L. is the third Burnet, the other two being members of the rose family. It is a salad plant known to the Greeks and found on meadows of Central Europe. Sir John Evelyn says of it in his Diary (1693), "Burnet Pimpinella is a common Sallet furniture." The seeds were sugar-coated and favored in the age of comfits, like coriander and caraway.

Chervil, *Anthriscus cerefolium* (L.) Hoffm.

Garden chervil is well known in Europe, being widely used in France and Switzerland to flavor soups, salads, in sauces for fish and shellfish, and in stuffings for fowl and red meats. However, it is but little used in this country and deserves to be better known, although it is true chervil is one of the lesser herbs. It is an eight-inch plant much branched, with finely-dissected but not capillary foliage, and tiny white flowers in the characteristic umbel. The species name *cerefolium* means "pleasant leaf," and the foliage has an odor somewhat like that of licorice but not rank or strong. Seed is readily available. From a spring sowing the plant flowers and goes to seed by the first of July even in our Northern states and must be planted several times for a suc-cession, although it reseeds itself. The seed is unusual, being exceedingly slender, needle-like, black, odorless, and large for an um-bellifer.

Chervil was known to the ancient Greeks and in Rome the foliage was eaten as greens, the root used as a vegetable. Charlemagne grew the plant under the name cerefolium and it was grown at the Benedictine mon-astery of Saint-Gall, in the ninth century. It is mentioned in Saxon literature and used by the English in medicine to a minor extent and as a potherb, "the young leaves im-parting flavour to soups, stews, and salades."

CHERVIL

Evelyn speaks of "chervil, whose tender tops are never want-ing from our sallads." As late as 1860 the foliage was being chopped fine for stuffings, salads, omelets and so on, but in recent years like many another old-time herb it has practically disap-peared from English cookery.

Coriander, *Coriandrum sativum* L.

Coriander is a pretty little annual almost worthy of a place in the flower-garden for its wealth of pinkish-white bloom re-sembling Queen Anne's lace and its dainty aromatic foliage. Seeds, or rather fruits, are large and round, finely corrugated, almost white, and strongly aromatic with a flavor all their own.

Although the foliage is sometimes chopped fine and used as

a garnish and flavoring in salads, it is the seed which has for long held popularity as an herb, used to-day in pickling spice, in bread and cakes, in sausages, and in the little sugar-coated candies called in England "comfits."

The original home of the plant was probably the cornfields of Tartary and across Asia to India. It was recognized very early in Hindustan and Burma for its culinary possibilities and became a constituent of Indian curry, "being as essential for the seasoning which flavored the dry rice of the pariah as for the dishes of his Mussulman lord." All alike chewed the seed for its pleasant flavor, it being second to anise in popularity for this use.

CORIANDER

The Chinese boiled the root as a vegetable and used the seed in beverages and confectionery even in ancient times.

"Coriander" means "having a buglike odor" but, as with many another aromatic plant, individual preference varies widely and the herb would not have held favor through long ages if most people had agreed with the man who gave it name. The plant was listed in the Ebers Papyrus, contemporary with the youth of Moses, and it was sufficiently familiar to the Jews of 1500 B.C. to be mentioned in the Bible (Exodus 16:31, and Numbers 11:7) as a simile: The hungry Children of Israel on their return from Egypt were commanded by Moses to gather the mysterious mushroom which appeared on the plains each morning called "manna, and it was like coriander seed, white."

The Greeks were familiar with the little round fruits and Anacreon mentions them in one of his lyrics. In Rome *polenta,* a barley bread, was flavored with coriander and it was pounded fine, mixed with cummin and vinegar, and spread over meat to keep it fresh.

The plant was taken north early and appears in a list of plants grown in France in the ninth century and also at the monastery of Saint-Gall. Saint Gall was a follower of the Irish missionary Saint Columba, and attracted to his hospice near the shores of Lake Constance so many followers that his institution became one of the most celebrated in all Europe. The Emperor Charlemagne was in close touch with the monastery and much of the knowledge we have of that great monarch comes through writings of a monk at Saint-Gall. Extant plans — the oldest extant architectural plans — of the whole magnificent institution show two gardens, one consisting of sixteen long rectangular beds of "physick" herbs adjoining the hospital, and one of similar very long beds of kitchen herbs adjoining the scullery, all encompassed by high protecting walls. In the vegetable beds were grown garlic, shallots, parsley, celery, chervil and coriander along with cabbage, beets, carrots and parsnips. Potatoes obviously are missing and food consisted for the most part of game animals and fish flavored with herbs and of soups and stews into which were thrown the vegetables and bunches of herbs for flavor.

During the fifteenth century the seed is mentioned as used in distilled liquors and the essential oil was extracted for this use as early as 1575. Our first colonists brought over the seed and to-day it is cultivated widely in Europe and South America for use in liquors and in medicine.

In Egyptian times the plant enjoyed favor as a remedy for pains in the head. In Rome it had many uses. It is mentioned in Saxon leechbooks, and was an ingredient in many of the secret nostrums of the Middle Ages. In the seventeenth century it was used like caraway to dispel wind and aid in digestion and it is still rather widely used as a carminative and to disguise unpleasant tastes and odors. It is also used in the perfume industry.

Coriander is easily grown in northern gardens and from spring-sown seed comes into fruit around August 1 when the whole plant may be pulled for winter use, the dry foliage crumbled for flavoring and the seed used in mixed spices. It readily reseeds itself.

Lovage, *Levisticum officinale* (L.) Koch.

Lovage or love-parsley is an old-time herb of lesser importance which has long since lost favor and become almost unknown except in the wild state. However, with a renewal of interest in the old herbs, plants are readily available in this country. A well-established plant will attain six feet in a season, with large coarse much-divided celerylike foliage of strong celery smell, and umbels of tiny yellow-green flowers. Fruits occur in pairs, like those of most of the carrot family, flat on the inner surface and strongly ribbed and curved on the outer, with oil tubes bearing a strong aromatic essential oil for which the plant was formerly noted.

FOR NORTHERN GARDENS

Lovage is a native of Liguria, in northwestern Italy. The Greeks knew it for its sweet aromatic roots and pleasantly flavored fruits, and so did the Romans. Galen says the root was used in medicine for alimentary complaints. Probably through his recommendation it was cultivated in physic-gardens of the monasteries

LOVAGE

along with rue and pennyroyal and tansy and sage and a host of other herbs, one old name for it being "lubestico." Both Charlemagne and the monks of Saint-Gall grew it under the name "leuisticum." Turner (1553) says lovage was good for "a cold stomach" and Culpeper (1656) that it aids digestion and eases pains and ague. He says the seeds were powdered and used for quinsy. Hill, a century later, says the fresh root is used for jaundice, the seeds to dispel wind like caraway and anise.

The plant was brought to New England very early but just when we do not know. Mrs. Alice Morse Earle in her charming *Old-Fashioned Gardens* says: "Old-fashioned folks kept up a constant nibbling in church, not only of seeds but of bits of cinnamon or lovage roots, or, more commonly still, of sweet flag. Many children went to brooksides and the banks of ponds to gather these roots." Charles Dudley Warner speaks of doing this when he was a boy in *On Being a Boy*. But the lovage which they gathered probably was not the Old-world species gone wild but one very similar to it and indigenous to this country, *Ligusticum canadensis,* or angelico, with similar large aromatic roots.

101

Scottish lovage or sea lovage (*Ligusticum scoticum*) is a sim-

ilar plant native to subarctic regions of both hemispheres, occurring in marshes along the seacoast from New York northward. This plant was known as early as 500 A.D., the stems and foliage used as a potherb or eaten raw in salads, having an aromatic flavor but also acrid and nauseous to those not accustomed to it as pottage. Withering (1787) says it is highly valued as greens and salad material in the rugged rocky isle of Skye.

SCOTTISH LOVAGE

Dill, *Anethum graveolens* L.

Dill (see Picture 5 at end of book) is one of the few umbelliferous herbs with a disagreeable odor, as the species name implies, but in spite of this fact it is one of the best known of all the herbs and one grown almost as commonly as parsley or sage. The word suggests pickles, and bunches of the ripening herbage appear in farmers' markets along with pickling cucumbers, the whole plant as well as the ripe seeds used to flavor pickling vinegar.

The herbage is also used to flavor pea and meat soups and chopped fine in salads and white sauces although rather rank in flavor, and it gives a pleasing variety to the usual parsley garnish. Seeds alone find fewer uses than most seeds of this aromatic family although they have for long been used to flavor gin and in India are sold in bazaars to be eaten as titbits like anise and caraway and also powdered for use in curries.

Dill is a tall annual resembling fennel, the flower cymes differ-

ing from fennel in being dull yellow rather than white. Fruits
are large, flattened, ovoidal, tan in color, with winged ribs which
carry the oil tubes, and they have a strong hot pungent flavor,
which characteristic gives the plant its genus-name, *Anethum,*
from the Greek "to burn." Dill readily
reseeds itself and, once planted, one is
never without it.

DILL

The plant is native to the Mediterranean countries, southern Russia, the
Caucasus and Egypt and was recognized
as of medicinal value by the author of
the Ebers Papyrus — the first medical
manuscript, which Professor Ebers purchased in 1850 on the steps of Shep-
heard's Hotel in Cairo. An Arab had
found it wrapped with a mummy and
had hawked it about the streets in vain
until he found a disinterested purchaser
in the German archaeologist. Professor
Ebers only later discovered that his cas-
ual investment of an insignificant sum was of inestimable value to
physicians the world over.

In Matthew 23:23 is reference to the three insignificant herbs
— "anethon," mint, and cummin — with which the Pharisees
were attempting to pay their tithes. The first word was formerly
translated "anise" but since the Greek word for dill was *aneton,*
modern commentators substitute "dill" for "anise" in the verse.

Dill was native to Greece and used there as a condiment.
Theocritus mentions it several times, a chaplet of dill crowning
the forehead several times in his Idyls. Moschus, Greek lyric poet
and follower of Theocritus, in his beautiful ode on the transito-

riness of human life says: "Alas, when once in a garden the mallows have died, or the green parsley, or blooming crisp dill, they live again after, and spring up another year. But we, the great, and brave, or wise of men, after we have once died, sleep a right long and boundless slumber from which none are roused" (Idyl III).

The Romans were familiar with the garland plant and condiment, and Horace, Virgil and Pliny all sing its praises. When the plant reached England we do not know but it was relatively late. Spenser in his *Muiopotmos* mentions "hed-purging Dill," and Culpeper says "the seed often smelled into stayeth the yexe or hiquet" (hiccough) and that it was used for wind on the stomach.

Dill was a plant hated by witches, and to be rid of them one had only to hang a bunch of the herb in the entry.

The plant contains an essential aromatic oil used like caraway as a carminative for children and as a vehicle for the administration of nauseous drugs. The production of the oil is still in an experimental stage in this country and the plant is grown to a limited extent in Maryland and in the Middle West — however, in increasing quantities.

Angelica, *Angelica archangelica* L.

In ancient times, plants were dedicated to the gods, the vine to Bacchus, the oak to Jupiter, and so on, and many herbs still retain such names as the herb of Jupiter (*Agrimonia eupatoria*), Jupiter's beard (houseleek, *Sempervivum tectorum*), Jupiter's staff (great mullein, *Verbascum thapsus*), Zeus' wheat (*Diospyros lotus*), Jove's flower (*Dianthus* sp.), Juno's tears (vervain, *Verbena officinalis*), Venus's looking-glass (*Campanula perfoliata*),

Mercury (*Mercurialis annua*), and all through botanical nomenclature, genus names of mythological characters are prime favorites, such as Adonis, Artemisia, Andromeda, Callirhoe, Cassiopaea, Phyllodoce, Circaea, Daphne, Helenium and Narcissus.

Then there is a class of plants named for Old-Testament characters such as Adam's needle (a wild chervil, *Scandix pecten-veneris*), Adam's rod also called Aaron's rod (great mullein, *Verbascum thapsus*), Solomon's seal (gen. *Polygonatum*), Aaron's beard (Kenilworth ivy, *Antirrhinum cymbalaria*) and Job's tears (*Coix lachrymae*).

Later, in the time of the saints and apostles, their names were given in profusion, and many of them still linger, such as St.-John's-wort (*Hypericum* gen.), St.-Peter's-wort (*Ascyrum stans*), St. Andrew's cross (*A. hypericoides*), St. Anthony's turnip (bulbous buttercup, *Ranunculus bulbosus*), St.-James'-wort (tansy ragwort, *Senecio jacobaea*), St. Bennet's herb (poison hemlock, *Conium maculatum*) and St. George's herb (garden valerian, *Valeriana officinalis*).

At some botanical period there was an epidemic of names such as the herb of grace (rue), the herb of friendship (*Sedum anacamperos*), the herb of the cross (vervain, *Verbena officinalis*), Our Lady's mantle (*Alchemilla pratensis*), Our Lady's shoes (*Aquilegia vulgaris*), Our Lady's bedstraw (*Galium verum*), and Our Lady's thistle (*Cnicus benedictus*) but the herb par excellence of all those used in early medieval times when religion was paramount in the thoughts of the people was the herb of the angels, the herb of the Holy Ghost, angelica. The whole name, *Angelica archangelica,* indicates the high place it held in herb lore. Death in the form of pestilence suddenly swooping down upon whole populations perhaps kept them overzealous in good works, and angelica, used to dispel the plague, came to be regarded with awe and reverence. Superstition, always closely allied to religion, and folklore abound with references to this plant.

Angelica is a large coarse biennial attaining six feet or more in height, with large hollow stems two or three inches across and compound pinnately dissected finely serrate foliage. Flowers occur in large terminal cymes of tiny whitish bloom. The whole plant is sweetly aromatic with odor resembling that of licorice.

It is native to northern Europe as far as Lapland and makes a good plant for the back of the border or better still on the bank of a stream. Seed may be purchased abroad and the plant in this country. Several species are native to this country, all tall coarse aromatics. The purple-stemmed angelica (*A. atropurpurea*), found in cool swamps and moist places in the north, is used in domestic medicine in this country.

Angelica first appears in literature during the Middle Ages and seems to have been unknown to the ancients. Turner says (1578), "It defends the heart against all poisons," and a contemporary, "Angelica, that happy counterbane, sent down from heav'n." Another writer, in 1676, says, "People do make a sprightful infusion in Angelico, against contagions." It had many other uses in medicine, all, however, minor.

But however useful in medicine, it is rather as a culinary product that angelica is known. A juice was distilled in 1640 and used as a flavoring. At this period the root of elecampane was candied as a popular sweetmeat, a citation reading: "Use elecampan root candied, or, for want thereof, anglice root." To-day angelica is a standard candied product retailing at around eighty cents per pound, and imported from France. The apple-green transparent stalks are sliced thin and used in tiny pieces to decorate pastries and confectionery, especially around the holiday season. Stalks formerly were blanched like celery and eaten as a relish and the root makes a good yellow dye.

Cummin, *Cuminum cyminum* L.

Cummin is certainly a fragile little plant as it behaves in Northern states, but because of its long and most honorable history, every modern herbalist should know what it looks like. Seed is readily available. The seedlings attain full growth within a few weeks, and the plant flowers, sets seed, and is gone before midsummer.

The plant seldom attains more than a few inches in height, the stem is weak and crooked, and the three or four comparatively large and compound leaves are divided into hairlike filaments. At the top is a heavy cyme of carrotlike white flowers which helps to bear it down, developing typically fusiform seed, the aromatic quality of which gives the plant its reputation as an herb. However, even in its native habitat cummin does not attain more than a foot in height.

The plant is supposed to have come originally from Abyssinia and western Asia and it has been cultivated in Egypt, Arabia, China, Palestine, and elsewhere since very early times. It occurs wild to-day in no part of the world. Wherever it has been grown, cummin has been regarded as a delicate plant, and if not kept well hoed was killed by a dodder, and was susceptible to fungus blights as well. Pliny says, "It seems to grow on the surface of the soil and seems hardly to adhere to it at all."

The seed was invaluable to the ancient Hebrews as a spread for their unleavened bread. A remarkable picture of agriculture in what we have regarded as an arid country occurs in Isaiah 28:25–27. "Doth he that ploweth to sow plow continually? Doth he continually open and harrow his ground? When he hath levelled the face thereof, doth he not cast abroad the fitches and scatter the cummin, and put in the wheat in rows, and the barley in the appointed place? For the fitches are not threshed with a sharp threshing instrument, neither is a cart wheel turned about upon the cummin; but the fitches are beaten out with a staff, and the cummin with a rod." (Fitches are also called black cummin or nigella or fennelflower (*Nigella sativa*). The sarcastic reference to coarse methods of harvesting the two condiments indicates their frailty and need of care.

Cummin is also mentioned in ancient Sanskrit and Persian manuscripts and it was well known in Greece. One Greek husbandman says to another in a Theocritan Idyl (X), "Don't cut your hand in splitting the cummin," for misers were called bean-splitters, and the cummin seed was far too small for even them to split. The smallness of the seed and its familiarity led to an old Greek proverb for stinginess and the appellation cummin-skimmers (*kuminopristes*), which are still in use.

The Romans likewise knew the little grain and ground it fine to spread on bread as the Indians still use sesame flour, in place of butter. Cummin was sold along with pepper as a substitute for that condiment, which was expensive in Rome. Pliny says people who ate too much cummin became pallid and thus had the appearance of being profound scholars. Horace and Persius likewise mention cummin-paleness.

During the early Christian era cummin continued in favor in the East and in southern Europe and gradually spread north. There is a record that a Norman monastery used 150 pounds of it a year and Saxon cooks in England had it imported at considerable expense, one such recipe stating that garlic could be used to season a goose but that a hen should be more delicately flavored, with cummin.

FOR NORTHERN GARDENS

At the enthronement of the Archbishop of Neville in 1466, no fewer than 104 peacocks were placed on the table in full panoply, the birds skinned and the head and tail feathers laid on the banquet table and then the fowl sprinkled over with cummin and roasted, sewed up in the rest of the skin, and brought to the table as a final course capping the feast.

After the fourteenth century, however, the seed lost much of its popularity, cheaper home-grown herbs taking its place, but it is still used in Indian curry and to a lesser extent in southern Europe.

The seed was used in medicine in ancient times and is cited in the Ebers Papyrus as a tonic and Hippocrates used a tonic of cummin and sesame seeds powdered and mixed with honey. Pliny mentions some seventy remedies in which it was used. It was grown in early convent gardens and mentioned in many electuaries of the Dark Ages and as late as the eighteenth century was regarded as a stimulant and remedy for stomach ailments.

One of the numerous treatments for sore eyes, a common complaint for hundreds of years, consisted of rose petals, fennel, rue and cummin foliage steeped in water, a linen cloth saturated with the juice and laid over the eyes upon retiring. Spenser speaks of "Rank smelling Rue and Cummin good for eyes" (*Muiopotmos*) and Emerson repeats the old belief thus:

> "Rue, myrrh, and cummin for the Sphinx
> Her muddy eye to clear."
> — *The Sphinx.*

Cummin is used widely to-day in India as an astringent, but in western Europe and America it is employed chiefly in veterinary medicine for ulcers from insect bites in cattle.

The oil contains two aromatic principles, cumic aldehyde and

109

cumene, which are used to a minor extent in the perfume industry and in flavoring liquors.

Smallage, *Apium graveolens* L.

Smallage or wild celery is native to salt marshes throughout southern Europe and the Caucasus; it was early recognized as of medicinal value but was too acrid and noxious for culinary use. It was prized as a garland plant, along with parsley and fennel, victors of the Nemean games being crowned either with smallage or parsley, which, we do not know for certain.

Theophrastus and Galen knew the weed and the Romans discovered that the wild plant could be hilled up and blanched, after which it was transformed into the mild fragrant plant we know as celery. They ate it raw in salads and boiled the root as a vegetable. Lucian says funerary meats consisted of eggs, beans, lettuce and smallage.

Celery was one of the first condiments to reach the country of the Gauls and Franks, being introduced into northern Europe by military men upon returning home from Roman conquests. Charlemagne grew *apium* and it became a standard monastic herb. Many medieval manuscripts mention smallage, small ach, smalache or smale ache, and Turner (1553) says, "Smallag hath suche a stronge savour that no man can eat it wyth hys meate." The Roman blanching custom had been lost through the passage of time and the plant reverted to ditches and brackish meadows.

However, the anonymous author of *The Complete Gardener* (1719) says, "We earth our celery plants quite up with earth from the high raised pathways," thus blanching the foliage and removing the strong weedy flavor and most of the toxic quality.

The cultivation of celery to-day is an exacting industry and the plant has passed from the class of luxury condiments to that of a staple vegetable. Seed is used in pickling spice, in cheese and sausage. It is very small, round, dark in color, and is sold by the ounce in city herb shops, coming mostly from France and high in price.

MINOR UMBELLIFERAE

Bishop's Weed, *Aegopodium podagradia* L.

Most gardeners are only too familiar with bishop's weed, having at some time introduced it as a pretty ground cover only to regret their action for, while the foliage is attractive, the plant soon gets out of bounds and spreads by runners which are difficult to extricate from the soil.

The genus name is from the Greek, meaning "little goat's foot," for the leaf is divided into three equal leaflets the pale green color of which is relieved by splashes of white which give the plant its colloquial name, "snow-on-the-mountain." The insignificant bloom is similar to Queen Anne's lace.

The plant had some reputation in medicine and in Europe the tender young foliage was eaten in salads. Goatweed is attractive as a foundation planting on the north side of a house between the wall and a driveway where it cannot escape. It thrives with a minimum of care and covers difficult areas satisfactorily.

Sweet Cicely, *Myrrhis odorata*

Children in rural America delight in finding sweet cicely in rich woodlands for its stems are sweet and pleasant in flavor although the foliage resembles that of poison hemlock. Four species of *Osmorrhiza* are found in our Eastern state, with fernlike foliage, hairy or smooth stems and long slender blackish fruits resembling those of chervil. All are strongly scented like licorice or anise.

However, the sweet cicely of old is another species, *Myrrhis odorata;* seeds are obtainable in this country and Mons. Correvon says the plant is a hardy desirable subject for the back border for its sweet aromatic much dissected foliage but that it demands rich moist soil. Seedlings are very slow to germinate, sometimes taking a whole year, and are very sluggish when once germinated.

Sweet cicely was known to the ancient Greeks who valued it in food and medicine, calling it *seseli.* Holinshed (*Chronicle,* 1577) says myrrh or mure was used in England in early Saxon times, "being not uncommon as a salad." Gerard (1577) speaks of "great cheruill or myrrhe," for its flavor is similar to that of garden chervil and was used for the same purposes. The root was used in medicine, the expressed juice drunk "against the plague" probably from a resemblance in taste to angelica.

There is one more usage, and this a most unusual one: the large dark-brown seeds nearly an inch long were ground fine and used in the north of England in the seventeenth century for polishing and perfuming oak floors and furniture.

BORAGINACEAE

Borage, *Borago officinalis* L.

The foliage of borage (see Picture 6 at end of book) is exceedingly rough and hairy not unlike that of *Anchusa italica,* but nevertheless the young foliage has been used as a potherb since

BORAGE

ancient Greek times and is still widely used for the cooling, cucumberlike flavor of its juice.

Borage is a member of a family known chiefly as noxious weeds, rank-growing plants often despised because of their small clinging burs. Plants attain a height of two feet, with large coarse gray-green foliage thickly beset with long stinging hairs. The individual flower is very beautiful — scarce to be matched in the whole plant kingdom — a sky-blue five-pointed star nearly an inch across, with long stamens meeting and tapering to a central black point. The flower is not unlike that of our wild "Shooting Star," *Dodecatheon meadia,* but since usually only a single one is out on a stalk at a time and is bent vertically downward and partly buried in a nest of long gray hairs, much of the individual beauty is lost. In spite of the habit of the flowers, however, a few plants or borage are well worth a place in the herbaceous border and are no more weedy than the highly prized anchusa, with the same porcelain-blue flower.

Borage is an annual, sometimes a biennial, and seeds are readily available. Seedlings afford mild but pleasantly flavored greens for the pot is thirty to forty-five days, for after flowering the foliage becomes rank and too hairy. The name borage is from the Latin *burra*, "rough hair," and is pronounced in England as indicated in the old couplet

"I borage
Give courage."

Borage is a native of Persia, Asia Minor, Greece and Italy, and is one of the conspicuous flowers of Sicily often described by writers. It may be the nepenthe of Homer, and Pliny says in wine it drives away sadness and brings pleasant forgetfulness. The late Egyptians and Arabians grew it for use in beverages, the physician Avicenna (980–1037 A.D.) mentioning its pleasant flavor. It was used during the fourteenth century in western Europe as a febrifuge, from the cooling sensation it gives, and also in the kitchen as indicated in this 1450 A.D. recipe for "cooking a hare in wortes": "Take colys, betus and borage, avens, violettes, malvis, parselie, betony, pacience, the whites of leeks, and the crop of the nettle, parboil and presse out the water, hew the hare small, and cook." Surely the rabbit flavor was well disguised!

William Turner, one of the greatest and earliest of the large school of herbalists and founder of Kew Gardens, says (1548) that "borage is an excellent sallet herb and also when eaten with bread and butter."

It had considerable reputation for use in "cool tankard," a light beverage frequently mentioned in literature, which consisted of water, cider, lemon juice, borage, clary, sometimes burnet, and various other herb juices. Richard Jefferies says in *Round About a Great Estate;* "The deserted house was rarely visited — only perhaps when some borage was wanted to put in summer drinks. For a thick growth of borage had sprung up by it, the plant with its scent of cucumber grew very strong, the blue flowers of which might be supposed to have been inserted exactly upside down to the real method of attachment."

Comfrey, *Symphytum officinale* L.

Comfrey and bugloss, boraginous pasture weeds of our East and Middle West, have long histories as herbs of minor importance. Comfrey is a coarse hairy perennial two to three feet tall, with large entire leaves and clusters of drooping yellowish-white to red-purple tubular flowers and a long stout root which is very mucilaginous even after being dried. It is to the last characteristic which the plant owes its reputation, going by these common names: healing blade, bruisewort, knitback, boneset, backwort and so on. The genus name, *Symphytum,* comes from the Greek meaning "to cause to grow together" in allusion to the mucilaginous character.

Comfrey comes from Asia and was known by 400 B.C., when Herodotus recommended it for mechanically preventing the flow of blood. The Romans likewise knew of this quality and the plant was taken to northern Europe as a valuable curative agent and appears in monastery lists and Saxon leechbooks of 1000 A.D. During the fourteenth century it was held in high esteem "to heal rasped throats," for quinsy and whooping cough, and was used as a poultice for bruises and open wounds.

Beaumont and Fletcher knew of its healing quality and mention it in *The Knight of the Burning Pestle* thus:

Jasper after beating Humphrey unmercifully says to him in derision:

> "Go, get to your night-cap and the diet
> To cure your broken bones."

Jasper's sister sighs:

> "Alas, poor Humphrey!
> Get thee some wholesome broth, with
> Sage and comfrey,
> A little oil of roses and a feather
> To 'noint thy back withal."

Our first colonists planted it at Salem and Governor Winthrop on Boston Common, and it was introduced into New Netherlands before 1649. Josselyn (1672) says it was in much repute as a plaster for wounds and as a cough medicine.

Viper's Bugloss, *Echium vulgare* L.

Viper's bugloss, "whose flowers can never decide whether to be blue or red," is one of the most beautiful flowers in the whole plant kingdom, with large showy petals of heavenly blue turning pinkish, and long curving daintily poised cerise stamens. The plant is not one for the flower-garden, however, because of the vicious thickly-set stinging hairs which beset stem and leaves and because of the long tap root which defies removal. Bugloss, like the hawthorns and thistles, is avoided by cattle and sheep and soon comes to take over whole pastures until, as Crabbe says (1783), "the blue bugloss paints the sterile soil the color of heaven above."

FOR NORTHERN GARDENS

Bugloss is a biennial from Asia by way of Europe. The name *Echium* is from the Greek for viper, either because these reptiles found a haven under its spiny canopy or, as Henslow says, from "a fancied resemblance of the foliage to the spots on the skin of the viper." The roots were used in ale and the potassium ash of the foliage for mouth ulcers and as a gargle for sore throat, but to-day bugloss is recognized only as a most pernicious weed of an exquisite blue.

VIPER'S BUGLOSS

The root of dyer's bugloss, *Anchusa tinctoria,* was formerly used as a dye for woollens, giving a rich blood-red color.

VERBENACEAE

Vervain, *Verbena officinalis* L.

Everyone knows the common vervain of roadsides and wet meadows which blooms at the same time as boneset and joe pye weed and makes of our lowlands in August and September a riot of white and rose and purple. Our vervain, *V. hastata,* is a collectable herb, used to a limited extent in medicine. During the Revolutionary War it was used to stanch the flow of blood, like New Jersey tea.

However, the Old-World herb was another species, *V. officinalis,* indigenous to the Mediterranean littoral but brought to this country for its medicinal properties and now gone wild and become a pernicious weed locally in cultivated fields from Maine to Texas. It resembles the native species, with similar wandlike spires of purple bloom.

The name vervain means in Latin "sacred herb" and as such the plant was regarded for centuries, common names being Juno's tears, holy plant, herb of the cross, herb of grace, pilgrim's cross and simpler's joy. In pagan times it was the purification herb par excellence and the altar of Jupiter was cleaned with it before the feast of the gods. Houses were purified with it in Greece and it may have been the plant used to cleanse the table of Baucis and Philemon upon the visit of the strangers although one of the mints is also regarded as the aromatic used.

Thus early symbolic, vervain was woven into garlands for special religious festivals and Virgil says priests in celebrating their rites

"In purest white . . . their heads attire,
And, o'er their linen hoods and shaded hair,
Long twisted wreaths of sacred vervain wear."
— *Aeneid,* Book XII.

It also decorated altars both in temples and the home:

Festoon these altars and fat vervain burn,"

says Virgil (Book I). This writer mentions vervain many times in his various works, the force of its powers indicated in this passionate appeal:

"Burn rich vervain and frankincense that I may array with magic spell to turn my lover's cold mood to passion!"
— *Eclogues,* Book VIII.

Horace in his charming Ode to Phyllis (Book IV), indicates its use in the home thus:

"I have in my garden, Phyllis, parsley for weaving garlands; I have a large abundance of ivy wherewith you bind your hair and brightly shine. The house is smiling with silver; the altar, twined with wreaths of holy vervain, longs to be sprinkled with the sacrifice of a lamb."

Virgil's love of quiet pastoral life is indicated in this quotation from the *Georgics* (Book IV):

"I saw a heavy Corycian swain, lord of a few acres of unclaimed soil, a domain too barren for the plough, unfitted for the flock, and ungracious to the vine. And yet, as he planted his potherbs here and there among the bushes, with white lilies and vervain, and fine-grained poppies about them, he matched in contentment the riches of kings."

Vervain was an herb of magic. Pliny tells of a messenger sent to a home to demand restitution of stolen goods, who carried with him a sprig of vervain to assure return of the goods lest the holder bring upon his head the wrath of the gods. Verbanarius, one of the ambassadors sent by the Romans to a certain enemy, wore a garland of this plant to insure his personal safety, as a modern warrior might carry a flag of truce (Sir Thomas Elyot, *Castell of Helth,* 1539). Livy says the ambassadors to a truce "should carry with them, one by himself, certain flint stones and likewise verven."

The Druids of Devon and Cornwall looked upon the plant as a magic herb; it was used in foretelling events and gathered at the rise of the dog star. On Midsummer's Eve, the turning-point in the sun's movement, in villages of Germany, says a sixteenth-century writer, people young and old gathered about fires wearing chaplets of mugwort and vervain, and performing ceremonies intended to work a charm upon the sun and lure it back again.

This rite performed on a sick man and copied from a fourteenth-century manuscript is part of a very old superstition:

"If a man lie sick, to know whether he shall live or die, take vervain in thy right hand and take his right hand in thine; and let the herb be between, so that he doth not know it. Ask him how he fareth and how he hopeth of himself. If he feels he is doomed, he will die, but if he be hopeful of recovery, so it shall be."

However, the plant has still another, and pleasanter role in literature, as depicted by John Fletcher in his charming pastoral drama *The Faithful Shepherdess* (1609), upon which Milton is said to have based his masque *Comus.* Clorin watching over her flocks and sorting over the various herbs she has collected on the mead recites the virtues of each as she mourns her dead lover. Of vervain she says:

FOR NORTHERN GARDENS

"Thou, light vervain, too, thou must go after,
Provoking easy souls to mirth and laughter,
No more shall I dip thee in water now,
And sprinkle every post and every bough
With thy well-pleasing juice, to make the grooms
Swell with high mirth, and with joy all the rooms."

Fletcher was well-versed in the virtues of various herbs and it is quite probable that Shakespeare's usage was gleaned from his close friend and one-time collaborator.

But the bitter is ever mixed with the sweet, and an old writer says of a lady:

"Thou art like the veruen, poyson one waye and pleasure an other."
— THOMAS LODGE, *History of the Duke of Normandy,* 1591.

Vervain had still one more usage — and no herb had more — it was a symbol of death:

"Sad cypress, vervain, yew, compose the wreath,
And every baneful green denoting death."
— VIRGIL, *Aeneid,* Book IV.

Our garden verbena is a species of the same genus, much improved from a South American wild flower by selection and cultivation.

Lemon-scented verbena, *Lippia citriodora,* belongs to a related genus, and while often called an old herb was introduced to the trade in 1785 from Buenos Aires. The foliage is sometimes used for tea, especially in Spain.

LABIATAE

Individuals of three great families comprise nine tenths of the medicinal and culinary herbs of former times, the Umbelliferae, the Compositae, and the Labiatae. The first contains plants of mild and pleasing aromatic quality used widely in the kitchen but in medicine chiefly to mask unpleasant tastes and odors; the second group is used widely in medicine and only secondarily in the kitchen; while the mints, comprising some two dozen well-known and easily-grown herbs, have long and most interesting histories both as recognized curative agents and because of their strong, invigorating, almost invariably pleasant aromatic odors used widely to enhance flavors of foods. With little decorative value in the garden, the mints are widely grown for their refreshing leaf odors and their often pleasing gray-green crinkled foliage. Most of the members of this family are hardy in northern gardens and very easily grown from seed or cuttings.

Germander, *Teucrium chamadrys* L.

During the great horticultural renaissance in the sixteenth century, gardens consisted of beds of plants set inside elaborate geometrically-patterned borders, and these minute hedges were often more interesting than the specimens they encompassed. Such hedge material must be hardy, as nearly evergreen as possible, capable of being kept down to less than a foot in height and still be bushy enough to make a dense growth. It must be compact and grow but slowly, staying within reasonable bounds.

Plants which could be adapted to these clipped borders were in great demand but few in number. Box, rosemary, lavender, lavender-cotton, hyssop and germander about completed the list, and no plant save box surpassed the last for the purpose, with its shrubby growth and woody stems, its neat, thick small and glossy foliage.

The species name *chamadrys* is from the Greek meaning "ground" or "low," for the plant rarely attains a foot in height, the common name, germander, being a corruption of this word through the old French and Middle English. The origin of the generic name *Teucrium* is unknown although, like that of many plants, it is probably mythological; Teucer was a son of King Scamander, mythical king of Troy from whom the famous Asia Minor river is named; his capital was Teucria and the inhabitants thereof Teucri, of which our words Troy and Trojans are corruptions.

No less than six *Teucriums* are native to this country, widely different from the old-time herb plant. *T. chamadrys* was totally unknown in northern Europe until the sixteenth century, when gardeners searched the known world over for unusual plants to enhance the elaborate gardens of the aristocracy. Rembert Dodoens, the Flemish physician and herbalist (1517–85), says that germander grew wild on the stony hills of his native Brabant and was transferred to English gardens during his lifetime, where it admirably fulfilled the demand for a tiny hedge plant.

This is one of the few members of the mint family to attain a woody growth and remain evergreen in character. The leaves are tiny, saw-toothed, very glossy and dark in color, and relatively thick. Also, unlike most mints, the foliage is almost odorless even when crushed fine. The plant grows very slowly and the new leaves which are produced all summer are much lighter in color than the older. Flowers are inconspicuous, red-purple, tiny, tubular, occurring in small terminal spikes in July and August.

Although it is listed in catalogs as hardy throughout our range, the plant needs generous protection in our northernmost states

GERMANDER

and even then the capillary stems will die off and an occasional plant be lost. It is being used as rock-garden material rather widely, but is difficult to grow from seed, being generally propagated by divisions and cuttings.

Some species of this genus have been used as remedies as far back as the time of Hippocrates, and Dioscorides and Pliny both mention the name. Galen copied a popular cure-all from the Greeks which contained germander, horehound, pennyroyal, lavender, saffron, fennel and carrot seeds, all macerated and the juice incorporated into wine and honey and eaten with a spoon — seemingly a very pleasant dose save for the fact that the ash of viper was added. Such formulae were called *theriaca* from the name of a venomous serpent, and later on "electuaries," and were sold in earthen pots throughout Europe and the Near East as antidotes against poisonous insects and reptiles as well as remedies for the known human ailments, the list of which was considerably shorter than at present.

A well-known gout remedy of the mid-eighteenth century was called "The Duke of Portland's Gout Powder," consisting of germander, aristolochia and centaury, the herbage powdered and taken daily in wine. But, adds a commentator, "along with every gout-remedy went a careful administration of the patient's diet."

Horehound, *Marrubium vulgare* L.

Horehound is one of the least interesting of all herbs because of its weedy habit and its propensity of filling the whole garden with seedlings. It is one of the few mints with an odor having no saving grace of sweetness, but none the less has been and still is an important plant which every home herb-gardener should have at least once.

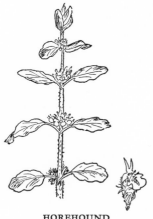

HOREHOUND

Seeds are readily available and the young plants thrive apace on the poorest and driest of soil, branching from the ground with weak, sprawly stems which root at the nodes so that a single plant comes to occupy several square feet of space. Leaves are round-ovate, bluntly-toothed with long petioles and resemble those of catnip but are more hoary. Flowers are tiny, white, tubular, and occur in dense whorls in the upper axils of the stems. The plant is a perennial.

The common name, horehound, comes from the soft white woolly coating of the young shoots and leaves and the accepted spelling from earliest times is horehound and not "hoarhound," which is often used to-day; this fact is easily traced. Other names are houndsbene, and marrube. The genus name is from the Hebrew *marrob,* meaning bitter-juiced. The plant has been used from early Greek times in medicine, but not as a culinary herb. It is a native of western Asia, northeast India, north Africa and the Mediterranean countries of Europe. Hippocrates used it to heal the circular sores which seem to have been common in Greece and difficult to cure; they may have been leprous sores.

Dioscorides says that in his time, the first century A.D., the plant was a roadside weed in Greece; nevertheless it was widely used in the treatment of phthisis. Pliny, in Rome, gives no less than thirty remedies in which it was used and says it was a plant of great utility in the treatment of coughs and pain in the chest, the same purposes for which it is widely used to-day. Few of the old drugs had any positive curative value but this is one of the few which was potent. Like many another odoriferous plant, horehound was used in Rome to repel serpents and scorpions which made life miserable to the ancients, even in cities. It is sad to note that in many of the recommendations against snake bite, the clause "except the asp" is added; for that serpent's bite, no herb was potent. Horehound was also used for jaundice and scrofula and in Nero's time was administered in large doses as a purge to counteract the vegetable poisons which were so convenient a mode of eliminating one's enemies.

The plant appears in Saxon leechbooks of 1000 A.D. under the name "haran haran" and in later works as harehune, horehune, and maruil. Like many other plants, it was first imported from the south by apothecaries and only discovered to be adapted to northern climates when the price became prohibitive and heavy duties assessed.

It was in medical use in Stockholm by 1400 and soon thereafter became very popular, for it is mentioned in numerous places. One herbal directs that the young shoots and flowering tops be boiled with honey to a thin syrup and used "for coughs, hoarseness of long standing, and all disorders of the lungs"; another, of 1607, reads, "Tak the fat of a calf and marrube with juyce of leeks" for coughs and colds, a remedy (save for the first ingredient) which is still in use.

In the nineteenth century and possibly before the plant juice was incorporated into a candy for the treatment of coughs and this confection became very popular — a use which only now seems to be dying out although horehound candy or lozenges may still be found on drug-store counters in winter.

Horehound is still used to a considerable extent in the manufacture of cough syrups, elixirs and lozenges, and is listed in the United States Pharmacopoeia and National Formulary. It is grown commercially to a limited extent in this country and is also collected from the wild growth before flowering and sold to drug houses. It contains a volatile oil, a resin and a crystalline bitter principle, marrubin.

It was introduced into America by our very first settlers and occupied an important place in their gardens and medicine cabinets. Unlike some of the herbs, horehound at once began to spread, and to-day may be found from Maine to California, in places a pernicious weed rooting deep and seeding readily. Cattle will not eat it.

Catnip, *Nepeta cataria* L.

A plant or two of catnip springing up spontaneously in the garden is rather a welcome addition than a weed to be promptly uprooted and it does not spread so widely as to become a pest. Cats love to chew the herbage provided the gardener has bruised it, for they seem totally oblivious of its presence until the aroma enters the air. They seldom actually eat it.

Catnip is not a native of this country but was brought over before 1620 by Captain John Mason who planted it among the eleven herbs he considered essential to the Newfoundland fisher-man's garden. It was planted at Salem soon thereafter for its medicinal value and Josselyn found it growing wild there fifty years later.

The plant comes from temperate parts of Asia and Europe and the genus name *Nepeta* (see Picture 7 at end of book) is said to refer to Nept, a town in Tuscany. As early as 1265 a Ger-man manuscript mentions *kattesminte,* and *katesmunze* is the German equivalent to-day; the Italians call it *herba catti,* the French *herbe du chat,* and the accepted name in England is cat-mint. American usage prefers cat-nept or catnep, of which catnip is a corruption.

This herb was familiar to the Romans, used for ailments of the nose and throat, and the herbage was incorporated into some of the early electuaries and hence retained in herb lore throughout the ages. Our American Indians learned from the whites that a tea steeped from the foliage produced restful sleep, and down to the present day a hot, aromatic infusion is a favored remedy for children's mild stomach disorders, restlessness and colic. It is used also as a diaphoretic in incipient colds and fevers.

Catnip is still a collectable herb of some importance and is listed in the National Formulary. The oil finds wide use in veterinary medicine, and is used by trappers as bait to attract wildcats and mountain lions. The green herbage is said to give relief to poison-ivy burns.

Besides its use in medicine, the plant was regarded as a culinary herb for soups and stews, along with fennel, parsley, marjoram, leeks and the rest, chiefly during the fifteenth century. Potatoes were still unknown and the list of vegtables a short one, and people craved greens, even bitter ones, in early spring to modify the heavy winter meats and suet puddings.

However widely it was used in pottage, catnip was very popular as a pleasant beverage in the centuries before tea from the Orient was foisted upon the English people, and oldsters may still be found who prefer native teas to that from the Far East.

Calamint, *Clinopodium calamintha* (L.) Kunze

Calamint, similar in name to catnip, is unfamiliar to American gardeners but can be obtained. It is a dainty low perennial with foliage smaller than catnip but similar to it and tiny pink and

white flowers covering the plant with a cloud during most of the summer. The odor is not unlike that of catnip, not as strong, pleasanter.

In Roman times the plant was rubbed over meat "to keep it sweet" and it was also used to flavor stews and roasts. In medieval ages it was highly prized as an herb tea to induce sweating in fevers, for colic in infants and for mild stomach disorders.

Edmund Spenser in *The Faerie Queen* (1596) says

AMERICAN CALAMINT

"The aged nourse had gathered rew and calamint"

but for what childish ailment we do not know.

While calamint is not found wild in this country, a similar species occurs in many states, *Clinopodium nepeta* (L.) Kunze, coming from Europe probably as a garden plant. It is similar to calamint and came into the writer's garden with seed of winter savory. It spreads widely by seedlings but makes a pretty terrace plant.

Ground-Ivy, *Glecoma hederacea* L.

Gill-over-the-ground, cat's-foot, Robin-in-the-hedge, alehoof, alecost, alehove, field balm — are only a few of the colloquial names for the humble and obstreperous little creeping mint which is a pest in damp lawns rather than a plant to be introduced into an herb-garden. Ground-ivy is difficult to eradicate, for it spreads rapidly by long weak-stemmed runners which break off when pulled, leaving many rooted nodes to start new plants.

The plant is native to middle Europe, Greece, and Italy, and long ago was taken to China and Japan. It has escaped from cultivation and is found in many parts of the world in forests and along shaded roadsides. The genus name *Glecoma* comes from the Greek meaning "thyme" or "pennyroyal." The small rounded

leaf is deeply incised and long-petioled and the tiny purple tubular flowers grow in clusters in the leaf nodes. The whole plant has a strong disagreeable odor.

The Greeks and Romans used it in herb teas to induce perspiration in incipient colds. It appears in English manuscripts around 1300 A.D. under the names heyhove and hale-

GROUND-IVY

houe, and was used to a minor extent in medicine. Most of the common names of the plant, however, come from its use in the brewing of ale. The name "gill" is from the French *guille* meaning "to ferment," and Turner (1597) says, "The women of our northern parts do turn the herb Alehove into their ale, but the reason thereof I do not know." Withering as late as 1787 says, "The leaves of Alehoof are thrown into the vat with ale to clarify it and give it flavour."

Almost any bitter plant which was not poisonous seems to have been used experimentally in the steeping of bitters and ales, sweet mary, tansy, sage, wormwood, sweet gale and others included. But after the introduction of hops all the old herbs lost favor and continued to exist out of sufferance and for household medicine.

Alexander Pope honors the little plant by bringing it within the sharp satire of his pen when he scorns the "art" of topiary gardening, at its height in the seventeenth century. All the animals that ever were and some that never existed were created out of yew and box; he commends to gardeners of the period: "St. George in box, his arm scarce long enough now, but will be in condition to stick the dragon by next April; a green dragon of the same, with a tail of ground ivy for the present; Edward, the Black Prince, in cypress; an old maid of honour in wormwood; and a quickset hog shot up into a porcupine, having been forgot during a week of rainy weather." * Quickset is privet.

Sage, *Salvia officinalis* L.

Every cook knows sage and regards it almost as essential a condiment as salt and pepper; if only one herb is grown in a corner of the vegetable garden it is generally this plant. A bundle of dry sage, one of summer savory, strings of onions, corn and apples seem to suggest the dusty attics of our forefathers, along with the spinning wheel and the long-horned beetle bootjack.

* S. Reynolds Hole, "Our Gardens." London, 1899.

Sage is easily grown from seed and is entirely hardy in our Northern states. It can be cut fresh in December in many states but loses little in drying. The plant is neat in habit, the gray-green crinkled foliage and large purple tubular flowers almost worthy of a place among the flowers. The two varieties, *S.*

officinalis rosea and *alba,* are very attractive, the one with rosy bloom and the other with white-mottled foliage.

The genus name comes from the Latin *salvare,* to save, in allusion to the reputed healing qualities of this, the type species. The genus is a large one comprising some five hundred species all indigenous to warm temperate climates.

Sage has been used in the kitchen since classical times and carried to all parts of the temperate world. It was widely grown in the early convent gardens and in eighth-century France was used "for potage," "for the coppe," and "to stylle."

SAGE

In Anglo-Saxon England fish was cooked in a sauce made of wine, sage, parsley, garlic and thyme, and a manuscript of 1393 described "pygges in sawse Sawge," an early mention of the custom of flavoring pork with sage. A cookbook of 1680 indicates that "sage is used commonly in sauces and to stuffe veal, pork, and roasting pigges." Charles Lamb in his essay upon roast pig says: "His sauce should be considered. Decidedly, a few bread crumbs, done up with his liver and brains, and a dash of mild sage." And sage has not lost any of its popularity with pork and is a staple ingredient in pork sausage.

"But where's the sage without the goose?" asks an herbalist

of 1750, for sage is just as necessary to the stuffing of goose as it is with pork, but obviously it is not used with meat with a delicate flavor.

Before the use of hops, it was a staple in brewing. Our New England forefathers brought from England the use of sage in cheese. Sage cheese, of pleasing color and aroma, is still made in the Netherlands. Dickens in *Bleak House* says grimly, "(The sea) is habitually hard upon Sir Leicester, whose countenance it greenly mottles in the manner of sage cheese."

Sage tea was the most important of the old-time herb teas and was used by Hippocrates. It is said that after a pestilence the people of ancient Egypt prescribed the use of sage tea for their women so as to make them more fertile and thus the sooner replenish their losses. The plant entered into many of the electuaries of the early Christian era although the mints did not attain the importance therein held by the seeds and herbage of the umbellifers.

However, the plant had medicinal virtues early recognized, especially as a diaphoretic in fevers and incipient colds. Charlemagne grew it, and Chaucer, who possessed considerable medical knowledge, infers that sage was used for broken bones:

"To use on . . . wounds and broken arms
  Some had their salves and others worked their charms,
  And sage they drank, and likewise remedies
  Of herbs, for they would save their limbs with these."
                                        — *Knight's Tale.*

From the fourteenth century sage seems to have been used for all sorts of ailments — sage wine, sage tea, sage bread — until the saying became prevalent, "How can a man die who has sage in his garden?

"Sage is for sustenance,
That should man's life sustaine." *

The noted herbalist, Gerard, who was head gardener to Lord Burghley during the reign of Queen Elizabeth and who grew 972 plants in the remarkable garden, says, "No man can doubt the wholesomeness of sage." He says, and it is oft repeated, that "sage ale quickens the memory and senses, good for the head and brain." John Wesley testifies to the value of sage tea thus: "Know that your having used it (China tea), it has brought you near the Chamber of Death." He was afflicted with palsy, but says, "The use of sage tea has fully answered my expectation: My hand is as steady as it was at Fifteen."

And if the sick in olden times could scarce avoid the use of sage in one semblance or another, so the dead were often laid away beneath it, for Samuel Pepys says he "observed between Gosport and Southampton a little churchyard where the graves were strewed with sage."

The essential oil of sage contains four terpenes which are used in the perfume industry, pinene, cineol, thuyone, and borneol; the plant is grown commercially in France and in our Southern states for these products. The field is mowed just before flowering time, the herbage dried and baled for shipment. One planting lasts four years.

Clary, *Salvia sclarea* L.

"Clary" (see Picture 8 at end of book) is a contraction of "clear-eye" by which name the plant was known for centuries;

* *A Handefull of Pleasant Delites,* Clement Robinson "and divers others," 1584. Reprinted many times, the most recent by the Spenser Society, London, 1781. Shakespeare was well acquainted with this book.

other names are see-bright and eyebright, indicating its chief use. Pliny says in Rome there were 253 diseases of the eye alone, which statement indicates one of his flights of fancy; but during the most unhygienic Dark Ages we know that people were afflicted with many eye troubles. Inflammation led to pus and many seeds were used to clear this film away, that of clary being mucilaginous in character. Even in ancient Greece the seed was used for this purpose.

In the Saxon leechbooks it appears as "sclareye," the "s" possibly an error due to copying, as several other errors in herb names have been perpetuated. Later the herb came to be called "Oculus Christi," indicating its chief use. However, it enjoyed some reputation as a sudorific, as a mild astringent, and as a cordial; it was "a great strengthener of the back and reins" (Turner, 1553) and a plaster made with the juice would draw out thorns and splinters.

However, after the sixteenth century other medicinals supplanted it, but it continued in use in beverages. Rhenish wine was made more "heady" by the addition of clary; it was used in muscatel and the plant is still called in Germany "muscatel sage." Home-brewed ales in Europe still often contain the plant. A cordial, clary water, was popular in the eighteenth century, made from clary flowers in wine. A recipe of 1751 uses brandy, sugar, cinnamon, and clary flowers with a little ambergris.

Although the whole plant has a very strong, disagreeable odor, it was formerly used as a potherb, and clary fritters was a well-known dish.

Clary is a six-foot biennial with a branched raceme of large subtly-colored flowers of attractive tubular shape and considerable size. Flowers are a pearly-mauve and the calyx pale rose. Together with the large crinkled gray-green foliage they are very effective in the back of a perennial border. The plant readily reseeds itself. It is a native of the eastern Mediterranean region and was brought to America around 1620. Josselyn comments on it in 1672: "Clary never lasts but one summer for the roots rot with the frost." This was but natural, for the plant dies after flowering once. However, new seedlings readily spring up and one planting generally suffices for a permanent display.

Bergamot, *Monarda* sp.

True bergamot is an Italian tree of the citrus family, the species name derived from the name of a city, Bergamo, around which its culture centers, the oil being extracted from the orangelike fruit and used widely in the perfume industry.

Several of the mints possess a lemonlike leaf odor, including the Monardas. The genus is a New-World one, half a dozen species being found from Quebec to British Columbia and on the arid plains of our Western states. All are pleasantly scented. The species generally grown for ornament in the garden is *M. didyma,* found on moist soil in the Eastern states, other names for the plant being Oswego tea, fragrant balm, bee balm, red balm and Indian's plume; it is a stout sharply four-square stemmed perennial two feet tall with soft downy serrate entire foliage and flat dense clusters of flowers with brilliant red tubular corollas.

The red monarda is an old-fashioned plant favored by our grandmothers and taken to Europe where it became very popular a hundred years ago. Mons. Correvon in *Rock Garden and Alpine Plants* says, "We had Oswego tea in my grandmother's garden in 1860 and my mother always used to have some branches or leaves of monarda on her table."

M. fistulosa, a species similar to the above but with soft lilac flowers, covers dry hillsides with its delicate bloom in August in our Midwest and readily hybridizes with *M. didyma.*

Horse mint, *M. punctata,* a native plant, was used rather extensively in medicine half a century ago as an aromatic stimulant to relieve colic. The American Indians used it as a hot infusion to induce sweating, in incipient colds, a practice taken up by the early whites. Monarda oil was used as a perfume in hair oil when this cosmetic was made at home from bear's grease, and many an American still living remembers when bear's fat was rendered for the oil which had many home uses.

The Monardas were taken to France and cultivated for their oil, which finds wide favor in soaps.

Balm, *Melissa officinalis* L.

(See Picture 9 at end of book.)

Some of the most beautiful passages in Shakespeare refer to balm. In *King Richard II* (Act III, Sc. 2) the rightful heir to the throne had himself liberally anointed with the consecrated balm-oil thinking thus to make himself secure in his new seat, saying:

"Not all the water in the rough rude sea
Can wash the balm off from an anointed king."

Later on the king resigns from the throne and is sent to the Tower, where he is later killed for weakness and extravagance. He says sadly,

"With mine own tears I wash away my balm,
With mine own hands I give away my crown."
— Act IV, Sc. 1.

King Henry IV bitterly assails his dissolute son whom he accuses of wanting to take the crown even before the father is in his grave:

> "Let all the tears that should bedew my hearse
> Be drops of balm to sanctify thy head."
> — Part II, Act. IV, Sc. 5.

King Henry VI likewise bemoans his trials in these words:

> "Thy place is fill'd, thy sceptre wrung from thee,
> Thy balm wash'd off wherewith thou wast anointed."
> — Part III, Act III, Sc. 1.

It is called a soothing ointment in *King Lear* when Cordelia is spoken of as "the balm of your age"; in *King Henry VI*, Part III, when "My pity hath been balm to heal their wounds," and in *The Rape of Lucrece*, "I'll . . . drop sweet balm in Priam's painted wound." In *Macbeth*, "sleep that knits up the ravell'd sleave of care" is called the "balm of hurt minds."

And Cleopatra dies with these exquisite words upon her lips:

> "Peace, peace!
> Dost thou not see my baby at my breast,
> That sucks the nurse asleep? . . .
> As sweet as balm, as soft as air, as gentle."
> — *Antony and Cleopatra,* Act V, Sc. 2.

Some of these references may be to the Oriental balm, balm of Gilead (*Balsamodendron opobalsam*), a tree of Upper India, but garden balm was also well known and favored in Shakespeare's time.

The balm mentioned in the Bible may be either, but the herb was undoubtedly meant when Homer speaks of "sweet balm and gentle violets" (*Odyssey*) for balm was native to rocky pastures and moist fields throughout southern Europe. Theocritus means meadow balm in this passage:

"My sheep have at hand balm to browse and the wild eglantine too blooms in abundance like roses."

—Idyl V.

The foliage steeped in wine was drunk by the Greeks for fevers and the crushed leaves as a plaster for the stings of scorpions and the bites of mad dogs.

Virgil took great pride in his bees and grew thyme, lavender and balm especially for their use. The Arabians knew the herb as well as the Oriental mastic gum, and the commercial trading companies distributed the dry herbage through much of Europe for use in medicine. Not until the early Renaissance did it arrive in abundance, appearing in a manuscript of 1440 as "herbe melisse" and "bawme." Turner, a century later (1562), calls it English "baume mint" and in the 1664 edition of his herbal is the statement that "Balm groweth in almost every Countery Housewife's garden. . . . It driveth away poisons arising from melancholly."

Sir Walter Scott has a character in *The Antiquarian* (Chapter 6) ask: "Would you take anything for your headache — a glass of balm wine?" Until a quarter century ago balm was considered a sudorific in good repute in rural England, one writer going so far as to say, "Balm tea is recommended as a remedy for all the ills that flesh is heir to."

A perfume was made in France and patents granted by Louis XIV, XV, and XVI, called Eau de Melisse des Cannes, and kept inviolate by the Carmelite Friars, consisting of balm flowers freshly gathered and free from stalks, coriander seed, angelica root, nutmeg, cinnamon, cloves, all pounded in a mortar and incorporated into wine. This aromatic spirit was used as a headache remedy, like lavender water.

OLD-TIME HERBS

Unlike some of the other herbs, balm was grown in the flower garden for its sweet odor; as early as 1600, a sprig of it was included with bouquets when given away. And just as old Baucis cleansed and sweetened her humble cottage board with "green mints" before seating her honored guests, so Mistress Quickly ordered the most important chairs in Windsor Castle to be prepared for the incoming friends:

> "The several chairs of order look you scour
> With juice of balm and every precious flower."
> — *The Merry Wives of Windsor,* Act V, Sc. 5.

It has been the custom in Roman times to rub furniture with aromatics to drive away evil spirits, although one commentator in an edition of Pliny adds facetiously: "No doubt they had learned that pennyroyal keeps away body lice," and balm was similar in odor.

Balm seems to have been a favorite herb of the poets, for it is often mentioned. Shelley, who seldom deigns to mention plants by name, uses it symbolically in two places:

> "The dew-mists of my sunless sleep shall float
> Under the stars like balm."
> —*Prometheus Unbound,* Act III, Sc. 3.

and in his verses "To Harriett: May 1814":

> "Thy look of love has power to calm
> The stormiest passion of my soul;
> Thy gentle words are drops of balm
> In life's too bitter bowl."

Lucy Larcom uses the word figuratively in these beautiful lines:

> "Breathe Thy balm upon the lonely
> Gentle Sleep!"
> — *Sleep.*

FOR NORTHERN GARDENS

The Savories, *Satureia hortensis* L.
Satureia montana L.

Summer savory is a spindly annual attaining eighteen inches in height with few branches all turned upward, minute entire leaves and small tubular white flowers characteristic of many mints. It is much used in poultry dressings.

Winter savory (see Picture 10 at end of book) is not as well known as it should be. It is a woody perennial, prostrate and spreading widely, and is an excellent hardy attractive plant for the rock-garden. Foliage is almost evergreen even in the North, small, entire, very dark green and shining. Flowers are like those of the former species and the plant is covered with bloom from the middle of August until frost; the bees love it.

These two savories by no means complete the list of those adapted to garden use. Seven species were known to the ancients, all dwarf, densely-matted aromatic shrubs, several used in medicine and for their bee-alluring propensities. Winter savory flourished on Mount Atlas and was known to the Greeks as *isope,* or hyssop.

There has been considerable discussion as to the hyssop used for sprinkling purposes in the Old Testament, the only point upon which savants agree being that it was not the herb we now know as hyssop, which was not native to Palestine. The plant which best fits the Hebrew *ezob* is *Satureia thymus,* which is abundant in that country and Syria.

Both our savories are from the Mediterranean region and were used by the Greeks in sausages, according to Lucian (*Epigrams*). Virgil says in his fourth Georgic, which treats of bee keeping: "Round their (the farmers') houses let the cassia blossom grow, and the wild thyme, with its far-flung sweetness, and a wealth of heavy-scented savory."

Savory reached Britain at the time of the Roman conquest and came to hold a high place in Saxon recipes when very few herbs were available. It was grown at the monastery of Saint-Gall and appears in Charlemagne's list as "Satureia," summer savory. It was an ingredient in the French *bouquet garni,* a combination of available herbs tied up in a cheesecloth bag and thrown into the soup or stew pot.

This elaborate recipe of the seventeenth century does honor to savory alone as seasoning: For Battalia Pie, take four small chickens, four squabs, four suckling rabbits. Cut them up, season with savoury, and put in a pie with sheep tongues, four lamb stones, twenty to thirty cockscombs, savoury-balls, and oysters. Lay on a crust and bake.

Savory was not favored by the poets with symbolic virtues ascribed to some of the herbs, but Perdita in *The Winter's Tale* (Act. IV, Sc. 4) gives the middle-aged distinguished king of Sicily who comes presumably a-wooing this gentle reproof:

> "Here's flowers for you:
> Hot lavender, mints, savory, marjoram;
> . . . these are flowers
> Of middle summer, and I think they are given
> To men of middle age."

Hyssop, *Hyssopus officinalis* L.

The word *hyssop* immediately calls to mind the Crucifixion, when Our Lord was handed a sponge soaked in vinegar dipped in hyssop (John 19:29). The first mention of the word, however, appears in Exodus 12:22 when Moses at the Passover directed his elders to wash the houses of the Jews so they should not be smitten like the Egyptians.

In Leviticus 14:4–6 and 49-52 Moses uses an aspergillum of hyssop dipped in blood for cleansing lepers, and in Numbers 19:6 and Hebrews 9:19 the herb figures in the rite of purification. Solomon's wisdom extended "even unto the hyssop that springeth out of the wall" (1 Kings 4:33) and in Psalms 51:7 a contrite sinner prays for pardon thus: "Purify me with hyssop, and I shall be clean."

The early Catholic Church abolished laurel twigs as aspergilla because of their close association with the spilling of blood and adopted hyssop instead, but the hyssop of the Bible and the Church is probably not the garden hyssop. Some eighteen herbs native to Palestine have been proposed as hyssop, including species of savory, marjoram and thyme.

True hyssop (see Picture 11 at end of book) is a low bushy plant not over two feet tall, with slender stems woody at the base, long slender dark-green leaves with a mild mint odor and spikes of closely-set dark blue-purple flowers. The plant is well worth a place in the flower-garden, for the flowers, while not bright, are a good blue which is

HYSSOP

scarce, and if kept cut back it will flower through most of the summer. Seeds are available and seedlings very easy to grow, flowering the second summer. An established plant readily reseeds itself.

Hyssop is a native of western Asia and southern Europe. As

an escape from early colonial gardens it has established itself along our eastern seaboard, and on the Pacific Coast it is found along roadsides and in waste places, able to sustain itself on arid soil.

The word "hyssop" from the Greek, means "an aromatic herb," although the odor is not strong, pleasant or repellent. The plant was used in ancient times as an emetic, in cough syrups made with honey, and in early compounds such as "The Salt of the Holy Apostles," this one to relieve difficult breathing.

The Anglo-Saxon leechbooks refer to the plant as "ysopo" and "isopo." The chatelaines of great manor houses in Plantagenet days considered the cultivation of herbs and a knowledge of their medical use an important part of their education, and an herb-woman became a part of many a large establishment, whose duty it was to grow, dry and store the multitude of herbs needed for winter use. When her lord returned from the joust with a bruised shoulder or hip, or when he came back from a battle with a gaping arrow or spear wound it was a part of his lady's duties to apply the proper herb and bandage the wound. Physicians were few and far away from the great estates and it was important that someone be at hand in every household to treat the family for all minor ills and most of the serious as well. *The Paston Letters* give abundant evidence of this fact during the period from 1435 to 1495 A.D.

After the dissolution of the monasteries, it became a part of the duty of the curate of a parish to grow the old herbs in his garden and succor the sick who came to his door as the monks had done in ages past. Such a custom is described in the biography of the English prelate and poet, George Herbert (1593–1633) * when the curate, his wife, and daughters grew and preserved many herbs

* Anon. *The Life of George Herbert of Bremerton*. London, 1893.

so that they could diagnose the ailment of a parishioner and apply the proper treatment.

During the eighteenth and nineteenth centuries the growing of herbs became in turn a part of the duties of every village and farm wife, and thus the knowledge of herb lore became widely disseminated. It is only now dying out in rural parts of England and America; now and then an aged woman can be found with a mind well stored with the lore of woodland and cultivated plants, but these gleanings, gathered over a lifetime, are not being passed down to her descendants, who scoff at them as nonsense not worthy of consideration.

Some of the old herbs are lost, only their names remaining, such an one being silphium of the ancients.

Hyssop never enjoyed a wide reputation in medicine and was not a culinary herb at all. However, in the Renaissance it enjoyed high favor as minute hedge material; and for this purpose it was brought to Virginia in the heyday of formal gardens.

Sweet Marjoram, *Origanum marjorana* L.

Sweet marjoram was a plant specially favored by the goddess Venus:

> "And though sweet marjoram will your garden paint
> With no gay colors, yet preserve the plant,
> Whose fragrance will invite your kind regard
> When her known virtues have her worth declared;
> On Simonis' shore fair Venus raised the plant,
> Which from the goddess' touch derived her scent."
>
> —PAUL DE RAPIN (1661–1725).

OLD-TIME HERBS

The word *origanum* is from the Greek *horos* or hill, and *ganos,* ornament, and means mountain joy or decoration, for marjoram covers otherwise barren slopes of its native rocky headlands along the Mediterranean shores. It is found also in Syria and as far east as Persia. There are about thirty species of the genus, mostly native to dry sunny and rocky hills around the *Mare Nostrum,* some of them of positive value in rock-gardens for their brilliant leaf bracts. Pot-marjoram is *O. onites* and winter marjoram *O. Heracleaticum,* both of culinary value.

The ancient physicians knew the plant and it was used in wreaths and in the kitchen as well. The coat of arms of the old lower Italian city of Marjori consisted of a sprig of marjoram on an azure field, for barrens about the city are redolent with the herb, and the blue seas form a part in every vista. Virgil refers to Idalia's lofty groves, where soft marjoram perfumed the air with flowers and fragrant shade (*Aeneid,* Book I) and Pliny with his encyclopedic grasp of facts as a horticulturist as well as observer of natural history gives careful directions for its cultivation in the garden. Other Roman writers, including Catullus and Columella, mention the plant.

We have no record that marjoram reached England until the thirteenth century when it was called variously marjoram, majorlane and majorane, the words probably corruptions of the Middle Latin *majorana,* referring to this, the greater *origanum,* as differentiated from another already known dittany or lesser *origanum.* A century later the word "marjorlaine" appears for the first time, the "r" added perhaps through an error in copying, as many another such mistake has been perpetuated. During the next several hundred years many spellings appeared, some with, others without the "r," until in the eighteenth century the spelling seems to have been fixed.

FOR NORTHERN GARDENS

Once introduced, marjoram became a prime favorite with the cook. Isaak Walton gives such elaborate recipes for the stuffings for his fishes, cooked as soon as removed from the stream, that even his humble carp was a dish fit for kings:

"Take sweet-marjoram, thyme, and parsley, of each a handful; a sprig of rosemary, and another of savory; bind them into two or three small bundles and put them to your Carp with four or five whole onions, twenty pickled oysters, and three anchovies. Then pour upon your Carp as much claret wine as will only cover him, and season your claret with salt, cloves, and mace, and the rinds of oranges and lemons."

After the fish was boiled it was laid on a platter, the herb broth poured over it, then egg yolks and shredded herbs.

Another seventeenth-century recipe called for a leg of mutton roasted over a spit and served with a sauce consisting of onions, savory, sweet marjoram, mushrooms, anchovies, and lemon. The mint, however, is missing.

The plant was chopped fine for salads but used sparingly, for marjoram, while sweet, is strong in flavor. Shakespeare mentions its use figuratively, when Lafeu eulogizes the dead Helen:

" 'Twas a good lady: we may pick a thousand salads ere we light on such another herb."

Whereupon the clown adds:

"Indeed, sir, she was the sweet-marjoram of the salad."
— *All's Well That Ends Well,* Act IV, Sc. 5.

Sweet marjoram was a favorite plant in the medieval cutting garden "for herbes of good smell," and sprigs of it were laid away with linens and with the winter's woollens to keep moths away. "Little glebs of fragrance" were plucked from the stems and dried for sachets.

147

The plant was little used in medicine, although the oil, anchusa root, camphor and alcohol formed a noted "cancer cure" of the eighteenth century. A tea is still used for incipient colds as with other mints. Externally, the herbage was bruised and applied to sprains and inflammations, including those of the eyes. The oil is still used for stiff joints and is still present in the United States Pharmacopoeia, used, however, more to disguise unpleasant odors and tastes than for any positive virtues.

It is said that Sicily abounds in herb-shops where nothing but dried herbs are sold, but one doesn't need to go to Sicily to find these quaint places; it was something of a surprise to the writer to find no less than six such shops surrounding one of the great city farmers' markets, where dried herbs in barrels and hampers and bags and boxes of all sizes were ranged in rows along the outside and again in windows within. Grass baskets of marjoram and sage tied in little bundles, large baskets of dried and curled rosemary leaves, smaller ones containing all sorts of herb seeds, and finally powders such as mustard and turmeric, not to mention the long strings of garlic dangling beside the door. Condiments may be purchased in a single shop from Italy, Crete, Greece, Syria, Persia, India, and even from Japan.

The reason for these shops is that seeds and foliage are used in quantity by meat packers, who use them in processed meats, and by pickling establishments, as well as by our great foreign populations familiar with their use at home.

Sweet-marjoram seed may be purchased, and the little plants attain size sufficient for cutting by fall, but do not live over our winters to flower another year. This herb deserves the highest praise, none being superior to it for culinary use fresh or dried.

Dittany-of-Crete, *Origanum dictamnus* L.

A plant of most unusual history and allied to sweet marjoram is dittany-of-Crete (see Picture 12 at end of book), the name meaning joy of Mount Dicte (in Crete). Homer mentions it, not by name, however, thus: Eurypylus is wounded in battle and "an arrow's head yet rooted in his wound." Then

> "Patroclus cut the forky steel away:
> Then in his hands a bitter root he bruised;
> The wound he wash'd, the styptic juice infused.
> The closing flesh that instant ceased to glow,
> The wound to torture, and the blood to flow."
> — *Iliad*, Book XI, ALEXANDER POPE translation.

Hippocrates knew this virtue of the herb; Aristotle, Dioscorides, and Pliny all describe its use. But somewhere in history its use as a simple astringent became distorted, no doubt through an error in translation, giving to the herb the power of drawing the iron out of the wound. It was a legend that if the goats of Crete were pierced by a javelin, they would seek out this plant on the hillsides and upon eating it the arrowheads would drop out and the wounds promptly close and heal over.

Virgil accepts the latter meaning in the *Aeneid* (Book XII). Aeneas was injured in battle but the simples of the priest-physician chosen by Apollo could not effect a cure. Venus, looking down from heaven, noticed her son's agony and, quickly descending in a cloud,

> "A branch of healing dittany she brought,
> Which in the Cretan fields with care she sought:
> Rough is the stem, which woolly leafs surround;
> The leafs with flow'rs, the flow'rs with purple crown'd,

Well known to wounded goats; a sure relief
To draw the pointed steel, and ease the grief.
This Venus brings . . . and brews
Th' extracted liquor with ambrosian dews,
[Venus prepares]
An od'rous panacee."

—Dryden translation.

Thus the simple herb took on supernatural power, a reputation it held for a thousand years and more. In 1398, Trevisia says: "Diptamnus is of so grete vertue that it dryeth and pulleth out yren out of the body." Another contemporary writer says, "If a man hunt the roebuck it will eat this wort and it puts out the arrow from its wounds," although the plant was totally unknown where the roebuck lived. Langley in 1546 says, "The Harte stryken with an arrow driueth it out with Detany." Michael Drayton, "The Fairies' Poet" (1563–1631), says

"And this is Dictam, which we prize
Shot, Shafts, and Darts expelling."
—The Muse's Elizium.

Similar statements are plentiful in early English literature, until the plant took on abstract significance as well. Sir Edward Digby in a speech made in 1623 said: "We shall receive from His Royal Hand that Dictamen which must expel divers Arrows that hang on the side of the Commonwealth." Bishop Hale, the very next year, followed up the idea thus: "The shaft sticks in thee! None but the Sovereign Dittany of the Savior's Righteousness can drive it out!"

As late as 1860, the legend persisted, when the Reverend Trench in *Sermons of Westminster Abbey,* obviously quoting from the seventeenth century bishop said: "The arrow which drinks up his Spirit, there is no sovereign dittany which will cause it to drop from his side."

Dittany had other, minor uses, for it was incorporated into the old Greek thericae copied from the temple at Cos by Galen and also in the Mithradates Antidote.  Charlemagne had it and it was used in Saxon kitchens as a pleasing aromatic, one such recipe using a sauce of parsley, dittany, thyme, garlic, pepper and salt to season fish. Its use can be traced consistently from that time to the present, and is not confused with sweet marjoram, dittany being used much earlier in northern countries.

DITTANY-OF-CRETE

Dittany is a "very pretty little plant, kept out of curiosity in gardens, six to eight inches in height, with white woolly leaves and tiny purple flowers in scaly heads" (Sir John Hill, 1756). Although it is difficult to obtain, the writer has seen plants of it in Detroit.

Thyme, *Thymus vulgaris* L.

Thyme is one of the old-time herbs which, instead of outgrowing its popularity, is used to a far greater extent to-day than ever before; it contains three essential oils, cymene, thymene, and thymol, which can be produced as efficiently and cheaply from the plant as they can synthetically in the laboratory. The most important, thymol, is an ingredient in numerous pharmaceutical preparations, in salves and ointments to clear the head in colds, catarrh and sinus infections, on cotton for earache and toothache, as an antiseptic for skin affections such as ringworm, eczema, psoriasis, and taken internally for the eradication of tape-worms. This oil was extracted in Germany as early as 1725.

It is used to a considerable extent in France in the perfume industry and in medicines to obscure disagreeable tastes and odors.

These are many species of thyme, mostly of southern European origin. The word "thyme" means incense, for the plant was used with other sweet-smelling aromatics for this purpose in ancient Greece. Mother-of-thyme (*T. serpyllum*) is abundant on the mountain slopes of Greece and Italy, on the Atlas mountains, on the Himalayas, and is even found on the high plateaus of Abyssinia where it forms a large part of the pasturage for the flocks and herds of the wandering tribes. It perfumes the rancid butter which dusky lords and ladies use to plait their hair into the innumerable tight little braids characteristic of their head-dress, and the national beverage, tetch, is flavored with this herb. It has spread to northern countries and is now found in rocky places over much of Europe as far north as Iceland and Green-land.

This species is a prostrate widely-branching little shrub only a few inches high with minute foliage and in June a profusion of purplish bloom tinting the hillsides like heather. Charles Kings-ley speaks of English "hills sweet with thyme and basil" and Robert Tannahill says

> "Now the summer's in prime
> Wi' the flowers richly blooming,
> And the wild mountain thyme
> A' the moorlands perfuming."
> — *The Braes o' Balquhither.*

Kipling speaks of the "blunt, bow-headed, whale-backed Downs covered with "the wind-bit thyme that smells of dawn in Para-dise" — a phrase scarce equalled even by the ancients.

FOR NORTHERN GARDENS

The garden thyme, *T. vulgaris,* is native to rocky outcrops along the western Mediterranean from Italy to Portugal. It is a taller plant, up to eight inches or more, with very dark green foliage and white bloom. It is easy to raise from seed, although the seed should be mixed with sand before sowing. As every rock-gardener knows, many other species are available for garden use hardy in our North.

Thyme is one of the most satisfactory of culinary herbs for winter use, for it is neither weedy in flavor nor too strong; enhancing rather than masking the flavors of foods. It is excellent in soups, white sauces, and in bread stuffings for roasts. The chief use of the plant in ancient times seems to have been its bee-alluring propensity, and poets for two thousand years have sung the praises of

> "Thick-growing thyme and roses wet with dew,
> . . . sacred to the sisterhood divine
> Of Helicon."
>
> — THEOCRITUS, *Idyls.*

Mahaffy, noted Greek scholar, says he could never find the Theocritan fields of Sicily, but he did discover on the mainland of Greece "here and there a plain or valley with great fields of thyme and arbutus, and there were herds of goats wandering through the shrubs and innumerable bees gathering honey from the thyme" (*Rambles and Studies in Greece*). A similar tract of seacoast on the east side of Italy has been used for ages and is still in use as temporary grazing ground for thousands of sheep brought there from afar to browse on the thymy fields and give to their mutton the peculiar but delightful flavor which is so highly prized.

The ancients prized highest the honey from Mount Hybla in

Sicily, and second best from Mount Hymettus in Attica. Martial, the Latin epigrammatist, scornfully asks, "You expect Hyblaean or Hymettian honey to be produced and yet you offer the bee nothing but Corsican thyme!" *Thymus corsica* was a miniature species with faint fragrance. Virgil sings praises of thyme throughout his works, especially in the Georgics as does Horace in his Odes and Epistles.

Mention of thyme is absent from the earliest writings in the North and seems first to appear around the year 1000 A.D. By the twelfth century it was an established potherb in England, and fish was cooked in water flavored with it and other herbs. A fifteenth-century work indicates its wider use in soups, sauces, salads, and in beverages. Isaak Walton uses it profusely in his fish sauces and stuffings. It is among the most popular herbs throughout most of Europe to-day, and deserves much wider use in this country, both fresh and dried.

In the garden, thyme has long been popular, used between stones in paths. Sir Francis Bacon says in his essay "Of Gardens":

"Those plants which Perfume the Aire most delightfully, . . . being Troden upon and Crushed are Three: That is Burnet, Wilde-Time, and Water-Mints. Therefore you are to set whole Allies of them, to have the Pleasure, when you walke or tread."

Besides its use in the kitchen, as a flavor for mutton-on-the-hoof and as a honey plant, thyme was a prime strewing herb in the ancient world. In *The Two Noble Kinsmen,* the play of unique authorship — John Fletcher and William Shakespeare — produced in 1610, little boys of Athens strew flowers and herbs before a marriage procession, singing:

"Maiden pinks of odour faint,
Daisies smell-less, yet most quaint,

FOR NORTHERN GARDENS

And sweet thyme true
Oxlips in their cradles growing,
Marigolds on deathbeds growing,
Larks-heels trim."

In the Middle Ages, floors of monasteries, churches, and great manorial halls were earthen or made of uneven stones or bricks, and difficult to sweep. In lieu of the broom, they were often strewn with sweet-smelling herbs. Rushes and meadow hay was deemed sufficient for ordinary days, but festival days, Sundays, wedding and funeral occasions, were honored with sweet flag, various mints, marjoram, thyme, basil, fennel and other herbs, all expensive plants to use. Bequests were frequently made in wills for the strewing of herbs in perpetuity in the chancels and even the naves of churches, and this charming custom is not entirely outmoded in rural England to-day.

Even in ancient Greece thyme was used as a funeral plant; Aristophanes says in *Peace*, "Will you not bury my body right away and pile a great heap of earth upon it and plant wild thyme thereon and pour perfumes on it?"

An herb as well-known as thyme could not escape the eye of the apothecary, and Hippocrates mentions its use. Oil of thyme was used by the Romans for coughs, colds, asthma, and bronchitis, for this chain of afflictions was prevalent in Rome. The oil was rubbed on the forehead for fainting, sleeplessness, and headache. Honey has stood high in medicine since ancient times, and thus thyme plays an indirect part of no little importance in medicine; in the Koran is the statement that "there proceedeth from the bellies of the bees a liquor of various colours, wherein is a medicine for men."

There are many references to thyme in medieval medicine.

Hill says in 1756, "Thyme is a better medicine for nervous

cases than most that are used." "The nightmare is a very trouble-some disease," he says, "and often puzzles the physician, but it may be perfectly cured by a tea made from this plant."

William Withering, in his four-volume *British Botany* of 1787, says "an infusion of thyme leaves removes the head-ach occasioned by the debauch of the preceding evening" and he notes what the ancients also recognized, viz. that "the flesh of sheep fed on thyme is superior to that of ordinary mutton."

Mints of the Genus *Mentha*

"Come, buy my mint, my fine green mint!" begs the flower-woman in one of the Cries of London, for up to the time of the Renaissance the various mints were undifferentiated, and several used as "mint sauce" and in medicine.

According to Theophrastus, Menthe, daughter of Cocytus, was beloved by Pluto, god of the underworld, but because of the jealousy of Prosperine she was changed by the latter into one of the humblest of plants, to be trodden underfoot by all. And thus mint came to be a favored strewing herb in Greece and later Rome. Baucis rubbed her humble board with the crushed foliage of this plant at the visit of Jupiter and Mercury:

"The table (she) sets; th' invited gods lie down, . . .
Then rubb'd it o'er with newly gathr'd mint,
A wholesome herb, that breathed a grateful scent."
— Ovid, *Metamorphoses,* Dryden translation.

Homer mentions mints, as does Hippocrates, and there is one reference in the Bible (Matthew 23:23). Pliny says "the smell of mint doth stir up in the mind and taste a greedy desire for meat." Down through the years, various mints appeared in monastery lists for culinary as well as medicinal use. Here is a fourteenth-century prescription for an ulcer cure which can scarce be equalled:

"For an ulcer, Take eggis that be rotyne undre an henne whane she sittes to bryng forth byrddes, and breke them and ley them on the sore and it schale sleye the worme for the stynche; and whoso hathe none eggis take thereof the Ius of mynte and it will do the same." *

Peppermint, *Mentha piperita* L.

Peppermint (see Picture 13 at end of book) and spearmint are very similar in appearance but when brought together the dif-

ferences are apparent; the former is a rich uniform deep green in color while the latter is yellower in tone; both species have stems and runners tinged with madder when grown in sunlight, these

PEPPERMINT

of the latter perhaps a little ruddier. Both have lanceolate leaves sharply serrate on the margins but spearmint leaves taper to more acute tips, peppermint leaves being broader and rather blunt at the ends and sometimes fine-hairy on the veins beneath. The one feature which best differentiates them, however, is the absence of a petiole in spearmint, while peppermint leaves have a short stem.

Peppermint is thought to have originated in Hindustan and been taken to Egypt early in written history and spread from thence. Again, it may have originated as a sport of the English hairy mint *M. hirsuta,* about 1696. Its superiority over other mints was recognized soon after this date, and by 1750 it was being

* G. Henslow, *Medical Works of the Fourteenth Century*. London, 1899.

cultivated on a commercial scale in Europe. It was introduced into this country shortly before the Civil War at Wayne, New York. By 1855 two acres were under cultivation in Saint Joseph County, Michigan; just before the depression this acreage jumped to 35,000, with 1500 pounds of oil to an acre an average yield, valued at $30 a pound. Other states opened up acreage to the plant and its oil came to be second only to turpentine among volatile-oil products in this country.*

This oil finds extensive use in the perfume industry, chiefly for soaps and toilet preparations; it is used as a flavor for confectionery, for cordials and chewing gum and is used widely in medicine for its soothing and antispasmodic effects in stomach disorders such as colic, diarrhea and dyspepsia, and also for its cooling effect in nose and throat preparations.

Spearmint, *Mentha spicata* L.

Spearmint (see Picture 14 at end of book) is not as agreeable in odor as peppermint and finds fewer technical uses; it is grown

SPEARMINT

in southern Michigan, where some forty thousand pounds of oil were produced annually before 1928, a far less yield than peppermint. The oil is used in medicine and also in chewing gum and perfumery.

Spearmint was brought to these shores very early and went wild before 1672. Its native home is Asia but it is now widely distributed over temperate portions of the globe. Peppermint likewise was introduced very early and is to be found throughout the country,

* A. F. Sievers, *Methods of Extracting Volatile Oils from Plant Material and the Production of Such Oils in the U.S.* U.S. Dep't. of Agriculture. Technical Bulletin No. 16, 1928.

but favors wetter places than spearmint. Spearmint is "lamb mint" and it also goes by such names as mackerel mint, Our Lady's mint, sage of Bethlehem, spire mint and brown mint. President Theodore Roosevelt planted a patch of it on the White House grounds, fifteen feet in length, to provide refreshment in beverages for his historic Tennis Cabinet. The bed was destroyed during the Hoover administration when the new office extension was added.

Water Mint, *Mentha aquatica* L.

Water mint, too, was introduced into this country early and is to be found in wet meadows and along streams in the Eastern states. It is a stout two-foot plant with finely pubescent stem and foliage, the latter petioled as in spearmint.

Horse Mint, *Mentha longifolia* (L.) Huds.

The coarse, hairy, sessile-leaved, low-growing horse mint occurs in wet places in our Eastern and Central states. It was known to the ancients and is supposed to be one of the bitter herbs with which the Passover lamb was eaten. During Pompey's time in Rome it was found that chewing this herb repelled or eradicated the parasitic worm which caused the dread elephantiasis.

Field Mint, *Mentha arvensis* L.

Field or corn mint is the only species of the genus in our country which favors dry places; it is an escape from Europe occasionally to be found on the Eastern seaboard from New Brunswick to Florida. This species was favorably known to the ancients and used in the kitchen and in medicine. A variety of this mint is widely cultivated in Japan for the high yield of menthol which is used extensively in medicine.

Our only native mint, *M. canadensis* L., is of no commercial importance, but was formerly used by the Indians for its cooling effect during fevers.

A very desirable rock-garden mint from abroad is *Mentha requieni,* Corsican mint, than which a more diminutive plant is scarcely to be found. Flowers are almost microscopic, pale lavender, appearing in June. Another minute mint for crevices is *Micromeria rupestris.*

Pennyroyal, *Mentha pulegium* L.

Few plants are more insignificant than pennyroyal (see Picture 15 at end of book) but few have enjoyed so long a reputation. There is an American pennyroyal, *Hedeoma pulegioides* (L.) Pers., but true pennyroyal is an herb of the Near East spreading through cooler parts of Europe to Finland. The Greeks used it in medicine and mention it in poetry; the Romans valued it as a good stomachic and perpetuated it in the Mithradates Antidote. Thus incorporated, the little plant held its own through the Middle Ages under the name "pulegium." As early as 1000 A.D. it was known that travellers who used a smelling salts of pennyroyal and wormwood could prevent seasickness, for which ailment it is still in use.

In the "Language of Flowers,"

> "Pennyriall is to print your love
> so deep within my heart,
> That when you look this nosegay on
> my pain you may impart."

But the unique value of the little plant is revealed by its species name, pulegium referring to its use in driving away *pulices* or body lice and fleas. The common name is a corruption of the old common name pulliol-royal (Latin *Pulegium regium*) and infers that royalty as well as common folk suffered from these pests. Other names for the plant are flea-bane and fleamint.

The oil of pennyroyal still enjoys a good reputation as a household remedy for mild complaints of children and is still used in pharmaceutical preparations.

PENNYROYAL

The plant is easily grown from seed and is a prostrate perennial, wide-spreading and rooting from the nodes. Flowers are tiny and red-purple in color. The plant readily reseeds itself.

Lavender, *Lavandula vera* L.

"Lavender blue and rosemary green,
When I am king you shall be queen,"

runs the old couplet and indicates the high regard for this plant in the past, for lavender has been cherished by the Egyptians, the Phoenicians, the Greeks, and the Romans, and is just as much prized to-day as ever, even in the face of competition from synthetic perfumes.

Lavender is no prosaic potherb of the kitchen-garden grown for the delectation of the gastronome, nor does it hold high place among medicinal plants; rather, like a beautiful lady it enhances its surroundings with a subtle suggestion of loveliness and refreshing purity, leaving to lesser things the homelier virtue of usefulness.

"Crossing the lavender slopes is one of the most pleasurable experiences of climbers in the southern Alps," says Mons. Henri Correvon,* "for the delicious odor of the sweet herb persists on clothing to remind them after returning home of the bright sunny regions they traveled over." This horticulturalist lists no less than eight species of the plant adaptable to garden use, all from the region of the Mediterranean but not all adapted to American gardens.

The species generally grown in our gardens is *L. spica* (see Picture 16 at end of book), a rather dwarf, compact shrub of whitened appearance, with long straplike foliage and short flower stalks of violet-purple bloom. *L. vera,* true lavender, is a taller plant, more spindly, with foliage less whitened, longer flower stalks, and lighter, lilac bloom. The former is the more hardy in our Northern states although both will come through an average winter with little loss. Both species like gravelly or stony soil with little enrichment and rather dry sunny positions for the greatest development of their essential oils. They are too slow from seed and it is advisable rather to purchase plants of blooming size.

LAVENDER

The beginnings of lavender in history are obscure; it apparently was not native to Egypt, but the people in that country had it in their walled-in gardens and shrines, and used it on sacrificial altars. The early Greeks decked their virgin victims with sweet-smelling flowers and foliage before offering them as human sacrifices to their savage gods. This custom was later supplanted by

* Henri Correvon, *Rock Garden and Alpine Plants.* New York, 1930.

animal sacrifices and still later by the burning of incense — fragrant herbs such as lavender, laurel and eucalyptus, for "of their sweet deaths are sweetest odors made."

It is conjectured that the plant which the Greeks called *nardos* from a Syrian city of that name was identical with lavender, although many other herbs vie with it for the honor; nard is frequently mentioned in the classics — by Ovid, Horace, Martial and others — as a very costly perfume. Pliny named a figure which compared with seventeen dollars a pound and Martial a still higher figure: "My mistress demands of me a pound of nard, or emeralds, or a pair of sardonyxes. That a girl should be worthy of these things I do wish" (*Epigrams,* XI:27).

The plant is still spoken of as spike, an old Roman synonym for it, one of the commoner Roman species being *L. spica.* Chaplets and garlands were woven of it, but one writer says it had to be gathered with care, a dangerous asp making its home under the shrubby little plant.

Virgil says beehives should be in beds of

> "Fresh lavender and store
> Of wild thyme with strong savory to flower."
> — *Georgics,* Book 4.

The ancients seemed not to have used the lavender of the Alps, and the first mention of *L. vera* in northern countries seems to appear in the twelfth century when it was grown in the garden of the Benedictine Abbess Hildegard (1099–1179), at Bingen on the Rhine. The widely-travelled and cultured Welsh physician of Myddavi (no more specific name has come down to us) who died in 1233 compiled a long list of medicinal plants with recipes for their use four hundred years before the writing of herbals became so popular, and this list included *L. vera,* thus authenticating its early use, probably, however, as the dry powdered drug or extract imported from southern countries by one of the great trading companies.

In 1387, satin cushions were stuffed and perfumed with lavender for the use of the Emperor Charles VI of France, no doubt considered a great luxury far beyond the use of the common people.

It was still highly prized in England in Chaucer's time, for this author associates it with royalty thus:

> "Envie is lavender to the court alway,
> For she ne parteth neither night ne daie."
> — Prologue to the *Legend of Good Women.*

But when lavender came to be more widely disseminated and was proven hardy it came into great popularity as a garden plant, as admirable little-hedge material, for strewing floors on special occasions, and for laying away with clothes. The perfume of the dried plant is practically permanent.

> "Sprays of gray-green lavender
> To keep 'till you're old."
> — Margaret Widdemer, *In My Mother's Garden.*

In his play *Friar Bacon and Friar Bungay,* Robert Greene (1560–1592), one of the lesser Elizabethan poets, has a king tell his son that in order to win his lady love he must turn himself into a smock, "Then she'll put thee into her chest and lay thee up in lavender, and upon some good day she'll put thee on," and the phrase "to lay up in lavender" has been in use ever since.

Sprigs were laid with church vestments ("The solemn clerk goes lavender'd and shorn," says Thomas Hood) and one's best silks and satins likewise were perfumed with its delicate scent.

FOR NORTHERN GARDENS

Sometimes the flowers alone were used, sometimes dried sprigs, and again both were twisted into "lavender pokes" with ribbons.

> "In a black oak chest all carven,
>   We found it laid,
> Still faintly sweet of Lavender,
>   An old brocade.
> With that perfume came a vision,
>   A garden fair,
> Enclosed by great yew hedges;
>   A Lady there,
> Is culling fresh blown Lavender,
>   And singing goes
> Up and down the alleys green —
>   A human rose."
>   — M. G. Brereton, *The Old Brocade.*

Hope chests were perfumed with the plant and Thackeray gives it a pretty line: "What woman, however old, has not the bridal-flowers and raiment stowed away, and packed in lavender, in the inmost cupboards of her heart?" (*The Virginians.*) And Scott comments on "the old maid, with her little romance carefully preserved in the lavender of memory" (*Sir Nigel*).

After it became plentiful, lavender was used in the linen closet as well, where its refreshing odor came to be a symbol of snowy whiteness and purity. In fact, the genus name *Lavandula* is supposed to have come from *lavare,* which means in Middle Latin "to lave or wash," and our modern washerwoman takes her name, laundress, from *lavandre,* because lavender was used to scent freshly-washed clothes. Little wonder, then, that lavender is so popular a scent for soaps, bath tablets, and toilet waters.

Sir Arthur Pinero wrote a sentimental story *Sweet Lavender* in 1888 in which the heroine is a laundress.

Two fishermen in Walton's *Compleat Angler,* considering

165

where they shall spend the night decide on a particular place thus:

"Let's go to that house, for the linen looks white and smells of lavender, and I long to lie in a pair of sheets that smell so."

Alfred Noyes has a whole poem devoted to lavender:

"Lavender, lavender,
    That makes your linen sweet;
The hawker brings his basket
    Down the sooty street."

An old-time writer says, "My winding sheet was taken out of lavender to be stuck with rosemary," rosemary being used during Renaissance times for embalming the dead, although lavender, too, was used "to scent the desert and the dead," from a note in *Lalla Rookh* that it was found on the Sahara Desert.

Lavender as a medicinal never attained a high reputation, although it was sometimes an ingredient in the electuaries, two species entering into the Mithradates Antidote. The herb has for long been regarded as a headache remedy and was the chief ingredient in the Queen of Hungary Toilet Water, in vogue for several hundred years. "Palsy Drops" in vogue in the eighteenth century also called for lavender flowers, rosemary tops, molasses spirits and water.

It is said that Queen Victoria loved lavender and that "the Royal Residences are thoroughly impregnated with the refreshing odour of this old-fashioned flower and there is no perfume that the Queen likes better." * Even to-day lavender is still popular in England and might almost be symbolic of the isle where there are

* Donald MacDonald, *Sweet-Scented Flowers and Fragrant Leaves.* New York, 1895.

FOR NORTHERN GARDENS

"Gay cottage gardens, glad,
  Comely, unkempt, and mad,
    Jumbled, jolly, and quaint;
  Nooks where some old man dozes;
  Currants and beans and roses
    Mingling without restraint;
  A wicket that long lacks paint; —
  Here grows Lavender, here breathes England."
                    — WILFRID BLAIR, *Lavender*.*

Rosemary, *Rosemarinus officinalis* L.

Rosemary (see Picture 17 at end of book) is native to the bold bleak, wind-swept headlands of the Mediterranean littoral, never found far from the splashing of the salt-sea spray. "The plant that delights in the spray of the sea" was translated into Latin *ros marinus, ros* meaning dew, thence corrupted to "ros maris," and in early Christian times rosmarie or *rosemary,* thus becoming associated with the Virgin Mary purely out of a fancied resemblance in the name.

It has enjoyed a reputation among peoples of various climes for almost three thousand years and has run the gamut of economic uses; for seasoning food, in medicine, in perfumes, as a strewing herb, in the brewing of beverages, as a "bees alluring plant," as incense, as a symbol at weddings and funerals, and even as an ingredient in the embalming of the dead.

Rosemary is a small shrub resembling lavender and often mistaken for it; the stem is woody, square in cross section when young, ordinarily less than two feet in height and sparingly branched, although in Sicily and the smaller islands where conditions are optimum for its growth the plant attains a height of

* *Punch,* April 4, 1917. Reprinted by permission of the proprietors.

five or six feet with a corresponding spread and rambles over ruins and garden walls in the greatest profusion and luxuriance.

The grayish-green rugose leaves are over an inch long, very narrow and revolute and whitened feltlike beneath. They tend  to slant sharply upward on the stem to resist drought. The foliage, like that of many drought-resisting plants, is highly aromatic and thus protected from the ravages of famished animals, for it is very difficult for a plant living in such a climate to replace the parts which have been destroyed. The flower, which people in colder climates seldom see, is bluish-lavender in color, tubular, inconspicuous, and occurs in small clusters at the nodes.

It is impossible to determine which has enjoyed the greater reputation among the ancients, rosemary or lavender, for both have been cherished

ROSEMARY

and a large literature has grown up around each. The early Greeks used both to adorn their virgins before sacrifice on the altar, and later used both as incense in place of their living sacrifices. The Romans used rosemary as hedge material around their sophisticated formal gardens because it lent itself to regular clipping. Pliny sums up its use thus:

"The garden avenue is bordered with box, and where that is decayed, with rosemary, for the box, wherever sheltered by the buildings, grows plentifully, but where it lies open and exposed to the weather and sprays from the sea, though at some distance from the latter, it quite withers up."

— *Natural History.*

But rosemary was quite at home in such exposed positions.

Wreaths of rosemary adorned the foreheads of youths and maidens at festivals in Rome, as mentioned by Ovid:

FOR NORTHERN GARDENS

"And (she) took especial pride to sleek
Her lightsome locks of hair;
With rosemary she wreathed them."
— *The Story of Cyllarus and Hylonome.*

The late Egyptians grew the plant in their formal and wall gardens and the Arabs prized it highly at Algiers and Morocco as a border for their rose gardens, clipped into low flat-topped hedges. It was taken to Britain by the Romans, and grew in the south of England as well as it had done in Rome, and has been grown there ever since. Its distribution north of the Alps was furthered by a "Kapitulare" of Charles the Great, 812 A.D., who ordered the rosmarinus to be planted in the Royal Gardens. The great trading companies, the Hanseatic League, the Easterlings, the Staple of Calais, and others, furthered its distribution, and returning travellers and Crusaders took the plant back with them.

The famous monastic orders planted it in both their kitchen gardens and medicinal plots and rosemary is mentioned among the very first in most extant lists of such plants. It came to occupy an even higher place than lavender, for while not as sweet it had more practical uses.

The plant was taken to England again in greater quantity at the time of the Norman Conquest when the new lords took over with them many condiment and medicinal plants which had grown in their Continental gardens. However, according to Dodoens (1578) "gardeners maintained it only with great diligence," for it was not an easy plant to grow in the north.

It appeared in the gardens of the nobility and only gradually filtered down to cottage gardeners over a period of several hundred years. In its heydey it was used in topiary work and was "sette by women for their pleasure, to grow in sundry proportions, as in the fashion of a cart, a peacock, or such things as they fancy" (Barnaby Googe, *Husbandry*, 1578). But by the seventeenth century the plant had fallen from grace, become too commonplace, as shown in *The Schoolmistress* by Shenstone (1714–63):

> "And here (is) trim rosemarine, that whilom crown'd
> The dainty garden of the proudest peer,
> Ere, driven from its envy'd site, it found
> A sacred shelter for its branches here."

Rosemary early took on a symbolic use which lifted it far above all others in affection and regard, as shown in this verse:

> "Rosemary is for remembrance,
>   between us daie and night,
> Wishing that I might always have,
>   you present in my sight."
> — CLEMENT ROBINSON, *"A Handefull of Pleasant Delites* (1584).

Little girls are often named Rosemary but almost never Lavender.

Sir Thomas More (1478–1553) says in *Utopia*, "As for Rosemarine, I let it run all over my garden walls not onlie because my bees love it, but because 'tis the herb sacred to remembrance, and therefore to friendship." By Shakespeare's time the plant was at the height of its popularity. Ophelia in the language of flowers distributes her posies culled in fancy with a dainty if satirical hand: "There's rosemary, that's for remembrance" (*Hamlet,* Act IV, Sc. 5), for the volatile Laertes certainly needed it, and Perdita in *The Winter's Tale,* also in graceful sarcasm, presents her distinguished guests with long-lived herbs, thus:

> "For you there's rosemary and rue; these keep
> Seeming and savor all the winter long:
> Grace and remembrance be to you both."
> — Act IV, Sc. 4.

FOR NORTHERN GARDENS

Rosemary made a capital strewing herb, although expensive and never abundant enough in the north to be used in quantity. Special items such as the following appear in old church accounts, indicating that this was a favored herb for strewing: "Item: Paid for hearbes and rosemary that were strewed in the church on the 24th day of October, being a day of thanksgiving, for the victorie over the Scots at Worcester, 8 s." "Rosemary, which had been wont to be sold for twelve pence an armfull went now for six shillings a handfull."

Because it was practically evergreen it was used for Christmas decorations as shown in Robert Herrick's poem:

> "Down with the Rosemary . . .
> Wherewith he drest the Christmas Hall."

It was also emblematic of the fidelity of lovers and occupied a prominent place among decorations at weddings. In a play of 1617, *A Fairie Quarrel,* one courtier inquires, "Your master is to be married to-day?" to which another replies, "Else all this rosemary is lost." Attendants at weddings carried sprigs of the plant, as shown in another contemporary play:

> "Know, varlet, I will be wed this morning:
> Thou shalt not be there, nor once be grac'd
> With a piece of rosemary."
> — *Roman Ally,* 1611.

During the ceremony,

> "Young men and maidens do ready stand
> With sweet rosemary in their hand,
> A perfect token of your virgin's life."
> — Old Ballad, *The Bride's Goodmorrow.*

OLD-TIME HERBS

When Anne of Cleves arrived at Greenwich as the bride of Henry VIII, she wore in her hair a coronet of gold and precious stones set full of branches of rosemary, and at a rustic wedding in Kenilworth attended by Queen Elizabeth "each wight had a branch of broom tied on his left arm for rosemary was scant there." In Germany also, well into the sixteenth century, brides wore sprigs of it in their hair and carried it in their bouquets.

The foliage was even gilded for weddings, along with bay leaves. Herrick says:

> "This done we'll draw lots
> Who shall buy and gild
> The baies and rosemary."
>
> — *Hesperides.*

However, Roger Hackett in a sermon of 1607 admonishes those who thus desecrate the natural foliage: "Smell sweet, O ye flowers, in your native sweetness: be not gilded with the idle arts of man." At the wedding feast also, a sprig of the plant was put into the wine and dedicated to the special good wishes for the bride's happiness.

However highly prized the plant was at weddings, it was just as indispensable at funerals, as Herrick says:

> "Grown for two ends, it matters not at all,
> Be't for my bridall or my buriall."

Speaking of a bride who had died of plague on her wedding day, says Decker in 1603, "Here is a strange altercation, for the rosemary that was wash't in sweet water to set out the bridall is now wash't with tears to furnish her buriall." *

* John Brand, *Observations on the Popular Antiquities of Great Britain,* London, 1849.

FOR NORTHERN GARDENS

"Dry up your tears," says Friar Lawrence to the mourners at Juliet's bier

> "and stick your rosemary
> On this fair corse; and, as the custom is,
> In all her best array bear her to church."
> — *Romeo and Juliet*, Act IV, Sc. 5.

"When the funeral procession is ready to set out, the coffin is nailed up and a servant presents the Company with sprigs of rosemary," says another sixteenth-century chronicler. "Everyone takes a sprig and carries it in his hand till the body is put into the grave, at which time they all throw in their sprigs after it."

George Sewell (d. 1726) has a beautiful poem, *The Dying Man in His Garden,* the last verse of which reads:

> "Thy narrow pride, thy fancied green
> (For vanity's in little seen),
> All must be left when Death appears,
> In spite of wishes, groans, and tears;
> Nor one of all thy plants that grow
> But Rosemary will with thee go."

To this day in England rosemary is prominent among funeral offerings for kings as well as for common people; the King places a wreath of it at the Cenotaph on Armistice Day, and it adorns the cemeteries of the war dead in whatever part of the world they be. Members of certain fraternal orders still drop a sprig of evergreen into the open grave.

However, the old custom of adorning corpses with rosemary and the carrying by mourners of a sprig of the aromatic shrub did not originate from mere sentiment but rather for a very practical one, viz. that the plant was regarded as a powerful disinfectant. The custom was begun in the era when pestilences were wide-spread and rosemary was carried in the hand whenever people walked in the streets and placed before the mouth when speaking, so it was only natural that sprigs of it be laid in the coffin "against the morbid effusions of the corpse" and carried by the mourners as protection against these "effusions."

Rosemary held a high reputation in medicine for various diseases; the Greeks and Romans used the herbage for pleurisy and colds, expressing the juice and administering it in honey. A gout remedy was concocted around 1235 A.D. and a queen is said to have been cured of paralysis by its use. It was called "Eau de la Reine de Hongrie," and consisted of the tops and flowers of rosemary soaked in water for fifty hours under gentle heat. The affected limb was washed with the water for a week, and the patient took a spoonful of it inwardly daily, after which the trouble was supposed to have disappeared. Another writer says the original "Water" contained rosemary oil, mint oil, and oil of roses, and that fistulas, gangrenes, and even cancers which would yield to no other treatment would dry up permanently at once. We have seen that the famed medicament was also made with lavender flowers.

Rosemary oil was distilled very early, itinerant herbalists setting up their stills where the plant was abundant and where water could be obtained to cool the condenser. The oil was used in numerous salves as well as in the making of perfumes. It was used in Rome in cosmetics. During the Middle Ages it was an ingredient in the pomander or little ball of spices and sweet-smelling herbs worn at the belt in an elaborate gold or ivory or silver container to mask body odors; later a compartment was added with a tiny sponge kept wet with aromatic vinegar made from rosemary or other herbs. In the eighteenth century the dried herbs were discarded and only the aromatic liquid retained, carried in a tiny vial or vinaigrette attached to the belt or worn on a fob. Even as late as the nineteenth century physicians and the clergy carried these aromatics to ward off diseases when they visited the sick.

The Eau de Cologne of Johann Maria Farina, developed in the early part of the eighteenth century, contained orange-peel and lemon-peel oils, neroli oil, bergamot and rosemary oil, compounded exactly and aged. Rosemary oil is used widely to-day in perfumes, soaps, hair oil, and in medicine, chiefly to mask unpleasant odors. It is also used to flavor alcoholic liquors; Chartreuse, concocted from various herbs culled from the slopes of the Dauphines in France and made by the Carthusian monks since 1607, is supposed to contain rosemary, although the secret has never been divulged or discovered by analysis of the beverage.

Sprigs of the plant have been popular for use in chests with woollens to keep away moths and the plant is sometimes called "guardrobe."

But with all its popularity in other uses, rosemary was also a culinary herb, especially to accompany roasts, for the flavor is strong. In *The Knight of the Burning Pestle,* by Beaumont and Fletcher, 1611, the host gives direction for the marriage feast of his daughter thus:

"I will have in only a couple of neighbours and their wives; and we will have a capon in stewed broth, with marrow, and a good piece of beef stuck with rosemary."

Sir Walter Scott describes a Christmas feast in old England:

> "Then was brought in the lusty brawn,
> By the old blue-coated serving-man;
> Then the grim boar's head frown'd on high,
> Crested with bays and rosemary."
> — *Marmion,* Introduction to Canto VI.

This custom of serving a boar's head at Christmas celebrations is very old, possibly of Norse origin, and is still preserved at Queen's College, Oxford.

In France and Germany rosemary has long been a staple condiment and large quantities of it are imported into this country from Italy to flavor sausage and other chopped meats and also for use in mixed pickling spices.

Rosemary was brought to our country before 1620 by Captain John Mason, who grew it, one wonders with what success, in Newfoundland! Josselyn says of it at Salem (1672), "It is no plant for this country." When grown in northern herb-gardens, it must be from glass-grown plants, which are readily purchasable in city markets in spring, for it is popular with people who have enjoyed it in their old European homes. It thrives, however, in Virginia, where it was brought in the seventeenth century for use as diminutive hedge material for it bears close clipping like lavender and hyssop and box. It flourishes also on the Pacific Coast and flowers there in winter with a blue "which has been likened to the blue of old-fashioned porcelain."

Sweet Basil, *Ocimum basilicum* L.

Basil (see Picture 18 at end of book) was a plant sacred to Vishnu and Krishna and in ages past "every good Hindu went to his long rest with a basil leaf on his breast. This was his passport to Paradise." And a sacred basil plant was placed upon his grave. The species of basil grown in India, *O. sanctum,* is called holy basil or *tulsi* and even yet the ground around the holy city of Pandharpur is wholly restricted to the cultivation of the *tulsi* plant. At one period the dead were interred beneath the floors of houses and a pot of basil was grown on a window sill and worshipped by the female members of the household every morning. To-day, although the dead are not so interred, the pot of basil is still grown, the sweet fragrance it diffuses representing the incense formerly burned in sacred memory of the deceased.

Boccaccio's tender story of Lisabetta burying the head of her dead lover in a pot of basil and watering it daily with her tears follows this Hindu reverence for the plant and is followed closely in Keats' *Isabella, or the Pot of Basil.* J. W. Alexander painted the well-known picture with the same title.

Sweet basil is native to the Near East and was well known in ancient Greece; Hippocrates used it as one of his four hundred simples but both Dioscorides and Galen held that it was unfit for human consumption. Pliny defends the herb, but remarks that the more it was abused the better it would prosper: "it must be sown with curses and ugly words." They thought the bruised leaves bred scorpions because these arthropods liked to rest under the plant. This is a translation which may not be typical of the medieval interpretation of ancient writers, but in 1586 Cogan wrote in *The Haven of Helth* that "a cer-

SWEET BASIL

tain Italian by often smelling to Basill, had a Scorpion bred in his braine."

Basil does not appear on Northern plant lists until 1387 and never captured the fancy of cooks as did many an humbler plant. It is a tall annual of rather weedy, rank appearance, growing up to thirty inches tall with a corresponding spread; foliage is light-green, large, heart-shaped, thin and crumpled, and rich in aromatic oil which to some is indescribable but to others reminiscent of licorice. Flowers are large for a mint, white, tubular, and appear amid generous green bracts in spikes at the top of the branches. The bees love basil flowers and a bed of a dozen plants will be visited by hundreds if not thousands of bees, yellow jackets, and wasps on bright sunny days, with a constant hum like that of the hive itself; it should produce honey of a most unusual flavor.

Seeds are readily available and the plant very easy to grow. Being an annual, the seedlings grow apace and need spacing in two or three weeks. Several strains seem to be sold as sweet basil which vary considerably in size of the plants and coloring of stems and foliage.

This is one herb which should be used fresh and not dried, for the large plant molds before it can be dried and loses its pleasant odor and taste. It adds a zest to the summer salad and it transforms pea soup into the feast of an epicurean. Chopped fine it may be used as a garnish instead of the ubiquitous parsley and a stalk cooked with a roast or stew imparts a different and most pleasing flavor. A writer of 1725 (Bradley) notes a fact concerning the flavor which should be remembered by the cook: "Basil imparts a grateful flavour if not too strong," and another a century earlier says: "Basil which being gently stroked on the hand, yields a pleasant smell, but crushed hard upon it, unsavoury" (Burton, 1627).

It is not strange that cooks are unfamiliar with basil, for Sir John Hill said as long ago as 1812 that it had long since gone out of use in England but that it deserved much wider popularity. It is used, however, on the Continent, finding favor especially in

Italy, while a Portuguese sauce for basting roast beef is made of basil, garlic, tarragon, thyme, marjoram and other herbs, simmered in oil and poured over the meat.

Like other mints, basil was used in medicine to induce sweating in fevers and colds, and also as an aid to digestion, but the best that most medieval physicians could say of it was that "basil produces a cheerful and merry heart."

It was taken to Newfoundland before 1620 but was not among the herbs of our first colonists. It has never escaped from cultivation here, for it seems not to reseed itself readily in the north.

In Italy basil is a love token, and in Crete it means "love washed with tears." The poet Shelley, who lived for long in Italy and who deigns to mention very few flowers or plants by name, was attracted by the virtue of this herb in his verses "To E-V," the Italian maid who was closeted in a convent and with whom the poet may have been enamored.

> "Madonna, wherefore hast thou sent me
>   Sweet-basil and mignonette?
>   Embleming love and health, which never yet
>   In the same wreath might be.
>   Alas, and they are wet!
> Is it with thy kisses or thy tears?
>   For never rain or dew
>   Such fragrance drew
> From plant or flower . . ."

The common name "basil" is from the Greek meaning "royal" and an English writer of 1860 says, "Sweet Basil is, as its name implies, one of the royalties among sweet herbs" (Delavan, *Kitchen Herbs*). It certainly deserves to be more widely grown.

An octogenarian lady visiting the writer's garden recently and coming to a patch of basil suddenly put her hands to her face and wept tears of joy, for it brought back happy memories of her girlhood days in Germany which she had not visited since. To many people, the memory of odors is far more vivid than of sights or sounds.

Minor Labiatae

Bugle, *Ajuga reptans* L.

A number of mints other than those above and which are hardy in northern gardens are classed as herbs, having been of some economic use in ages past; in fact, if one were to describe  all such plants through the plant kingdom he would include practically the whole category, for few plants there are which have not found some use.

Bugleweed is a familiar rock-garden perennial desirable for carpeting bare spaces where little else will grow, but it spreads apace and is liable to become a pest. It is native to shaded areas of temperate Europe and was used on the field of battle by Roman legions for agglutinating wounds.

BUGLE

The cook learned to spread the macerated foliage over roast meats to congeal the flesh and thus keep in the flavor. In medieval times *Ajuga* was useful and stood high among healing herbs. An infusion was used in tuberculosis to arrest the "spitting of blood"—a phrase met all too often in medical works of the period. Like digitalis and convallaria, bugle also lowers the pulse rate and it was valuable in allaying coughing and as a mild narcotic.

The root gives a good black dye for woolens, formerly widely used.

Self-Heal, *Prunella vulgaris* L.

The old name for this little prostrate perennial pest of damp lawns was "Brunella," from the German *Bräune,* meaning "quinsy," and, during the early Middle Ages the herbage was macerated and bound on the throat for that affection. Being mildly astringent, it was used as a gargle for sore throat. Our American Indians used it in cases of dysentery, especially for babies.

SELF-HEAL

But the plant has now lost all its virtues and is known simply as a weed, of world-wide distribution.

Rabbit's Ear, *Stachys lanata*

The exceedingly soft furry mint called rabbit's ear, cat's ears, and similar names is familiar to many rock-gardeners who use it as a delightful contrast to green foliage. The plant is from southern Europe and was used by the Greeks for its value in healing open wounds, hence one of its common names, woundwort. It was taken to northern Europe for this exclusive purpose in the Middle Ages and occupied an important place in cottage-garden medicine.

Motherwort, *Leonurus cardiaca* L.

Motherwort is a coarse roadside perennial weed from two to five feet tall, naturalized from abroad and now spread to most

MOTHERWORT

parts of the country. It comes from Siberia. The common name refers to its former use, in "female complaints," especially hysteria. Hill says in 1756 it was a famous medicine "for palpitation of the heart when that arises from a hysteric cause but there are some palpitations which nothing can cure."

Cobbler's Bench, *Lamium maculatum* L.

The little creeping mint of old-fashioned gardens with bad odor and little madder-red flowers was a favorite of our grandmothers because of the white-mottled foliage, but it soon overstepped its bounds and came to fill the roadsides and vacant places. Old cemeteries are sometimes overrun with it, as are the sites of homesteads long gone to ruin. It is being reintroduced into shady places difficult to cover but should be used with care and a ruthless hand.

Old names are red nettle, variegated dead nettle, and spotted dead nettle, although it is not a nettle and not in the least offensive even if the calyx teeth are sharp when the plant has matured.

The plant comes from temperate Asia and was used medicinally at least by the first century A.D. for Pliny includes it among the nettles and ascribes to it the virtue of curing erysipelas and says that it was employed against superficial cancer. During the Middle Ages it was used as a poultice for the King's Evil (scrofula), a common disease recognized by the hard kernels in the armpits, neck, and groin, and which we term tuberculosis of the glands and bones. The plant juice was drunk "for spitting of blood."

One can read between the lines, by the frequent mention of the White Plague in its many forms, of the dreadful conditions under which people were forced to exist, and one wonders just how well-placed was the profound faith in the curative properties of herbs for such troubles as gangrene, mad-dog bite, tuberculosis and cancer. So many herbs were used for the same ailment, often as many as a hundred plant and animal ingredients composing a single electuary, and a single one was often used for so many ailments that one must conclude the physician used every medicament available and let Nature take her course. If the patient died he was beyond help when they were used, but if he recovered, the herbs were given the praise and the faith in them went on. However, we should realize that if the faith in herb medicines was lost the sick had no other reliance, and the optimism which they bred no doubt had much to do with the cure.

SCROPHULARIACEAE

Bene, *Sesamum orientale* L.

Bene or sesame (see Picture 19 at end of book) is a plant of great antiquity and great practical importance, and modern herbalists should grow it at least once, if only out of curiosity.

BENE

"Open, sesame" of the Arabian Nights refers to the grain of this plant.

Sesame is a weedy-looking little plant about eighteen inches tall characterized by lovely but fugacious white tubular flowers an inch long appearing late in August from May-sown seeds. The foliage is entire, long and tapering gracefully, dark green in color, and the whole plant including stems is very soft-fuzzy to the touch. Stems are four-square and at the junction of stem and bud is a peculiar hard tiny orange circle. Although the flowers drop within a few hours after opening, the buds increase in size so rapidly that one can practically watch them develop.

From the species name of bene, one might infer that the plant is unadapted to cultivation in our Northern states, but it is an annual of rapid growth which can be grown satisfactorily, although seed will not ripen save in very long summers. Seed is readily available, and is large, tan in color, flat and shining, and is familiar to most people from the bread and buns which are a standard product of bakeries. When parched the seed has a rich nutty flavor. The first frost, however, takes the whole plant for it is very tender.

Growing bene has neither odor nor taste, but the leaves are heavily charged with mucilage which makes them valuable in medicine for cholera, dysentery, and diarrhea, and in cough medicines. The seeds, which are rich in oils, are used in Oriental countries as a substitute for butter and are used in large quantities in the manufacture of oleomargarine and soaps. The oil which has no taste or odor, is a substitute for olive oil, and is used as a base for emulsions, ointments and poultices.

In India sesame is called *til*. It was introduced from islands in the Pacific before the Aryan invasion and for ages has been one of the most valuable of cultivated products. The seed was taken to China in ancient times and is used there as widely as in India for food, medicine, in cosmetics, the oil-cake to fatten cattle, and the residue to enrich the soil. No plant save the soy bean has been of more value to the Chinese.

The Egyptians were familiar with the plant, and the Hebrews in the days of Israel cultivated it along with cummin, for the Biblical reference to "fitches" being threshed not with a sharp instrument, but with a staff (Isaiah 28:27) is taken by many commentators to refer to sesame, while some regard fennel-flower (*Nigella sativa*) as fitches. Herodotus saw sesame grown in Babylonia and Egypt (400 B.C.) and it was familiar to the Greeks. The poet Menander says it was a custom in Greece to give the bride a sesame cake as a symbol of fruitfulness "because sesame is the most fruitful of all seeds." Aristophanes mentions it in *The Birds*.

The Romans made a paste of the macerated seeds as a spread for bread, as they also used cummin seeds.

Foxglove, *Digitalis purpurea*

The foxglove of our gardens (see Picture 20 at end of book) furnishes one of the most valuable of all medicines, digitalis, an essential drug in every physician's kit as a specific for heart afflictions. No drug, natural or synthetic, has been advanced to supplant it as a heart sedative.

The plant is a native of Europe, the name given by the noted botanist Fuchs in allusion to the thimblelike corolla. Dodoens, the Belgian herbalist (1578) says "digitalis is found in dark shadowy valleys and coombes where there is mining for iron and smith's coal." He says boiled in water the foliage was used for liver and spleen complaints, no mention made of its use as a heart sedative. An old Italian proverb says "Digitalis cures every wound." Gerard (1597) advocates its use for a variety of complaints, and Parkinson (1650) omits all mention of its action on the heart.

In fact, the first paper to receive attention on its use for this purpose appeared in 1785, by the British botanist, William Withering, "An Account of the Foxglove." Four years later it was taken up by Guy's Hospital, London, to lower the pulse in scarlet fever and tuberculosis without diminishing the patient's strength. Its use was soon furthered by physicians, and case histories were reported in the medical journals. Thornton in 1810 says, "It is a new medicine used experimentally and not yet understood." But for the last hundred years the drug has been one of the specifics, in use the world over, and nothing has been able to supplant it, although convallaria, from lily-of-the-valley, is sometimes prescribed where digitalis fails.

The plant is widely cultivated to-day for use in medicine, strains having been developed which are richer in the chief constituent, digitalin, than the wild plant.

Digitalis is a biennial not reliably hardy over winter in Northern gardens, the seedlings needing generous protection. Strains with several color variations are obtainable. The plant was brought to this country very early for its decorative quality and has gone wild to a limited extent, especially in the far Northwest where it occurs in fence corners and on the border of woodlands, and is protected from molestation by state laws.

Culver's Root, *Veronica virginica* L.

CULVER'S ROOT

No more beautiful plant can be grown in the perennial border than the native Culver's root (see Picture 21 at end of book) which is often seen growing along roadsides. The numerous tall willowy wands of white foamlike bloom give to the garden an air of delicacy scarce equalled in any other plant. It is entirely hardy, spreads very slowly, and blooms in July after the great spring outburst is over. In rich soil the plant will attain fully six feet in height and if cut back after blooming will send out a second but minor display.

187

Culver's root is an American plant used by the Indians as a laxative, although the fresh root is a violent, ofttimes dangerous, purge. One name, Beaumont's root, refers to the fact that its value was recognized by the noted physician of that name, known best as the first to watch the working of the human stomach through a pane of glass which he inserted into the open wound of a French-Canadian trooper who had been shot in action. The physician was stationed at Mackinac Island, Michigan, at the time, as surgeon in the United States Army.

Its best-known name, Culver's root, perpetuates that of an early Illinois physician who learned of its value from the Indians.

The plant is a collectable herb and is rapidly disappearing from the American scene.

PLANTAGINACEAE

Plantain, *Plantago major* L.

"Oh, sir, plantain, a plain plantain! . . . no salve, sir, but a plantain!"

Thus begs the clown with a broken shin in *Love's Labour's Lost* (Act III, Sc. 1), and Romeo says much the same:

Rom. "Your plantain-leaf is excellent for that."
Ben. "For what, I pray thee?"
Rom. "For your broken shin."
— *Romeo and Juliet,* Act I, Sc. 2.

Plantain was one of the few herbs reputed to heal broken bones.

"These poor slight wounds need not a plantain," says a player in *The Two Noble Kinsmen* (by John Fletcher and William Shakespeare), inferring that the herb was used for serious injuries rather than for mere minor ones. The schoolmistress grew in her dame's garden in William Shenstone's long poem "plantain ribbed, that heals the reaper's wound," which undoubtedly was a deep, serious, sickle-blade wound.

Thus it is seen that the ubiquitous weed in almost every lawn was once held in high regard, however far it may have fallen at present.

Plantain is of world-wide distribution although the Indians claimed the white man brought it to America. In spite of the fact that one of its common names is "white man's foot," **Kalm,** one of our earliest botanists, thinks it was a native.

The weed can be traced back at least to Chaucer, who mentions it along with pellitory, an herb reputed at that period to heal broken bones. It is one of the few herbs mentioned in Holinshed's *Chronicle of England* (1577–8) upon which Shakespeare drew for his historical material, some nameless plant being referred to as "a kind of herbe like unto plantain."

The Chinese used the herb as greens and in the sixteenth century they were thrown into the stew pot. But to-day the plant is no more than a pernicious weed which even the lawnmower misses, although the seed affords valuable bird food.

PLANTAIN

RUBIACEAE

Woodruff, *Asperula odorata* L.

Woodruff owes its chief virtue to its sweet odor; it was never a potherb and was of minor importance in medicine, but it was one of the best of the strewing herbs, due to the presence of coumarin, a phenol, salicylaldehyde, which is also present in new-mown hay, in the tonka bean, and in yellow clover. Coumarin was one of the very first of the coal-tar derivatives to be synthesized in the laboratory and was discovered by Sir William Perkin in 1868, revolutionizing the whole of organic chemistry.

The plant is a low creeping one with fragile stem, whorled leaves, and a loose raceme of minute white flowers in June and July. It is native to dark shady forests of temperate Asia and Europe and first appears in Saxon leechbooks of 1000 A.D. as "wuderofe," its strong odor making it valuable in smelling salts for headaches. German references occur as early as 1265 and by the fourteenth century it was used in Sweden and England in an ointment and called "herb Walter," for Walter de Elvesdon, of whom nothing further is known, the name being soon contracted to herb water. Woodruff was an al-

WOODRUFF

leviate plant only, hence it never sank very deeply into medical lore.

It was a favorite garden plant for its odor which is released only upon crushing the foliage. It was fairly abundant, easy to grow, and hence a capital strewing herb for the floors of manors and churches.

> "As aromatic plants bestow
> No spicy frangrance while they grow,
> But crush'd or trodden to the ground,
> Diffuse their balmy sweets around."
> — GOLDSMITH, *The Haunch of Venison.*

·An item appears among the churchwardens' accounts of a London church during the reign of Edward IV (1442–1483):

"For Rose garlondis and Woodrove garlondis on St. Barnabe's Daye, 11 pence."

St. Barnabas' day occurs on June 11.

A sprig of the sweet-smelling herb was taken to church by maidens along with sweet mary and other aromatic leaves and when held in the warm hand a pleasant aroma filled the region of the holder. It was also a favorite guardrobe and one writer says "when drawers are opened, the sweet breath of cowslips and new-mown hay will give a welcome to a feast of reason and a flow of soul."

Ladies' Bedstraw, *Galium verum* L.

Why should a fragile little trailing vine be called ladies' bedstraw? For exactly the reason the name implies; men could sleep on coarse straw, but high-born ladies of the late Middle

Ages demanded the softest available material for their couches and the matted herbage of this plant exactly fitted the purpose. The dried stems are soft and springy and do not readily crumble to dust. The plant first went by the name Our Lady's bedstraw — and this name is sufficient to date the first use of the plant. Our Lady's mantle, Our Lady's shoe-laces, Our Lady's glove, and so on *ad nauseam* were given humble plants during the Middle Ages when ritualism was strong and people were pious.

YELLOW BEDSTRAW

Ladies' bedstraw is native to meadows of Europe, from Greece to Lapland, and established its reputation on a very different usage. As early as 50 A.D., Dioscorides wrote of its use in Greece in the dairy to coagulate milk, the word *Galium* coming from the Greek *gala,* meaning milk. The plant seems to have escaped the Saxon writers and to appear first in the fifteenth century when Matthiolus, the first of the great school of Renaissance herbalists, says the people of Tuscany used the plant to curdle their sheep's and goat's milk for cheese making. Dodoens (1576) says, "The herbe gallion may serve for rennet to make cheese." Gerard goes still further and notes that "divers sorts of herbes are called cheese-renning or Ladies Bedstraw" and that the crushed plant was used to make Cheshire cheese. Withering, three centuries later, says "the best Cheshire cheese is still being prepared with the flowers of ladies' bedstraw."

In modern cheese making, however, the plant is not used, the rennet from the cow's stomach being the only source, but bedstraw was brought to this country for that purpose, when, we do not know, save that the early chroniclers do not mention it. The plant occurs locally in Massachusetts, thence westward through New York and Ontario to eastern Michigan, where it occurs locally abundant but not widely distributed.

The plant is a rather desirable one in the rock-garden for its wealth of dainty matted foliage but the yellow-gold flowers in a large loose receme are dull and muddy. It spreads rapidly, however.

Madder, *Rubia tinctoria* L.

Madder is perhaps not obtainable for the herb-garden and is not adapted to Northern climates, although it is grown in our southern states to a small extent and on a larger scale in central Europe. The large root, three or four feet long, stout and slender, is the source of one of the oldest known dyestuffs, being the only red dye known to the Egyptians. The Greeks and Romans also used it for woollens, cottons and leather.

However, the ancient art of dyeing was lost to history until the time of the Renaissance when, like many another "lost art," it was revived to compete with the newly discovered cochineal and dyewoods. The plant was grown extensively by 1507 in Germany, France, and the Netherlands. Holinshed says in his *Chronicle of England* (1587) that "madder, for long neglected, is now a little revived and offereth itself to prove no small benefit unto our country." He notes further that the commerce in madder and woad to the Continent stood next to wool and tin in English exports.

Dyers were men of importance at this period and among the most respected of professional men. In Saint David's churchyard, in Exeter, there lies a Sir Thomas Jefford, dyer to King James II, who presented to that monarch a piece of woollen goods dyed a deep blue on one side and a scarlet on the other, a remarkable feat at the time. The dyes used were undoubtedly woad and madder.

VALERIANACEAE

Garden Heliotrope, *Valeriana officinalis* L.

The herb valerian is a common plant in the perennial border for its wealth of tiny fragrant flowers blooming with iris and pe-

onies. The plant is a hairy perennial spreading slowly by rope-like white runners, and bears coarsely-toothed long light-green foliage mostly near the ground and a three-foot stalk of bloom spreading out at the top in a flat cyme of pinkish-whitish tiny tubular flowers.

The herb portion of the plant is the root and stout runners which are dug and dried in the fall, comprising the "valerian" of the druggists. Valerian was used by the Egyptians, the Greeks, and the Romans, being an ingredient in the

GARDEN HELIOTROPE

Mithradates Antidote. It reached the North as early as the ninth century under the Old-English names "setuale," "setwell," and "setwall," these names occurring frequently in medical works for the next few hundred years, although it seems always to have been of only minor importance, used for fevers, for aches and pains, for ulcer of the mouth, as a sedative, and as an antispasmodic.

However, the drug is still used by physicians for hysteria, epilepsy, nervous diseases, whooping cough, and in the delirium of low fevers, and it is considered a good nerve tonic. It is said to induce sleep where opium fails. The plant is cultivated in Saxony, the Netherlands, and in Shropshire, England, on a commercial scale, and to a small extent in Vermont and New York state.

Cat's valerian is one name for valerian, and Charles Lamb speaks of "the cats, when they purr over a new-found sprig of valerian." However, the writer has yet to find a cat who notices the plant at all. Still, like catnip, it is used to bait traps for wildcats and even rats.

Centranthus ruber (see Picture 22 at end of book), known also as *V. ruber,* commonly called red valerian and Jupiter's beard (from the character of the stamens), is a most desirable perennial for the northern garden. It bears a raceme of bloom like that of *V. officinalis* but of a most beautiful crushed-raspberry color and the foliage is gray-green, glaucous, thick, and very smooth. The plant attains two feet in

RED VALERIAN

height, blooming late in June in the North, but if the old flowers are cut off immediately, it will bloom for most of the rest of the summer. Seeds are available and the plant easy to grow from seed.

The plant is odorless and not strictly an old herb, for it had no reputation as a useful plant. It was known very early in history, however, and comes from Persia and the Near East. It has no medical or culinary use.

Little valerian, corn salad and fetticus are old names for *Valerianella lacustra,* a plant cultivated for centuries in England and on the Continent as a salad plant. It was brought to this country early and has escaped to fields in the East, an inconspicuous weed less than a foot tall, with a cyme of tiny blue flowers.

Greek valerian (*Polemonium reptans*) is a member of the phlox family and bears no relation to the above plants save for a resemblance in name. The yellow lady's-slipper (*Cypripedium pubescens*) is sometimes called American valerian from the strong odor of the root, as is also the exceedingly rare ram's head lady's-slipper (*C. arietimum*), both of which should be protected in all states but which are collected and sold as valerian in many.

COMPOSITAE

The third largest group of herbs comprises the Compositae, often strong-odored, daisylike plants which were brought to this country for food or medicine but which have now spread from coast to coast as pernicious weeds.

Elecampane, *Inula helenium* L.

Julia, the daughter of Augustus Caesar, is said to have eaten the candied root of elecampane daily as a sweetmeat, which Pliny calls an "extremely wholesome" sweet, although the root has a powerful odor and bitter taste. It was cooked and preserved in honey and was also dried and reduced to a flour and mixed with honey or vinegar, or it was cut into small chunks and molded with raisins or dates, affording Roman epicures a delicious dessert.

Horace describes an epicure's dinner consisting of sea-eel elaborately dressed and "in the sauce green rockets and bitter elecampane" were boiled (*Satires*, Book 2).

Trace of the confection is lost until the late Renaissance when a writer says, "I noticed every child without exception had a bottle of elecampane — the younger ones having one tied round their necks — all sucking away at this curious compound of

Spanish juice, sugar and water with great assiduity. I was informed by a very old man that the custom had always obtained on this day (Easter Monday) as long as he could remember." *
Nineteenth-century writers comment on the sweet thus: Thackeray in *The Newcomes* says, "I don't know how he spent his pin money except in hard-hack and alycompaine"; Beresford speaks of "some long-forgotten bonbon of your boyhood — treacle, elecampane, stick licorice"; an anonymous writer of 1875 says of the molded confection, "I have admired Nelson in marble and eaten him in elecampane."

But the plant has enjoyed a reputation in medicine as well. Hippocrates prescribed it for specific ailments of the brain, stomach, kidneys and uterus; the Romans used it for indigestion — which may account for its use in candied form; and during

ELECAMPANE

the Middle Ages it was regarded as a valuable tonic and stimulant. It was in sufficiently good repute when our first colonists came to America for them to bring it as soon as possible. Josselyn, writing fifty years after the first colonists arrived, discovered that the plant was "excellent for stuffings of the lungs upon colds, shortness of wind and the ptisick-maladies that the natives are often troubled with." He says he helped several Indians make a drink of the root, with sassafras root, catnip, anise seed, fennel seed, and "molasses spirit," the whole simmered down to a thick syrup, bottled, and taken a few spoonfuls at a time.

The plant is no longer used in candied form but is listed in

* T. F. T. Dyer, *British Popular Customs,* London, 1876.

the United States Pharmacopoeia and National Formulary and used rather widely in cough medicines to-day, just as it was in the time of Hippocrates.

Elecampane is a six-foot perennial scarcely adapted to the home garden unless it be a large one, as it spreads rather rapidly. The leaves are often very large, rugose and leathery above and soft and velvety beneath. Flowers occur sparingly in racemes and might be taken by the uninitiated for dingy little sunflowers. The foliage is bitter but has very little odor.

It came originally from the region of the Caucasus and thence to Siberia and spread early through much of Europe. It was a weed in this country before 1672, now to be found in fence corners and along roadsides from Nova Scotia to Minnesota and south as far as North Carolina.

Camomile, *Anthemis nobilis* L.

When a garden visitor is given a sprig of camomile to smell, he expects to be met with a strong rank disagreeable odor like that of the dooryard mayweed for the foliage is similar, but is agreeably surprised to find instead that it smells like a ripe mellow apple. The word "camomile" is from the Greek *chamaimelon* meaning "earth apple." *Anthemis* is also from the Greek, *anthemion* meaning "flower."

Camomile (see Picture 23 at end of book), is a low creeping plant spreading by runners, with parsleylike much crisped dark-green pinnate foliage not two inches long with delightful odor, and white daisylike almost odorless flowers standing up on long stems. The plant flowers sparingly. It is a hardy perennial easily raised from seed.

OLD-TIME HERBS

A bed soon becomes compact, as a medieval writer discovered who said:

> "A camomile bed
> The more it is trodden
> The more it will spread."

This fact made the plant a useful one in horticulture and it was used for walks, between stones in paths, and for banks. "Large walks like the Temple Gardens of Thessaly, raised with gravel and sand, having seats and banks of Camomile; all this delighteth the mind and bringeth health to the body." Thus spoke one of the noted gardeners of Renaissance times, Lawson, in *The Orchard*.

John Lyly says in *Euphues or the Anatomy of Wit* (1578), "Camomile, the more it is trodden and pressed down, the more it spreadeth," and this expression became popular and was repeated many times during the next two hundred years. Shakespeare, ever ready to pick up a sprightly bit, says in *King Henry IV,* Part I:

"I do not only marvel where thou spendeth thy time, but also how thou art accompanied: for though the camomile, the more it is trodden on the faster it grows, yet youth, the more it is wasted, the sooner it wears." — Act. II, Sc. 4.

Only a few years later, in a play of anonymous authorship, the same idea appears:

> "The Camomile shall teach thee patience
> Which riseth best when trodden most upon."
> — *The More the Merrier.*

Other similar usages might be cited up to 1748, and the plant made capital strewing material even though minute in size, for the odor is strong and permeating.

Camomile was never a kitchen herb but has enjoyed a long reputation in medicine. The Egyptians used the flowers in ointments; the Romans used them internally for liver and bladder troubles and wove them into garlands for festivals. The tenth-century Saxon leechbooks say of it, "Let hym (that hath sore eyes) take the ooze of Chamaimelon and smere the eyes therewyth." The name varies considerably in literature from 1265 to 1450 — camomella, camamyle, cananilla, canemille and so on.

CAMOMILE

Not until 1568 does its chief virtue appear, when a physician used it as a sudorific to induce perspiration. Gerard says, "It easeth the peine in the chest coming from winde," and in Germany the dried flowers are still made into a tea and given for children's colic and for dysentery. A camomile tea or tisane is widely used in Europe as a mild sudorific in place of coffee or tea, and the beverage is served regularly on the French Atlantic liners.

Thomas Hood (1799–1845) in complimenting the various professions in *Wreaths for Ministers* regards camomile as the badge of the physician:

> "How the doctor's brow should smile,
> Crown'd with wreaths of camomile!"

Camomile is of considerable value in the perfume industry, and is grown in Belgium, France, Germany, and England for the essential oil which is distilled and the various fractions — ethers and acids — used separately. A double flower gives a

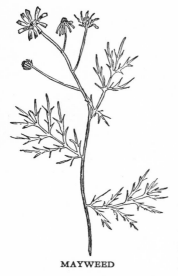

MAYWEED

milder oil which is more reliable in strength and more constant in quality than the single.

Our dooryard mayweed (*Anthemis cotula* L.), a native plant widespread throughout the world, similar in appearance to camomile but with a much-branched flower stem, is also of medicinal use in spite of its rank odor and bitter taste. "Stinking Camomill" was well named and used in cases of hysteria; it was introduced into California before the advent of the English, and called "Spanish manzanillo" or "manzanitta." A tea was steeped from it for children's colic.

Feverfew (*Matricaria parthenium* L.) (see Picture 24 at end of book), a similar composite with strong not unpleasant odor, was formerly used for the purpose implied in its name. The Emperor Charlemagne grew it under the name *Febrifuga* and down through history this usage can be traced. It saved the life of the hero in Charles Reade's *The Cloister and the Hearth,* "when the grand medicines of the physicians came up faster than they went down."

It was also used for quinsy, for the ague, as an antispasmodic in hysteria, and in Roman times for erysipelas and warts.

FEVERFEW

Feverfew is an almost indispensable perennial in the garden for its constant supply of bloom from spring to frost and for the pleasing white mass-effect it lends to the border. The plant reseeds itself and it is the seedlings coming along all summer that give fresh bloom. The old plants are liable to die out after blooming unless frequently topped. The old single daisy has been supplanted by much improved bloom with no dull yellow center. There is even a yellow-headed *Matricaria* of dwarf nature and shorter blooming period.

Yarrow (*Achillea millefolium* L.) is a close relative of the camomiles and has been used in medicine at least since 1000 B.C. for agglutinating blood. The Greeks used it on the field of battle and Pliny says the genus name comes from the fact that Achilles used it to stop the flow of blood in the arrow wounds of his men.

It was used in the North as early as 725 A.D. and in the Saxon leech-

YARROW

books of 1000 A.D. appears as "millefolium." In Stockholm in a 1425 citation it is called "neseblod." Other old names are soldier's woundwort, sanguinary and nosebleed, which indicate its chief use.

There is a rose-colored yarrow and also one with deep red bloom which are desirable garden plants, but the field yarrow, with finely dissected foliage and muddy white flat cyme of flowers, is too weedy for the perennial garden. It belongs, however, in that portion devoted to herbs.

Lavender Cotton, *Santolina chamaecyparissus* L.

Santolin was introduced into northern Europe at the time of the Renaissance when diminutive hedge material was sought which would withstand close clipping. It seems to be mentioned first in 1538, by the horticulturist, William Turner, who may have introduced it from southern Europe where it thrives on poor arid soil. It was still scarce a hundred years later, for Parkinson writes in 1629, "The rarity and novelty of this herb, being for the most part but in the gardens of great persons, doth cause it to be of great regard."

The plant offered a varied color note to the garden, for it is well-named, lavender cotton (see Picture 25 at end of book),

LAVENDER COTTON

the foliage similar in size to that of lavender but considerably whitened, although it is finely dissected; it grows slowly, is bushy from the base, and makes a compact little hedge, more hardy than several other plants used for the purpose. It was brought to Virginia by the Cavaliers for their gardens imitative of those grown in England at the time.

Santolin is perfectly hardy in our Northern states and, while it grows but slowly, will form a plant of considerable size and spread. Flowers occur in racemes over the top of the plant, which in June may appear to be a mass of golden-yellow. It is very slow from seed and is generally purchased from nurserymen in pots although not at all common with them. It likes full sun and rather arid soil, and makes a good front-border plant for several years, or permanently if kept clipped.

The foliage has a strong aromatic odor and bitter taste and seems admirably adapted to some medicinal use, but it was introduced after the heydey of herb medicines was over. It was laid away with the winter woollens, however, to repel moths and for its aroma. It was frequently called French lavender. It has no connection with santonin, or Levant wormseed, the latter being a drug obtained from the flowerbuds of *Artemisia maritima* and *A. pauciflora,* and used to eradicate roundworms.

Sweet Mary, *Chrysanthemum balsamita tanacetoides* L.

"Who cares now to find out what costmary may be," writes an English garden author, "which used to be grown in every farmhouse garden?" and still later another says, "By now (1933) its cultivation has practically ceased and the plant become very rare."

However, it has by no means died out in this country, for the watchful eye can often find it in fence corners or on clay banks along roadsides on back-country roads near farmhouses. Almost every old farmhouse site in the East or Middle West if it has been left alone will yield several old-fashioned plants, always including this one (see Picture 26 at end of book). Ribbon grass, gill-over-the-ground, carpenter's bench, flowering currant, common purple lilac, an occasional pear tree, a scrawny double red rose, a clump of tansy and another of sweet mary frequently remain to denote former habitation after the little cellar hole has disappeared and the last vestige of log and shingle have disintegrated. Sweet mary is often found in old cemeteries, a fact which is true of a great many of the old-time herbs.

Sweet mary is one of the very nicest of the old herbs for its pleasing odor, and for this reason alone worthy of a place in every herb-garden. It has no present economic use, although the wife of a market gardener who sold the writer a plant a few years ago remarked, "You can put a few leaves in the bottom of a cake pan and they will flavor your cake," the gardener adding, "And you can crush a leaf and lay it on a sore or bruise and it will heal it at once."

The plant is a hardy perennial, attaining some five feet in height in good soil, and spreading all too rapidly by runners. Foliage is tongue-shaped, hence one common name for it, tongue plant, and flowers occur in loose heads, consisting of little golden buttons. The foliage has an odor all its own, sweet but strong,

SWEET MARY

often called balsamitic, hence the species name. It is bitter to the taste.

Sweet mary probably originated in Kashmir, India; it was grown in the gardens of ancient Egypt for its pleasing odor. The thick aromatic root of some "cost" was used by the Greeks and Romans as a spice, but it is not certain that this was the plant. The plant reached Switzerland, France, and Spain before the ninth century and is mentioned in the Emperor Charlemagne's list as "cost." It was used in medicine in England by the year 1000, imported from the Continent. A manuscript of

1400 A.D. mentions the plant thus: "Anoint the wound with hote oiles as the oile of coste." In 1585, "Cost or detyn (dittany-of-Crete) stampt and mixt with oyle" was used as a salve.

The sweet-smelling foliage was used in the kitchens of the aristocracy of France by 1400. Chopping tables were a part of the kitchen equipment in large establishments and one recipe of the period begins: "Take parsel, and myntes, and costmaryn, and sauge, and mince the fresh foliage on the chopping table." Another recipe begins: "Take a leaf of costmarye, a clove of garlycke."

Sweet mary was introduced into English gardens around 1578 A.D. and soon thereafter references to its use became frequent. Dodoens says "Coostmarie is used in meetes as Sauge, and other hearbes, and especially in salades and sawces, for which purpose it is excellent as it yieldeth a proper sent and Taste."

Most of the colloquial names for sweet mary refer to its use for another purpose — alecost, alecoast, costmary, and cost, the last from the Latin *costum,* an aromatic plant. Being fragrant and bitter, the plant was a favorite of brewers who used it to flavor and give head to ale. References such as these are frequent: "Alecost if it be steeped a while in Ale . . . maketh a pleasant drink" (1620); alecost is "famous for dispatching the parturition of ale and beer" (1676): "Costmary that so likes the Cop" (1630). After hops were introduced, all the old herbs which had been used in ale were dropped, but sweet mary had by now become established in cottage gardens and was beloved for its odor. Maidens carried a leaf or two to church in lieu of perfume, it was tied up in sachets with rosemary and lavender, and it was used as a flavoring when spices were beyond a poor man's purse.

The plant was used in medicine for a variety of ailments —

from eliminating worms in children and killing head lice, through several digestive disorders, to this use: "It is good for them that have eaten hemlocke." However, by 1756, Sir John Hill says, "More virtues have been said of it than it deserves," and soon thereafter it was dropped from the British Pharmacopeia. Even as early as 1788 a writer said, "Although once greatly esteemed as a garden plant, costmary is at present much neglected."

Tansy, *Tanacetum vulgare* L.

Tansy (see Picture 27 at end of book) has been one of the old standbys in the herb-garden for centuries and practically every farmyard in our Eastern and Mid-West states could display a clump of this strongly aromatic medicinal herb. Most people who have lived in the country or in villages recognize the plant

TANSY

and many have drunk tansy tea in their childhood days, remembering the bitter draught with repugnance.

Tansy is fairly common even yet along roadsides and the writer recently saw a fine clump of it in the clay abutment of a bridge in the Upper Peninsula of Michigan, surely a test of its hardiness. The foliage of tansy is attractive if one can avoid the odor, being large, feather-veined and dissected as finely as that of yarrow, and very dark green in color. The flowers occur in large flat cymes and consist of numerous hard little dull-golden buttons. They are being used by city florists to an increasing extent when in bloom in July. "Bitter buttons" is one old name for the plant.

Tansy is a native of Greece and the Crimea but is omitted from ancient records, at least in recognizable descriptions. Charlemagne grew it at Aix-la-Chapelle (830 A.D.) and the Benedictine monks of Saint-Gall cultivated it in their physic-garden; in 1265 it was called *tanesie* in Germany; and Sir A. Conan Doyle says in *Sir Nigel* that the peasants of 1348 A.D. used many "tea-like drinks which cost not a penny — mallow tea, tansy tea, and others, the secret of which has passed."

During the fifteenth century there are records that tansy was used in the curing of ale both in France and England; at this time it occupied a high place among medicinal herbs, the tender foliage, fresh or dried, being steeped and the tea given for flatulence, children's colic, and abdominal cramp, in seizures of the gout, and even for the plague. One such prescription reads: "Do take sauge, tansey, sorrel, saint mary gouldes (marigold), stamp these erbes in a mortar and drink the iouise (juice) of hem in ale or clere water and it schalle distroye the pestilence be it never so felle."

Tansy has for centuries been a young girl's medicine, tansy tea alleviating slow and painful menstruation. It was considered a splendid cathartic, a gentle stimulant to the digestive processes, and even a sedative.

During the fifteenth century small cakes containing bitter tansy juice were eaten at Easter as an annual reminder of the bitter herbs eaten by the Jews at the Passover Feast. Later the cakes gave way to puddings:

> "On Easter Sunday be the pudding seen
> To which the tansy lends her sober green."

From this annual penance rose the custom of serving tansy puddings at other times during spring, as a gentle cathartic and blood cleanser after a winter of foods deficient in vegetables. Later, a dish made from eggs and flavored with tansy came to be a popular main course and was called simply a "tansy." These lines from an old book corroborate this custom:

> "Praying you suppe with us this night,
> And ye shall have made, at your devis,
> A great pudding, or a round haggis,
> A French moile, a tansie, or a froise."

The *moile* was a dish of marrow and grated bread; the tansy an omelet with tansy juice; and the *froise* an omelet with strips of bacon in it.

A recipe of 1420 reads: "Take faire Tansy and grinde it in a mortar. And take eyern, yolkes and white, and draw hem through a streynour and straw al o the iuice of the Tansey; and meddle the egges and the Iuise togidre." It does not say whether this is fried or baked. Many of the old manuscripts mix Old German with the English words and many of the long English words are spelled as they are to-day while shorter ones are not. A recipe of 1513 calls for "a tansaye fryde, and other bake metes," indicating that the tansy held equal importance with the meat.

Samuel Pepys (1666) says he "spent an hour or two with pleasure with her and ate a tansy," and Izaak Walton used it to flavor some of his fish. He says: "In the spring (the cooks) make of them (minnows) excellent Minnow-Tansies; being fried with yolks of eggs, the flowering cowslips, and of primrose, and a little tansy; thus used they make a dainty dish of meat." One writer of 1683 comments dryly that "whereas a cod could be bought for fourpence, the seasonings for its stuffing were not to be had for less than nine shillings!"

Even as late as 1860 an apple-tansy is mentioned in cookbooks; how it was made is left to the imagination. It is said that the city of Chester, England, still clings to its tansy pudding of old.

Tansy was one of the herbs of colonial times in America and by 1785 it had become widely naturalized over New England. One wonders whether tansy cakes, puddings, omelets, and apples were New England dishes as well.

The plant is still listed in the United States Pharmacopoeia, chiefly for its use as a tea to avert colds, a cold decoction to be used during convalescence from fevers and jaundice, as an anthelmintic, and externally for use on bruises, tumors, and inflammations. The drug is a powerful one, too strong doses resulting in vomiting, convulsions, and even death. It is cultivated in some states and the herbage distilled for the use of pharmacists.

Wormwood, *Artemisia absinthium* L.

"Bitter as wormwood" is a simile often used in the Bible. The Israelites hated bitter flavors and gall and wormwood (see Picture 28 at end of book) were the most disagreeable tastes they could conceive. The plant is mentioned no less than twelve times in the Bible, sometimes obscurely, but many of the references are well known. "For her lips drop honey, and her mouth is smoother than oil, but in the end she is bitter as wormwood, sharp as a two-edged sword" (Proverbs 5:3-4).

The plant is native to the region of the Ural Mountains, but was taken to Egypt very early in history, being listed in the famous Ebers Papyrus as used for headaches and to eliminate pinworms from the alimentary tract, for which purposes it is still valued to-day.

Artemis, the Greek goddess, is said to have "delivered these flowers to Chiron, the Centaur, who first from their worts set forth a leechdom," i.e. the centaur found them good for human

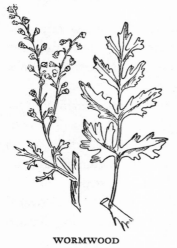

ailments. The Greeks used the bitter plant for many diseases and Dioscorides says also to keep moths from clothing — perhaps the first record of such a use.

The Romans used it as an anthelmintic and stomach tonic and also wove the graceful branches and flowers into garlands and decorated their altars with it and burned it as incense for the fragrant odor. In the early Middle Ages it was used as a "sovereign remedy against seasick-

WORMWOOD

ness." "If anyone proposes a Journey," reads an old Herbal, "then let him take to hold in his hand the wort artemisia, then he will not feel much toil in his journey." Pennyroyal was also a remedy for this malady and the two were often combined. Even in our early colonies, a conserve was made of wormwood, rose petals, ginger, and lemons and used for seasickness.

"Men are seldom in a hurry to drink their wormwod," says Charles Reade in his fifteenth-century romance *The Cloister and the Hearth,* but while disagreeable to take, it is mild in its action and very effective. Linnaeus says it was taken as a bitters for gout, liver complaints, and for scurvy. Outward application gave relief to sprains and bruises, and the herb is of sufficient value to be included in the United States Pharmacopoeia, chiefly for children's pinworms.

It was used in the Middle Ages as protection against insect

vermin as shown in this verse from Tusser, one of the large school of herbalists:

> "While wormwood hath seed get a handful or twaine
> To save against March, to make flea to refraine,
> Where chamber is sweetened and wormwood is strowne
> No flea, for his life, dare abide to be knowne."

It was also used as powder sprinkled in books and manuscripts to keep out book lice, sometimes mixed with powdered cedar-wood and valerian.

It had another practical use, in the brewing of beverages. Wormwood wine is mentioned in Holinshed's *Chronicle of Elizabethan England* (1577) in the interesting chapter on "Food and Diet." The powerful French drink, absinthe, was named from the old Greek word for wormwood, *Apsinthos*. A quaint reference of 1626 says that "a draught of ale and wormwood wine mixed in a morning comforts the heart, scours the maw, and fulfills other beneficial offices."

Wormwood, like tansy, was used in the seventeenth century to flavor cakes.

It did not escape notice of the poets, and Shakespeare refers to it at least four times. The nurse in *Romeo and Juliet* reminds the maiden of the wormwood that was used in her weaning (Act I, Sc. 3). Hamlet, watching the Player King and Queen, remarks aside, "Wormwood, wormwood" (Act III, Sc. 2). In *Love's Labour's Lost* (Act V, Sc. 2), Rosaline says: "To weed this wormwood from your fruitful brain, . . . Visit the speechless sick." And in *The Rape of Lucrece* the victim scourges the villain thus:

> "Thou ravisher, thou traitor, thou false thief,
> Thy honey turns to gall, thy joy to grief! . . .
> Thy sugar'd tongue to bitter wormwood taste."

"May all your good luck turn to wormwood," is the farewell spoken in *It's Never Too Late to Mend,* Charles Reade.

Our early settlers knew the value of the plant and from their introduction it has spread as a weed from Newfoundland and even Hudson's Bay to the Dakotas and south-ward. While a weed, wormwood makes an attractive appearance even in a perennial border, for a single specimen given room is a beautiful shrub, with its silvery, intri-cately-dissected foliage and pyramidal flower stalk. While hardy, much of the top will die back in winter, but it springs up anew from the base. Seeds are obtainable and seed-lings grow apace.

Many other species of *Artemisia* make capital garden material, *A. lactifolia* one of the best, a six-foot plant with a graceful raceme of milk-white sweetly-scented flow-ers in late summer, *A. albidum,* silver king (see Picture 29 at end of book), one of the best of perennial plants and excellent winter decoration when dried, and *A. frigida,* a low rock-garden silky-silvery plant much in demand.

LEAF OF ARTEMISIA
FRIGIDA

Southernwood, *Artemisea abrotanum* L.

"The garden border where I stood
Was sweet with pinks and southernwood."
— JEAN INGELOW, *Reflections.*

Southernwood, lad's love, old man, is an old garden plant well known for the invigorating odor of its skeletonized silvery foliage. No bouquet from our grandmothers' gardens was complete without a sprig of it.

It, too, was a medicinal plant of old, even in Roman times. Horace, bemoaning the decay of the sturdy Romans of old and the rise of a new class of poetasters, says, "Learned and unlearned, we scribble verses, all alike; whereas he who was never on board fears to steer a ship, artisans alone handle tools, physicians alone undertake physicians' duty, and none but a professional man dares prescribe southernwood for a patient" (Epistle II, 1).

Charlemagne grew it in France (812 A.D.) under the name *abrotanum,* the Saxons knew it as "suthe-wurt," and the physicians of the Middle Ages called it, among other versions of the name, "sithen wode" and "sothren wode," from which is derived our common name for the plant. Like so many herbs, it had a multitude of uses for unallied ailments, all the way from "spitting of blood" to relieving serpent bites.

It was an admirable strewing herb, not too expensive, for it grows apace and is entirely hardy in the north.

> "Oft in churches breathing fragrance,
> The sweet and pungent southernwood."
> — SARAH N. CLEGHORN, *A Puritan Lady's Garden.*

Even as late as the last century it was hung about courtrooms in London to avert jail fever which might taint the judges from the poor prisoner brought before the bar. There is no record, however, that either rue or this plant was hung about the cells of the prisoners to destroy the fever at its source.

Southernwood may often be found in old cemeteries, but it is rather uncommon in gardens to-day. It was introduced by our first colonists and may be found in fence corners and waste lands from Massachusetts to Nebraska, and some horticulturists

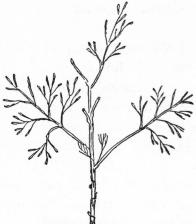

LEAF OF ROMAN WORMWOOD

have it for sale with other old-time herbs. It spreads rapidly from runners.

Roman wormwood, *Artemisia pontica* L. (see Picture 30 at end of book), has foliage even more skeletonized than southernwood and a much pleasanter odor. It, too, was used in olden times for a variety of ailments.

"Old woman," *Artemisia stelleriana* Bess. (see Picture 31 at end of book), is frequently used in rock-gardens for its thick, feltlike, almost white foliage, which is broad and blunt, quite unlike many of the wormwoods. It is a prostrate little shrub, entirely hardy, with a flower stalk a foot high consisting of relatively large hard buttons of a dull muddy-gold color. It is readily available from nurserymen. It comes to us from Asia by way of European gardens and was introduced very early and has gone wild, even on Atlantic sea beaches whence comes one common name, beach wormwood.

Tarragon, *Artemisia dracunculus* L., is one of the most useful of the wormwoods and immediately suggests vinegar. The bitter principle of most members of the genus is missing from this one, which has a pleasant taste, similar to that of sweet basil, chervil and licorice.

The plant is hardy, but seldom flowers and sets seeds in the North, consequently it is generally propagated by cuttings or divisions. It is

TARRAGON

native to southern Siberia and Russia, but was grown in Greece and known to Hippocrates and cultivated in Egypt for its peculiar flavor. The Emperor Charlemagne grew it under the name *draganeta*. The Arabian physician, Avicenna (980–1037 A.D.) used tarragon in medicine, and Elyot, an English physician, wrote in 1538, "Tragonia has a taste lyke gungyr." Langham, another English writer (1579), says "Tarragon is good in sallads with lettuce."

Sir John Evelyn puts its virtues thus (*Diary*, 1693): "Tarragon is one of the perfumery or spicy Furniture of our Sallets." Abercrombie, noted horticulturist, says of it, "Tarragon is a fine flavoured aromatic plant to improve flavour of soups and sallads." (*Everyman His Own Gardener*, 1767.)

Tarragon was used to flavor beverages, and to-day it is widely used in home-made vinegar, the tender foliage and flowering tops made into a pickle. In the south of Europe it is popular in sauces for fish and soups and is used to flavor mayonnaise dressings.

Mugwort (*Artemisia vulgaris* L.) is a homely weed with foliage similar to that of wormwood but broader in all parts and sharp-pointed at the tips of leaf divisions. The foliage is green and smooth above and cottony-white beneath. Flower heads are like those of the whole genus. The plant occurs wild from Nova Scotia to Michigan but is not common in its western range. It came from northern Asia and has been used since early times in Europe, and later in this country, for women's complaints. One of its old names is "motherwort," from which the common name is a contraction. Drayton puts its chief use thus:

"The belly hurt by birth by mugwort to make sound."
— *Polyolbion* (1613–1622).

Besides being of value as a uterine remedy, it was an antispasmodic for many diseases and used as a substitute for quinine in fevers, and as a counterirritant for ulcers. Other old-time usages were these: "If it be placed under the saddle of a horse, it will make him travaile fresh and lustily"; "If a footman take mugwort and put it into his shoes in the morning, he may go forty miles before noon and not be weary"; "If any propose a journey, then let him take in his hand this wort Artemisia and let him have it with him and then he will not feel much toil in his journey."

Pot-Marigold, *Calendula officinalis* L.

One has only to visit flower shops to realize that the cultivation of marigolds of almost saucer size, fine colorings, and long-keeping qualities has become a sizeable industry in this country. The old-time herb marigold has indeed come into its own.

Marigold is classed as an herb because of the coloring matter which can be extracted from its petals. In Roman times, foods colored a golden yellow were highly prized and a badge of luxury. The color used was saffron, and saffron was one of the most expensive products of the realm. Two other plants were sometimes used, false saffron, *Carthamus tinctorius,* which gave a reddish tint, and *Calendula officinalis,* which seems to have been less well known for some reason, perhaps for its detectable distinctive flavor.

However, calendula came from eastern Asia and was known to the ancients and used in India, in Egypt, and at Constantinople for the same purpose, the dried flowers used to color and flavor soups, syrups, and conserves.

When the Romans went to Britain they found true saffron too difficult to obtain and resorted to substitutes. When calendula was first used there we do not know, but there are records that it was used in Saxon times. However, thus early the name — merscmear-gealla — is taken to refer to the marsh marigold (*Calthra palustris*) as well. A name used soon thereafter is *spousa solis,* bride of the sun, and for reasons given below there can be no doubt that this refers to calendula. Other names included Mary Gowles, "gowl" being a general term for daisy, easily transferable into "gold," hence "marigold."

By the eleventh century there are definite proofs that this marigold was used as food coloring, although it is quite probable that it had been in use in England since the Romans first arrived. Fifteenth-century records in France and England indicate that marigolds were used in beverages, both for flavor and for color. Macaulay says in his *History of England* that people in this century "brewed gooseberry wine and cured marigolds." The plant gives unusual color and flavor to cheese and is still used for this purpose.

When the name "pot-marigold" first came into use is not known. John Gay (1685–1732), the Devonshire poet, says:

> "Fair is the gilly flow'r, of gardens sweet,
> Fair is the mary-gold, for pottage meet."
> — *The Shepherd's Week.*

Our first colonists brought marigolds with them, and Josselyn says (1672), "Of such herbe among us which do thrive are parsley, marigold, chervil, burnet, winter savory, summer savory, time, and sage," but marigolds never went wild like some of their plants. We should like to know the use our forefathers made of marigolds.

For marigolds enjoyed a medical reputation with more basis in fact than many an old-time herb. In the fourteenth century, the flowers were dried and pounded in a mortar with the root of the Madonna lily and used in some base as a plaster for felons; the former was incorporated into honey and taken "to cure trembling of the harte"; the flower was used for ague, toothache, headache, red eyes, jaundice and sundry other ailments. Hill (1786) says, "A tea made of the fresh flowers is good for fevers, promoting perspiration and throwing out anything that ought to appear on the skin."

The flowers have for long been used as a hemostatic, and as such Miss Gertrude Jekyll gave over a large part of her noted Sussex garden to the cultivation of the flower during the Great War, sending innumerable bushels of the flowers to first-aid stations in France to be used as dressings for wounded soldiers.

Calendula ointment is still prescribed by a few physicians in this country as a mild astringent and soothing paste for skin affections. A fluid extract is manufactured by pharmaceutical houses as a carminative and the plant is listed in the National Formulary. In country districts in this country a syrup is made from the flowers for ulcers of the mouth.

The Marigold has enjoyed far wider literary associations than fall to the lot of many of the old-time plants, for it has the unusual quality of turning with the sun.

"The Marigold observes the Sun
More than my Subjects me have done."
— Turner's *Herbal*, 1553.

Thus spoke King Charles I during his kingly meditations on "A Walk In A Garden on the Isle of Wight." Francis Quarles (1592–1664) calls the flower "The sun-observing Marigold."

"A Wife" in 1613 said of her husband, "His wit, like the Marigold, openeth with the sun," and John Cleveland (1613–1659) says:

> "The marigold, whose courtier's face
> Echoes in the sun, and doth unlace
> Her at his rise, at his full stop
> Packs and shuts up her gaudy shop."

Nicholas Breton, an obscure Elizabethan writer, says in *Six of the Clock*:

"It is now the sixth hour; the sweet time of the morning; and the sun at every window calls the sleepers from their beds. The Marigold begins to open her leaves, and the dew on the ground doth sweeten the air."

Shakespeare several times mentions the "winking Mary-buds" which begin to "ope their golden eyes" and Keats perhaps gives the opening flower the finest lines of all:

> "Open afresh you round of starry folds,
> Ye ardent marigolds!
> Dry up the moisture from your golden lids."
> — *I Stood Tiptoe upon a Little Hill.*

Many others write of the opening of the flower, but it also retires with the Sun. Perdita gives to men of middle age the flowers of midsummer:

> "Hot lavender, mints, savory, marjoram;
> The marigold, that goes to bed wi' the sun
> And with him rises weeping."
> — *The Winter's Tale,* Act IV, Sc. 4.

Critics have questioned whether marigold or the sunflower is meant in the last reference, but Ellacombe, authority on Shakespearean flowers, says, "There can be no doubt that pot-marigold was meant, for it was always a great favorite in our forefathers' gardens."

Marigolds had been used as funeral offerings in ancient Greece, and Shakespeare uses this knowledge in *Pericles:*

> "The purple violets, and marigolds,
> Shall, as a carpet, hang upon thy grave
> While summer days do last."
>
> — Act IV, Sc. I.

"Marigolds on deathbeds blowing" are mentioned in *The Two Noble Kinsmen* (the play by Shakespeare and his friend John Fletcher).

However, as early as 1523 marigolds were so widely grown as to have become weeds, for "Golds is an yll wede and groweth commonlye in barleye and pees" fields, although the *gold* may refer to some other flower, like the buttercup. Dickens says in *Dombey and Son,* "The small front-gardens had the unaccountable property of producing nothing but marigolds."

Chicory, *Cichorium intybus* L.

From the maze of tough ropelike stems almost devoid of foliage, one would scarcely realize that the common roadside "Blue Sailors" was a desirable salad herb, but as such it was cultivated for at least six hundred years. However, one of its old names was *Barbe de Capuchin,* suggesting that the stems were as tough as the beard of a Capuchin monk. The tough stem, however, was never used, but always cut away at the crown, and tender root leaves allowed to develop. These basal leaves, grown to large size, were bleached to avoid any trace of strong bitter flavor and to enhance

the tenderness, and were popular as "sallet-furniture" in the heydey of herbs.

Chicory and the plant we call endive were confused in classic
literature, both being used in salads. Dioscorides records two sorts
of chicory, and Lucilius contrasts
the simplicity of fare among the
frugal Roman forefathers with
the depraved luxury in his own
time. His ancestors had been content to dine on "the tear-produc-
ing onion with its lacrymose
shells, the endive besides, stretch-
ing out with feet like horses,"
which a critic says "probably al-

CHICORY

ludes to the wide-spreading fibres of the Intybus." Virgil mentions chicory also, and Ovid says Baucis and Philemon set before their distinguished visitors at least three courses:

> "A garden salad was the third supply,
> Of endive, radishes, and succory."
> — *Metamorphoses,* Book VIII.

Chicory is native to most of Europe, including England,
although like many another plant it may have had an Asiatic
beginning far back in history, for the name is from the Arabic,
of unknown meaning. Its long taproot makes the plant adaptable
to many soils and conditions of drought, for it is found on arid
gravelly and chalky hillsides as well as along sterile roadsides.

In medieval medicine the plant was used as a narcotic, sometimes administered before operations, but its chief use was in
spring salads. Both root and foliage were used. However, its
chief use, discovered some one hundred thirty years ago, was

225

as a coffee substitute or adulterant, or as an independent beverage with considerable reputation of itself. It came into use in England when the tax imposed on coffee became too high and various substitutes were tried, acorns, horse-chestnuts, turnips, rye and others, chicory giving a beverage most nearly like coffee. However, it lacks the stimulant caffein which makes an infusion of coffee more agreeable to most tastes.

The plant is grown rather widely in Europe for this use and to some extent in this country, notably near Bay City, Michigan. Chicory used with coffee gives a better color, and adds a trace of bitterness from the presence of inulin, the bitter principle of many composites. It is said to have been brought to America by Governor Winthrop as food for his sheep. In Belgium, a variety of chicory called *witloof* has long been grown for use in salads. It is transferred to trenches in the greenhouse in the fall, and the heads cut off before tops develop. The root is eaten during the winter sliced in salad or boiled as a vegetable.

Endive, *Cichorium endivia,* is thought to have originated in China, but it was known to the Romans as a favorite salad ingredient, and Virgil sings its praises. It was long used in the south of Europe but seems not to have reached England until the sixteenth century. Gerard (1597) refers to the plant and Gilbert White (*Natural History of Selbourne*) quotes from an article written in 1663 that "curled endive bleached is much used beyond the seas" and "for a raw sallet seemed to excel lettuce itself."

Endive is coming into favor with Americans for winter salads.

Dandelion, *Taraxacum officinale* Weber

Dandelion root has been used in medicine from ancient times. "It is one of the drugs overrated, derogated, extirpated, and rein-

stated time and time again from Theophrastus' time to to-day." *
It is supposed to be a native of Greece and Asia Minor but very
early became a weed and followed civilization to all parts of the
world.

The Chinese have for ages used the plant as a potherb, and
called it "earth nail" and "golden hair": gardeners who have tried
in vain to extirpate the plant from the lawn will appreciate the
former.

In the Middle Ages, when vegetables were scarce and every
green thing of the fields was investigated for its antiscorbutic
value, dandelion was used as a potherb and in salads, the leaves
often bleached to remove much of the bitter principle, and it is
superfluous to state that it is widely favored to-day especially by
Italians who visit the suburban areas in spring with trowel and
basket for both foliage and flowers, the latter used principally in
wine.

The root is dried and roasted as a coffee substitute and is similar
to chicory in content and flavor. The root also is a valued pharmaceutical product, collected in fall when the milky alkaloidal juice
is most abundant and less bitter than when the plant is flowering.
It is a mild laxative and tonic, and is used in household medicine
for torpid liver and dyspepsia.

Lettuce, *Lactuca sativa* L.

The origin of lettuce is lost in pre-history; it is supposed to have
come from the Himalayas and Siberia, or from Upper Egypt,
but may have had its beginnings on the Mediterranean littoral.
The Egyptians used lettuce, peppermint flowers, and the resin
from the acanthus plant to exterminate worms. Wycliffe translates

* C. F. Millspaugh, *Medicinal Plants*. Philadelphia, 1892.

the "bitter herbs" with which the Jews ate the Passover Feast as "wylde letise," but other herbs claim this distinction.

In Greece lettuce was a food only for the highest classes and was served with olive oil and saffron, and funeral meats consisted of eggs, beans, smallage and lettuce. It was still a luxury in Roman times. Horace asks a friend, "How did you enjoy yourself at the dinner of Nasidiemus, the wealthy? Tell me, what dish first appeased the anger of your appetite?" To which the other replies, "First was served a Lucanian boar . . . ; garnished with pungent rapes, lettuces, radishes, all things suited to rouse the sated stomach." (*Satires*, Book 2.)

Martial, epigrammatist who tells in his short, pithy, often frivolous remarks of everyday life in decadent Rome more than many a serious writer, says, "At the warm baths, Aemilius takes lettuces, eggs, lizard-fish, and says that he is not dining at home. (What he takes at the baths is all he will get)." (Epigram XII.) "Tell me," he inquires, "why is it that lettuce which used to end our grandsires' dinners, ushers in our banquets?" A commentator adds that it relaxed the alimentary canal, getting it ready for the feast to come. Martial mentions lettuce many other times.

The plant entered into several early electuaries and was thus perpetuated unbroken through the Dark Ages. In the eighth century it was one of the limited number of kitchen herbs available to cooks; it is mentioned in the first English book on gardening, 1217 A.D., and Holinshed says in Elizabethan England lettuce and oil were served for supper, the second meal of the day, after the heavier earlier meal of numerous courses of meat and fish.

Vegetable pies were popular in the fifteenth century, and one writer describes such a pastry consisting of spinach, sorrel, parsley, and eggs; another of samphire, lettuce, onions, vinegar, oil, and sugar. "Compound sallets" served for special occasions consisted of tender buds and flowers — violets, various mints, sage flowers, marigolds and lettuce.

Leigh Hunt says of the height of a man's friendship:

"Then an egg for your supper with lettuces white
And a moon and a friend's arm to go home with at night."
— *To William Hazlitt.*

"Lettuce is to me a most interesting study," says Charles Dudley Warner in his delightful essay "My Summer in a Garden." "Lettuce is like conversation; it must be fresh and crisp, so sparkling that you scarcely notice the bitter in it. Lettuce, like most talkers, is, however, apt to run quickly to seed. Blessed is that sort which comes to a head, and so remains, like a few people I know; growing more solid and satisfactory and tender at the same time, and whiter at the center, and crisp in their maturity. Lettuce, like conversation, requires a good deal of oil, to avoid friction, and keep the company smooth; a pinch of attic salt; a dash of pepper, a quantity of mustard and vinegar, by all means, but so mixed that you will notice no sharp contrasts; and a trifle of sugar. You can put anything, and the more things the better, into salad, as into conversation; but everything depends upon the skill of mixing. I feel that I am in the best society when I am with lettuce. It is in the select circle of vegetables."

During the Middle Ages lettuce was regarded as a valuable narcotic and its milky juice, from which the name *Lactuca* is derived, was used with opium to induce sleep. One fourteenth-century direction is this: "For to make a man sleep three days so that his woundes will heal" he should drink a liquid composed of lettuce, henbane, and poppy — all violent and dangerous to use. Another suggestion of the same century reads that "bread steeped in white broth with sodden lettuce or cyckorie are good to be used for a man injured in battle."

THE THISTLES

The Holy Thistle, *Carduus marianus* L.

Several thistles were used as medicinal or culinary herbs in the past, including the holy thistle. During the Middle Ages when religion was paramount in the minds of the people and common things were given symbols of worship, the white splotches on the foliage of this plant were said to be the milk of the Virgin Mary and the herb was called, among other names, milk thistle, the Virgin Mary's thistle, Our Lady's thistle, and holy thistle.

The plant is a native of Greece and Italy, and is an annual with large irregular foliage, deep-green in color blotched with white. The edges are sharp and irregular in outline but not prickly or spiny. It was formerly gathered in quantity in Italy and used as a potherb and salad plant and is so used even to-day. It is often cultivated in flower-gardens in this country for its large deep-purple heads of flowers, and has escaped to waste places in various parts of the country.

St. Benedict's Thistle, *Cnicus benedictus* L.

Another thistle well known during the Middle Ages is St. Benedict's thistle, a plant with a head of yellow rather than deep purple. It is named for the Italian Saint Benedict of Nursia (480–543 A.D.), founder of the great Benedictine order. During the Middle Ages almost magic virtues were ascribed to this plant for it was supposed to be capable of curing every disease, including the plague. One herbalist says it is a salve for every sore, another, more doubtful, that "it may be one of the Sub-Committee in curing the French pox (small-pox) but it can never cure it of itself."

The plant was so widely publicized that in Elizabeth's time, every cottage garden is said to have boasted a plant. Hill says (1778) the thistle was still used as bitters and as a stomachic but that it had lost much of its reputation.

It is found wild in this country, having come accidentally with grain seed, and occurs from

ST. BENEDICT'S THISTLE

northeastern Canada to Alabama and again on the West Coast. It is still collected for medicinal purposes. The plant is not a true thistle, being nearer the *Centaureas* or bachelor-button tribe. The plant is an annual with dark green, veiny and hairy leaves, very sharp-pointed and spiny.

Shakespeare refers to its virtues once, thus:

MARGARET: "Get you some of this distilled Carduus Benedictus and lay it to your heart; it is the only thing for a qualm."

HERO: "There thou prickest her with a thistle."

BEATRICE: "Benedictus! why Benedictus? you have some moral in this Benedictus."

MARGARET: "Moral! no, by my troth, I have no moral meaning; I meant, plain holy-thistle."

—*Much Ado About Nothing*, Act. III, Sc. 4.

Sow Thistle, *Sonchus oleraceus* L

Sow thistle is a vile-smelling weed of some ten feet in height which often fills vacant lots in suburban areas. It is not a true thistle but belongs rather to the wild lettuces and hawkweeds, being topped with tiny pale yellow dandelionlike heads of bloom, and with the bitter milky juice of the Lactucas.

However, the plant very early attained a reputation as a medicinal and even as a potherb. It appeared in English medicine in 1387 as "sowe-thistel" and is mentioned frequently during the next century as a tonic. One herbalist says of it, "The prolonged use of sow-thistle preserves vitality and youth."

When the Hon. John Josselyn came to this country to visit his brother in 1638 and again in 1669, he recorded in detail his observations on the native plants and animals he saw, on the European plants which had been introduced by the settlers, and also on his many contacts with the friendly red men. His remarks are the very first records of American life and are very informative and highly valued to-day. Josselyn learned much from his friendly contact with the Indians, including their treatment of diseases to which they were particularly vulnerable — common colds, asthma, and pneumonia. He introduced European treatments of the last-named to them; for instance, he says, "I helped several of the Indians with a drink to be taken for stuffing of the lungs," a complicated medicine containing a multitude of herbs, some native, others from the colonists' gardens, all put into a kettle and simmered down to half or less the original volume with molasses spirits, bottled, and drunk diluted with ale or water. One of these contained, among other ingredients, sow-thistle foliage, fennel seed, anise seed, sassafras root, elecampane, catnip and chenopodium.

Safflower, *Carthamus tinctoria* L.

No less than three plants yield what is called in commerce "saffron," and the one which concerns us first here is not the true Oriental product but rather the "bastard" or "false" saffron, which is a member of the composite family. Safflower has sunflowerlike seeds, and a head of bloom with red ray flowers and a central disc of golden yellow. The plant is some two feet tall, with a weak, soft-bodied stalk and long, narrow, incised foliage. It will set seed in the North if planted early.

The plant is often called saffron thistle from the spiny appearance of the foliage, which, however, is soft instead of prickly.

Safflower is a native of the East Indies but was taken to all parts of the known world very early in historic time; Homer knew it as differentiated from true saffron; Dioscorides said the seeds were purgative, and the foliage was used in Greece as a potherb. The Greek women also used the flower as a cosmetic stain, for it was fugitive and not a permanent dye. It was taken to China by 115 B.C., and reached Japan by the first century A.D. and is still highly valued in the Orient. It was cultivated in Egypt before the first century B.C. and grave clothing has been found dyed with it, which gives a very different red from that of madder, the commoner red dye. Fragments of the flowers have been recovered from Egyptian tombs, used in funeral wreaths.

Pliny says the plant was imported into Rome from Egypt in his time, the flower used as a dye and the oil of the seeds as a cathartic.

Classic learning was transplanted first to Asia Minor and then to Persia, and from thence it was slowly disseminated to the whole Mohammedan world, entering Europe by way of Spain. It is in precisely this order that many of the herbs known to the ancient world have come to us, for we trace them from Rome to Asia

Minor, Persia, Arabia, and thence to southwestern Europe, slowly pushing upward through France to England, and from thence to Scandinavia and the New World. A few filtered further to the east, to India, China, and thence to Japan.

Safflower, called *Gartoon,* is recorded from Turkey in the tenth century, used by a physician named Mesu; Avicenna, the noted Arabian physician (980–1037 A.D.) used the seed, which was called *Kurtum.* Early Sanskrit writers knew the plant as a dye and used the seeds in medicine; it was cultivated very early in the Deccan and in Burma as the best yellow dye available, and for centuries its cultivation in the Orient was a large industry. Indeed, the dye has only been replaced in India during the last half century by aniline colors which are not fugitive. In India, the discontinuance of its culture was a serious matter, for not only was the dye extracted but the seed-oil was a valued crop for use in soap-making, and the refuse used as a fertilizer. "Sweet-oil" of the apothecary shop consists of safflower oil, earthnut oil and til or sesame oil. Hair oils consist largely of safflower oil.

Safflower was grown in England by 1540, called bastard saffron. Like true saffron, a powder of the petals was sprinkled over meats to give the desired golden color, for safflower owed its chief virtue to its resemblance to true saffron. A writer of 1662 says, "No precious drug is more adulterated than Saffron with Carthamus."

Safflower is still a valued cosmetic dye, because few dyes of the proper color are fugitive.

> "You give your cheeks a rosy stain,
>   With washes dye your hair;
> But paint and washes both are vain,
>   To give a youthful air."
>   — WILLIAM COWPER, *On a Similar Character.*

True Saffron, *Crocus sativus* L.

While safflower is a weedy thistlelike plant of the composite family, the true saffron of commerce comes from quite a different plant; from the autumn crocus, a member of the iris family. The genus Crocus is native to arid regions of southeastern Europe and west-central Asia, and this species is a fall-blooming one with a lilac flower only now coming into favor in American gardens. It is not to be confused with the autumn-blooming colchicum, also with a lilac to mauve flower.

SAFFRON CROCUS

Crocus sativus is the source of the true saffron which has been used since earliest recorded time as a culinary product, as a delicate perfume, and as a beautiful yellow dye. Saffron is one of the plants mentioned in the Ebers Papyrus and was one of the most precious products of the East, a luxury used as a simile in song and story.

In the Song of Solomon (4:14), the bridegroom's apostrophe to his beloved reads:

> "A garden . . . is my bride, . . .
> Thy shoots are an orchard of pomegranates,
> With precious fruits;
> Henna with spikenard plants,
> Spikenard and saffron."

The bride says of herself, "I am the rose of Sharon, a lily of the valley" (2:1). The rose of Sharon is translated more literally from the Hebrew, "autumn crocus of the plains."

There is little doubt that saffron gained much of its reputation from its similarity to gold, the royal metal, thus bringing the royal color into raiment as well. In Greece young virgins wore saffron-hued robes to denote their chastity, and also at their sacrifice on the altar.

Aeschylus (b. 525 B.C.) uses the word in like fashion in *Agamemnon:* Iphigenia being sacrificed at the altar by her father (see Picture 32 at end of book) to propitiate the gods of the adverse winds, "trailing on the earth her robe of saffron dye," was raised "above the altar-stone from where amid her robes she lay."

Later Greek writers mention the plant — Euripides, Aristophanes, Theophrastus and Moschus. Hippocrates lists it among his four hundred medical agents, for sore eyes and skin affections.

In Rome the product was used as incense, burned upon public and private altars with frankincense and myrrh and other sweet-smelling aromatic woods. Vicinius in *Quo Vadis* (Chapter VII) says when he builds a house for his beloved he will erect an altar as to a divinity and offer myrrh and aloes and in springtime saffron and apple blossoms.

The powdered saffron is soluble in water and upon special occasions the yellow fluid was sprayed about Grecian and Roman halls, courts, and theaters for the delicate perfume which filled the air. In Rome it was used also in private apartments although it was still very costly and a mark of sophisticated living.

Martial, Spanish-born epigrammatist, speaks of "the pale streams of red saffron" which were sprinkled about the theaters and amphitheaters. The patrons did not always escape the ruddy stream, for he says, "Who is loth to pass, all unknown, to the lake of Styx? Is not this, I ask, better than to sprinkle the stage with a ruddy shower and be drenched with streams of saffron?" Again he says, "Breath of balm, shed from foreign trees, of the last effulgence that falls from a curving jet of saffron" (*Epigrams,* Books V and XI).

In *Quo Vadis* again, the air at a riotous feast was "filled with the odor of flowers and the perfume of oils with which beautiful boys sprinkled the feet of the guests" and soon became stifling, "permeated with the saffron and the exhalations of the people." Guests blew the golden powder from each other's hair, for at the feasts of the wealthy it was an indication of station and luxury (Chapter VII).

In extravagant fashion typical of his reign, Nero caused saffron powder to be sprinkled on the pavements in his path when he made a triumphal entry into Rome.

Besides its use as a perfume, the yellow powder was used on food, both for its rich golden color and for its delicate flavor. Horace describes the importance of making a compound salad dressing, to tempt the palates of his guests, of "sweet olive oil, wine, pickle, chopped herbs, and Cicilian saffron sprinkled over the whole" (*Satires,* II).

The saffron used by the Romans was grown largely in Sicily and in Persia but not widely in Italy although Pliny gives minute directions for its cultivation at home and encourages its growth. Virgil says, "Let there be gardens redolent of saffron flowers" (*Georgics,* IV). Ovid says a certain maiden went into the field with Mercury to reap. She was accidentally hit on the head by a flying missile, with fatal results, and from the blood which spurted over the ground from her wound there sprang up a mead of saffron.

OLD-TIME HERBS

The plant was grown in India very early, chiefly in Kashmir, and while too expensive for wide usage, was the perfume of princely feasts, marriages and religious ceremonials.

During the early Middle Ages, saffron was one of the chief commercial products of Arabia and its transport kept fleets on the Red and Mediterranean seas. From thence its culture spread to Spain, where it was grown as early as 961 A.D. Returning Crusaders introduced its growth into France and England.

The plant is said to have been introduced into China about 1300 A.D. although Marco Polo says that China produced ginger, camphor, silk, cotton, salt, and saffron, much earlier. Cultivation was revived in Italy in the fourteenth century and it was soon grown in Germany and Switzerland as well. Thus its cultivation became almost world-wide. The coloring was used for more purposes than almost any other herb, being a flavoring for salads and sauces, a color for soups and meat stews, a medicinal of high rank, a favorite perfume and cosmetic ingredient, and a golden-yellow dye indicating the height of luxury.

The importation of saffron was subjected to heavy duties and thus its cultivation was begun in England very early and found to be successful. It was grown early at the ancient town of Walden, in Essex, forty miles from London. Later the town became known as Saffron Walden from this, its chief industry, a name it still retains. Hakluyt * when he visited Walden was told that a returning pilgrim had brought a corm from the Levant during the reign of Edward III (1327–1377) secreted in a hollow of his staff. And "so he brought the root into this realm with venture of life; for if he had been taken, by the law of the country from whence it came, he had died for the fact."

* Quoted from *Abbeys, Castles, and Ancient Halls of England and Wales.* John Timbs and Alexander Gunn. London, n.d.

FOR NORTHERN GARDENS

A large industry grew up in Cambridgeshire and Essex during this reign and continued for more than four hundred years, and it was also grown early at Walsingham, Norfolk, and gave name to Saffron Hill, near London, where it was also cultivated. The beds in all cases needed constant and expert care. Thomas Tusser in his *Five Hundred Pointes of Goode Husbandrie* (1573) says:

"Pare the saffron plot
 Forget it not
His dwelling made trim
 look shortly for him
When harvest is gone
 then saffron comes on
A little of ground
 buys saffron a pound."

Mention is often made of this condiment in monastery account books, one item of the Durham establishment in 1539 being for 6½ pounds of saffron at seven pounds eight shillings! Thus well did the monks live. An ounce sold at this time for twelve pence, and a pound for from ten to twenty shillings! The Corporation of Walden paid five guineas for a single pound of the powder, worth many times that amount in to-day's money, to present to Queen Elizabeth when she visited the village.

In spite of its gradually increasing culture, saffron continued to be expensive because of the small amount of product obtained from a field of bloom, for the "saffron" consists of the heavy mass of orange-red pollen which clings to the slender three-inch anthers inside the lavender cup when in full bloom. The anthers are clipped with tiny forceps and laid out in a single layer to dry. When dried, the strings of material become dark orange-red in color and are preserved in small boxes. This is called "hay saffron"; the anthers are also pressed into cake form while drying.

239

Saffron is readily adulterated in undetectable form by adding to the hay form bits of shredded beef dipped in saffron water and by adding grease and butter to the cake form. Penalties, however, were always severe even including the death sentence from the easy temptation to cheat.

Like most vegetable products, saffron was used by the ancients in the treatment of diseases, but its value has always been more psychological than physiological; in the Middle Ages a little saffron water was prescribed for many ailments, among them jaundice, for by the Doctrine of Signatures any yellow-juiced plant was by nature given for such an ailment. Even yet the jaundice of new-born babies is treated with it, although it disappears of itself within a few days.

Saffron was a highly-prized culinary product, giving a rich golden color to foods from soups to puddings. English-grown saffron gave a better color than that grown in the Near East. Here is a strange fourteenth-century recipe for a pudding: "Take hens and pork, and boil them together. Hew the flesch small, and grind it all to a dust. Take grated bread and mix it with the broth and add to it the yolks of eggs. Boil it and put therein powdered ginger, sugar, saffron, and salt, and look that it be stiff."

In the Paston Letters, source of much of our knowledge of life in the fourteenth and fifteenth centuries in England, Mistress Paston writes in 1471 from her Norfolk estate to Sir John in London to send her a long list of condiments for her kitchen, including saffron.

The plant was in its heydey during Shakespeare's time and he mentions it often. "I must have saffron to colour the warden's pies" says a clown in *The Winter's Tale* (Act IV, Sc. 3), the warden pear being a baking-pear; in others words the phrase means pear-pies made richly golden with saffron.

FOR NORTHERN GARDENS

In *The Comedy of Errors* Antiphlobus inquires of his wife:

> "Did this companion with the saffron face
> Revel and feast it at my house to-day?"
>
> — Act IV, Sc. 4.

The word saffron is so thoroughly inculcated into language that it is frequently used as an adjective, as above. Even as far back as the time of Aristophanes the expression was used:

> "Beautifully dressed and wearing a saffron-colored gown
> To the end that I may inspire my husband with the most ardent
>   longings."
>
> — *Lysistrata.*

The spirit of Ceres before Prospero's cell in *The Tempest* enters addressing Iris:

> "Hail, many-colour'd messenger, . . .
> Who, with thy saffron wings upon my flowers
> Diffusest honey-drops, refreshing showers."
>
> — Act IV, Sc. 1.

The adjective is often used figuratively in place of the noun, as in these lines from Walter Savage Landor (1798):

> "Go early, ere the gladsome hours
> Strew saffron in the path of rising morn."

"Aurora is robed in saffron" (Addison, *Spectator,* No. 265), and this and countless other metaphors go back to the original of Homer "when the sun once more is saffron steep'd." The word is even used as a verb, to saffron a cake, to saffron a robe, and so on, old recipes directing the cook "to saffron it well." In Ireland, "they saffron'd all their wearing linen" (1622). Nature saffrons the hills and azures the mountains to delight him," reads a phrase in *Blackwood's* (1833).

Saffron pastry was common in England and is made even yet in Cornwall. Saffron is widely in use in Spain for many dishes.

Besides these usages of the product, it was a dye of great value, going back to ancient Greece. It was a favorite dye for Oriental carpets and, along with madder, indigo, onion skins and turmeric, was a standard dye until the recent advent of aniline dyes.

In old Ireland, the king's mantle was dyed with it; "When the Irish chieftains came to make terms with Queen Elizabeth's lord-lieutenant, they came to court in saffron-coloured uniforms"; and in the seventeenth century a saffron-dyed shirt was worn by those of high rank in the Hebrides.

However, saffron was fugitive as a dye and has now all but disappeared. The crocus is still cultivated in France, Spain and Sicily, as well as in the Far East, but on a much reduced scale. It is no longer grown at Saffron Walden but is cultivated to a limited extent in other parts of England. It is no longer used in medicine.

Fall crocuses are coming into favor in American gardens for fall bloom and becoming reasonably priced. Many shades are available along with the original *Crocus sativus*.

Meadow Saffron, *Colchicum autumnale* L.

Colchicum is becoming known to American gardeners, although it is still high in price. When purchased, generally in September, the corm will bloom at once, in water or without. Planted in the fall, it sends out an eighteen-inch stalk in May with large parallel-veined foliage. This dies down by midsummer, and some day in fall the gardener is agreeably surprised to note a close cluster of half a dozen mauve white-based buds which open in a few days to eight-inch mauve crocuslike flowers. Individual flowers last several days and the cluster continues to bloom for several weeks.

Meadow saffron was known to the ancients, not as a golden powder, to be used on foods, but as a rank poison, eating the corm often proving fatal. Pliny recommended milk as an antidote.

The alkaloid, colchicum, was a convenient method of eliminating one's enemies.

However, the plant had other uses. Alexander of Tralles, a sixth-century physician of Asia Minor, used it in a gout treatment which is still in use, almost a specific for the ailment. During the Middle Ages it was used for gout and rheumatism and even as late as the eighteenth century corms were strung around the neck as an amulet to ward off these ailments.

COLCHICUM

To-day the alkaloid is separated into two constituents, one of which stimulates the flow of the bile and is still used for gout but must be administered with great care. It still appears in the United States Pharmacopoeia.

Cooking reduces the virulence of the poison and the corms were sliced and cooked by Egyptian women a century ago to develop *embonpoint,* considered a desirable feminine asset in that country.

Colchicum now grows wild over much of Europe, hence the common name.

A List of Herbs according to Their Use

Condiments	Medicinals	Perfume Industry	Dyes
The Onion Tribe	Onion	Sage	Woad
Garden Sorrel	Garlic	Bergamot	Dyer's Green-
Mustard	Madonna Lily	Balm	weed
Water-Cress	Lily-of-the-Valley	Peppermint	Weld
Horseradish	Nettle	Spearmint	Madder
Wall Pepper	Wild Ginger	Lavender	Safflower
Caraway	Garden Sorrel	Rosemary	Saffron Crocus
Parsley	Sour Dock	Woodruff	
Fennel	Wood Sorrel	Camomile	
Anise	Burdock	Saffron Crocus	
Chervil	Rhubarb		
Coriander	Monkshood		
Lovage	Hellebore		
Dill	Opium Poppy		
Angelica	Celandine		
Smallage	Bloodroot		
Sage	Mustard		
Savories	Woad		
Sweet Marjoram	Houseleek		
Thyme	Burnets		
Peppermint	Agrimony		
Spearmint	Flaxseed		
Sweet Basil	Hemp		
Tarragon	Rue		
Saffron Crocus	Caraway		
	Fennel		
	Anise		
	Dill		
	Cummin		
	Comfrey		
	Horehound		
	Catnip		
	Thyme		
	Peppermint		
	Pennyroyal		
	Lavender		
	Bene		
	Foxglove		
	Culver's Root		
	Garden Heliotrope		
	Elecampane		
	Camomile		
	Tansy		
	Wormwood		
	Pot-Marigold		
	Dandelion		
	Colchicum		

INDEXES

of Herbs mentioned in the book

INDEX OF LATIN NAMES

[Family Names in Roman]

247

INDEX OF LATIN NAMES

Linum usitatissimum L., 67.
Lippia citriodora, 121.

Malvaceae, 78.
Marrubium vulgare L., 125.
Matricaria parthenium L., 204.
Mercurialis annua, 105.
Mentha, 156–180.
Mentha aquatica L., 159.
Mentha arvensis L., 159.
Mentha canadensis L., 160.
Mentha longifolia (L.) Huds., 159.
Mentha piperita L., 157.
Mentha pulegium L., 160.
Mentha requieni, 160.
Mentha spicata L., 158.
Melissa officinalis L., 137.
Micromeria rupestris, 160.
Monarda sp., 136.
Monarda didyma, 136, 137.
Monarda fistulosa, 136.
Monarda punctata, 137.
Myrrhis odorata, 112.

Nepeta cataria L., 127.
Nigella damascena, 93.
Nigella sativa L., 93, 108, 185.

Ocimum basilicum L., 176.
Ocimum sanctum, 176.
Origanum dictamnus L., 149.
Origanum Heracleaticum, 146.
Origanum marjorana L., 145.
Origanum onites, 146.
Osmorrhiza, 112.
Oxalis acetosella L., 27.

Papaver somniferum L., 38.
Papaveraceae, 38–41.
Petroselinum hortense Hoffm., 82.
Pimpinella anisum L., 93.
Pimpinella saxifraga L., 96.
Plantaginaceae, 189–190.

Plantago major L., 189.
Polemonium reptans, 198.
Polygonaceae, 25–29.
Polygonatum, 105.
Poterium sanguisorba L., 59.
Portulaca oleracea L., 31.
Portulacaceae, 31.
Potentilla procumbens Sibth., 61.
Prunella vulgaris L., 181.
Pulsatilla patens (L.) Mill., 37.

Radicula armoracia (L.) Robins, 49.
Ranunculaceae, 33, 93.
Ranunculus bulbosus, 105.
Ranunculus ficaria L., 41–42.
Reseda luteola L., 65.
Resedaceae, 65.
Rhum officinale L., 28.
Rhum rhaponticum L., 28.
Rosa centifolia, 57.
Rosa gallicia, 58.
Rosaceae, 58–62.
Rosemarinus officinalis L., 167.
Rubia tinctoria L., 194.
Rubiaceae, 191–195.
Rumex acetosa L., 25.
Rumex acetosella L., 25.
Rumex crispus L., 26.
Ruta graveolens L., 70.
Rutaceae, 70.

Salvia officinalis L., 131.
Salvia officinalis alba, 132.
Salvia officinalis rosea, 132.
Salvia sclarea L., 134.
Sanguinaria canadensis L., 42.
Sanguisorba officinalis L., 60.
Santolina chamaecyparissus L., 206.
Satureia hortensis L., 141.
Satureia montana L., 141.
Satureia thymus, 141.
Scandix pectenveneris, 105.

INDEX OF LATIN NAMES

Scrophulariaceae, 184–188.
Sedum acre L., 56–57.
Sedum anacamperos, 105
Sedum purpureum, 56.
Sedum telephium L., 55.
Sempervivum arboreum, 54.
Sempervivum tectorum L., 54, 104.
Senecio jacobaea, 105.
Sesamum orientale L., 184.
Sisymbrium nasturtium-aquaticum L., 47.
Sonchus oleraceus L., 232.
Spinachia oleracea, 30.
Symphytum officinale L., 115–116.

Tanacetum vulgare L., 210.
Taraxacum officinale Weber, 226.
Teucrium chamadrys L., 122.
Thymus corsica, 154.
Thymus serphyllum, 152.

Thymus vulgaris L., 151, 153.
Trigonella foenumgraecum L., 93.

Umbelliferae, 79–112, 122.
Urtica dioica L., 21.
Urticaceae, 21–22.

Valeriana officinalis, 105.
Valeriana officinalis L., 196.
Valeriana ruber, 197.
Valerianaceae, 196–198.
Valerianella lacustra, 198.
Veratrum album L., 35.
Veratrum viride Ait., 35.
Verbascum thapsus, 104, 105.
Verbena hastata, 118.
Verbena officinalis L., 104, 105, 118.
Verbenaceae, 117–120.
Veronica virginica L., 187.

Zingiber officinale, 23.

INDEX OF ENGLISH NAMES

INDEX OF ENGLISH NAMES

Mustards, 4, 5, 43–53.
Myrrh, 28, 58, 109.

NARROW dock, 26.
Nettle, 4.
Nettle family, 68.
Nettles, 21.
New Jersey tea, 59.
Nigella, 108.
Nosebleed, 205.

OLD man, 216.
Old woman, 218.
Onion, 12, 14–15, 17, 242.
Onions, 6, 11, 18, 84, 228.
Opium poppy, 6, 38–40.
Orache, 30.
Oswego tea, 136.
Our Lady's glove, 193.
Our Lady's bedstraw, 105, 193.
Our Lady's mantle, 105, 193.
Our Lady's shoelaces, 193.
Our Lady's shoes, 105.
Our Lady's thistle, 105, 230.

PARSLEY, 12, 82–87, 99, 104, 110, 119,
    132, 147, 151, 221, 228.
Pasque flower, 37.
Pea family, 63–65, 93.
Pennyroyal, 95, 101, 124, 160–161.
Pepper, 80.
Pepper grass, 56.
Peppermint, 6, 157–158, 227.
Pilewort, 42.
Plantain, 4, 73, 189–190.
Pilgrim's cross, 118.
Poison hemlock, 105.
Poor man's leaf, 54.
Poor man's pepper, 56.
Poppy, 3.
Poppy family, 38–41.
Pot-marigold, 220–224.
Pot-marjoram, 146.

Purple-stemmed angelica, 106.
Purslane, 4, 31–32.

QUEEN Anne's lace, 97, 111.

RAM's head lady's-slipper, 198.
Ramsons, 18.
Red balm, 136.
Red nettle, 183.
Red sorrel, 25.
Red valerian, 197.
Rhubarb, 28–29.
Ribbon grass, 207.
Rock leek, 18.
Robin-in-the-hedge, 130.
Roman fennel, 91.
Roman wormwood, 218.
Rose, 6, 57.
Rose burnet, 59–61.
Rose family, 58–62.
Rose mallow, 3, 78.
Rosemary, 3, 5, 58, 74, 75, 76, 123,
    161, 167–176, 209.
Rue, 3, 6, 16, 25, 70–77, 91, 101,
    105, 109.
Rush onions, 17.

SAFFLOWER, 233–234.
Saffron, 5, 6, 28, 58, 124, 235–242.
Saffron thistle, 233.
Sage, 3, 84, 101, 116, 131–134, 221,
    229.
St. Andrew's cross, 105.
St. Anthony's turnip, 105.
St. Benedict's thistle, 230–231.
St. Bennet's herb, 105.
St. George's herb, 105.
St.-James'-wort, 105.
St.-John's-wort, 105.
St.-Peter's-wort, 105.
Salad burnet, 59–60.
Salem woodwax, 65.

INDEX OF ENGLISH NAMES

Winter marjoram, 146.
Winter savory, 3, 4, 141–142, 221.
Woad, 4, 51–53, 65, 195.
Woadwaxen, 64.
Wood sorrel, 25, 27.
Woodruff, 3, 191–192.
Woodwax, 64, 65.
Wormseed, 30.

Wormwood, 6, 131, 213–216, 218–220.

YARROW, 205.
Yellow dock, 26.
Yellow lady's-slipper, 198.
Yellow rocket, 65.

ZEUS' wheat, 104.

A CATALOGUE OF SELECTED DOVER BOOKS
IN ALL FIELDS OF INTEREST

A CATALOGUE OF SELECTED DOVER BOOKS
IN ALL FIELDS OF INTEREST

AMERICA'S OLD MASTERS, James T. Flexner. Four men emerged unexpectedly from provincial 18th century America to leadership in European art: Benjamin West, J. S. Copley, C. R. Peale, Gilbert Stuart. Brilliant coverage of lives and contributions. Revised, 1967 edition. 69 plates. 365pp. of text.
21806-6 Paperbound $2.75

FIRST FLOWERS OF OUR WILDERNESS: AMERICAN PAINTING, THE COLONIAL PERIOD, James T. Flexner. Painters, and regional painting traditions from earliest Colonial times up to the emergence of Copley, West and Peale Sr., Foster, Gustavus Hesselius, Feke, John Smibert and many anonymous painters in the primitive manner. Engaging presentation, with 162 illustrations. xxii + 368pp.
22180-6 Paperbound $3.50

THE LIGHT OF DISTANT SKIES: AMERICAN PAINTING, 1760-1835, James T. Flexner. The great generation of early American painters goes to Europe to learn and to teach: West, Copley, Gilbert Stuart and others. Allston, Trumbull, Morse; also contemporary American painters—primitives, derivatives, academics—who remained in America. 102 illustrations. xiii + 306pp.
22179-2 Paperbound $3.00

A HISTORY OF THE RISE AND PROGRESS OF THE ARTS OF DESIGN IN THE UNITED STATES, William Dunlap. Much the richest mine of information on early American painters, sculptors, architects, engravers, miniaturists, etc. The only source of information for scores of artists, the major primary source for many others. Unabridged reprint of rare original 1834 edition, with new introduction by James T. Flexner, and 394 new illustrations. Edited by Rita Weiss. 6⅝ x 9⅝.
21695-0, 21696-9, 21697-7 Three volumes, Paperbound $13.50

EPOCHS OF CHINESE AND JAPANESE ART, Ernest F. Fenollosa. From primitive Chinese art to the 20th century, thorough history, explanation of every important art period and form, including Japanese woodcuts; main stress on China and Japan, but Tibet, Korea also included. Still unexcelled for its detailed, rich coverage of cultural background, aesthetic elements, diffusion studies, particularly of the historical period. 2nd, 1913 edition. 242 illustrations. lii + 439pp. of text.
20364-6, 20365-4 Two volumes, Paperbound $5.00

THE GENTLE ART OF MAKING ENEMIES, James A. M. Whistler. Greatest wit of his day deflates Oscar Wilde, Ruskin, Swinburne; strikes back at inane critics, exhibitions, art journalism; aesthetics of impressionist revolution in most striking form. Highly readable classic by great painter. Reproduction of edition designed by Whistler. Introduction by Alfred Werner. xxxvi + 334pp.
21875-9 Paperbound $2.25

CATALOGUE OF DOVER BOOKS

VISUAL ILLUSIONS: THEIR CAUSES, CHARACTERISTICS, AND APPLICATIONS, Matthew Luckiesh. Thorough description and discussion of optical illusion, geometric and perspective, particularly; size and shape distortions, illusions of color, of motion; natural illusions; use of illusion in art and magic, industry, etc. Most useful today with op art, also for classical art. Scores of effects illustrated. Introduction by William H. Ittleson. 100 illustrations. xxi + 252pp.
21530-X Paperbound $1.50

A HANDBOOK OF ANATOMY FOR ART STUDENTS, Arthur Thomson. Thorough, virtually exhaustive coverage of skeletal structure, musculature, etc. Full text, supplemented by anatomical diagrams and drawings and by photographs of undraped figures. Unique in its comparison of male and female forms, pointing out differences of contour, texture, form. 211 figures, 40 drawings, 86 photographs. xx + 459pp. 5⅜ x 8⅜.
21163-0 Paperbound $3.00

150 MASTERPIECES OF DRAWING, Selected by Anthony Toney. Full page reproductions of drawings from the early 16th to the end of the 18th century, all beautifully reproduced: Rembrandt, Michelangelo, Dürer, Fragonard, Urs, Graf, Wouwerman, many others. First-rate browsing book, model book for artists. xviii + 150pp. 8⅜ x 11¼.
21032-4 Paperbound $2.00

THE LATER WORK OF AUBREY BEARDSLEY, Aubrey Beardsley. Exotic, erotic, ironic masterpieces in full maturity: Comedy Ballet, Venus and Tannhauser, Pierrot, Lysistrata, Rape of the Lock, Savoy material, Ali Baba, Volpone, etc. This material revolutionized the art world, and is still powerful, fresh, brilliant. With *The Early Work,* all Beardsley's finest work. 174 plates, 2 in color. xiv + 176pp. 8⅛ x 11.
21817-1 Paperbound $2.75

DRAWINGS OF REMBRANDT, Rembrandt van Rijn. Complete reproduction of fabulously rare edition by Lippmann and Hofstede de Groot, completely reedited, updated, improved by Prof. Seymour Slive, Fogg Museum. Portraits, Biblical sketches, landscapes, Oriental types, nudes, episodes from classical mythology—All Rembrandt's fertile genius. Also selection of drawings by his pupils and followers. "Stunning volumes," *Saturday Review.* 550 illustrations. lxxviii + 552pp. 9⅛ x 12¼.
21485-0, 21486-9 Two volumes, Paperbound $6.50

THE DISASTERS OF WAR, Francisco Goya. One of the masterpieces of Western civilization—83 etchings that record Goya's shattering, bitter reaction to the Napoleonic war that swept through Spain after the insurrection of 1808 and to war in general. Reprint of the first edition, with three additional plates from Boston's Museum of Fine Arts. All plates facsimile size. Introduction by Philip Hofer, Fogg Museum. v + 97pp. 9⅜ x 8¼.
21872-4 Paperbound $1.75

GRAPHIC WORKS OF ODILON REDON. Largest collection of Redon's graphic works ever assembled: 172 lithographs, 28 etchings and engravings, 9 drawings. These include some of his most famous works. All the plates from *Odilon Redon: oeuvre graphique complet,* plus additional plates. New introduction and caption translations by Alfred Werner. 209 illustrations. xxvii + 209pp. 9⅛ x 12¼.
21966-8 Paperbound $4.00

DESIGN BY ACCIDENT; A BOOK OF "ACCIDENTAL EFFECTS" FOR ARTISTS AND DESIGNERS, James F. O'Brien. Create your own unique, striking, imaginative effects by "controlled accident" interaction of materials: paints and lacquers, oil and water based paints, splatter, crackling materials, shatter, similar items. Everything you do will be different; first book on this limitless art, so useful to both fine artist and commercial artist. Full instructions. 192 plates showing "accidents," 8 in color. viii + 215pp. 8⅜ x 11¼.   21942-9 Paperbound $3.50

THE BOOK OF SIGNS, Rudolf Koch. Famed German type designer draws 493 beautiful symbols: religious, mystical, alchemical, imperial, property marks, ines, etc. Remarkable fusion of traditional and modern. Good for suggestions of timelessness, smartness, modernity. Text. vi + 104pp. 6⅛ x 9¼.
                                                20162-7 Paperbound $1.25

HISTORY OF INDIAN AND INDONESIAN ART, Ananda K. Coomaraswamy. An unabridged republication of one of the finest books by a great scholar in Eastern art. Rich in descriptive material, history, social backgrounds; Sunga reliefs, Rajput paintings, Gupta temples, Burmese frescoes, textiles, jewelry, sculpture, etc. 400 photos. viii + 423pp. 6⅜ x 9¾.   21436-2 Paperbound $3.50

PRIMITIVE ART, Franz Boas. America's foremost anthropologist surveys textiles, ceramics, woodcarving, basketry, metalwork, etc.; patterns, technology, creation of symbols, style origins. All areas of world, but very full on Northwest Coast Indians. More than 350 illustrations of baskets, boxes, totem poles, weapons, etc. 378 pp.
                                                20025-6 Paperbound $2.50

THE GENTLEMAN AND CABINET MAKER'S DIRECTOR, Thomas Chippendale. Full reprint (third edition, 1762) of most influential furniture book of all time, by master cabinetmaker. 200 plates, illustrating chairs, sofas, mirrors, tables, cabinets, plus 24 photographs of surviving pieces. Biographical introduction by N. Bienenstock. vi + 249pp. 9⅞ x 12¾.   21601-2 Paperbound $3.50

AMERICAN ANTIQUE FURNITURE, Edgar G. Miller, Jr. The basic coverage of all American furniture before 1840. Individual chapters cover type of furniture—clocks, tables, sideboards, etc.—chronologically, with inexhaustible wealth of data. More than 2100 photographs, all identified, commented on. Essential to all early American collectors. Introduction by H. E. Keyes. vi + 1106pp. 7⅞ x 10¾.
                          21599-7, 21600-4 Two volumes, Paperbound $7.50

PENNSYLVANIA DUTCH AMERICAN FOLK ART, Henry J. Kauffman. 279 photos, 28 drawings of tulipware, Fraktur script, painted tinware, toys, flowered furniture, quilts, samplers, hex signs, house interiors, etc. Full descriptive text. Excellent for tourist, rewarding for designer, collector. Map. 146pp. 7⅞ x 10¾.
                                                21205-X Paperbound $2.00

EARLY NEW ENGLAND GRAVESTONE RUBBINGS, Edmund V. Gillon, Jr. 43 photographs, 226 carefully reproduced rubbings show heavily symbolic, sometimes macabre early gravestones, up to early 19th century. Remarkable early American primitive art, occasionally strikingly beautiful; always powerful. Text. xxvi + 207pp. 8⅜ x 11¼.   21380-3 Paperbound $3.00

ALPHABETS AND ORNAMENTS, Ernst Lehner. Well-known pictorial source for decorative alphabets, script examples, cartouches, frames, decorative title pages, calligraphic initials, borders, similar material. 14th to 19th century, mostly European. Useful in almost any graphic arts designing, varied styles. 750 illustrations. 256pp. 7 x 10.
21905-4 Paperbound $3.50

PAINTING: A CREATIVE APPROACH, Norman Colquhoun. For the beginner simple guide provides an instructive approach to painting: major stumbling blocks for beginner; overcoming them, technical points; paints and pigments; oil painting; watercolor and other media and color. New section on "plastic" paints. Glossary. Formerly *Paint Your Own Pictures*. 221pp.
22000-1 Paperbound $1.75

THE ENJOYMENT AND USE OF COLOR, Walter Sargent. Explanation of the relations between colors themselves and between colors in nature and art, including hundreds of little-known facts about color values, intensities, effects of high and low illumination, complementary colors. Many practical hints for painters, references to great masters. 7 color plates, 29 illustrations. x + 274pp.
20944-X Paperbound $2.50

THE NOTEBOOKS OF LEONARDO DA VINCI, compiled and edited by Jean Paul Richter. 1566 extracts from original manuscripts reveal the full range of Leonardo's versatile genius: all his writings on painting, sculpture, architecture, anatomy, astronomy, geography, topography, physiology, mining, music, etc., in both Italian and English, with 186 plates of manuscript pages and more than 500 additional drawings. Includes studies for the Last Supper, the lost Sforza monument, and other works. Total of xlvii + 866pp. 7⅞ x 10¾.
22572-0, 22573-9 Two volumes, Paperbound $10.00

MONTGOMERY WARD CATALOGUE OF 1895. Tea gowns, yards of flannel and pillow-case lace, stereoscopes, books of gospel hymns, the New Improved Singer Sewing Machine, side saddles, milk skimmers, straight-edged razors, high-button shoes, spittoons, and on and on . . . listing some 25,000 items, practically all illustrated. Essential to the shoppers of the 1890's, it is our truest record of the spirit of the period. Unaltered reprint of Issue No. 57, Spring and Summer 1895. Introduction by Boris Emmet. Innumerable illustrations. xiii + 624pp. 8½ x 11⅝.
22377-9 Paperbound $6.95

THE CRYSTAL PALACE EXHIBITION ILLUSTRATED CATALOGUE (LONDON, 1851). One of the wonders of the modern world—the Crystal Palace Exhibition in which all the nations of the civilized world exhibited their achievements in the arts and sciences—presented in an equally important illustrated catalogue. More than 1700 items pictured with accompanying text—ceramics, textiles, cast-iron work, carpets, pianos, sleds, razors, wall-papers, billiard tables, beehives, silverware and hundreds of other artifacts—represent the focal point of Victorian culture in the Western World. Probably the largest collection of Victorian decorative art ever assembled—indispensable for antiquarians and designers. Unabridged republication of the Art-Journal Catalogue of the Great Exhibition of 1851, with all terminal essays. New introduction by John Gloag, F.S.A. xxxiv + 426pp. 9 x 12.
22503-8 Paperbound $4.50

CATALOGUE OF DOVER BOOKS

THE ARCHITECTURE OF COUNTRY HOUSES, Andrew J. Downing. Together with Vaux's *Villas and Cottages* this is the basic book for Hudson River Gothic architecture of the middle Victorian period. Full, sound discussions of general aspects of housing, architecture, style, decoration, furnishing, together with scores of detailed house plans, illustrations of specific buildings, accompanied by full text. Perhaps the most influential single American architectural book. 1850 edition. Introduction by J. Stewart Johnson. 321 figures, 34 architectural designs. xvi + 560pp.

22003-6 Paperbound $3.50

LOST EXAMPLES OF COLONIAL ARCHITECTURE, John Mead Howells. Full-page photographs of buildings that have disappeared or been so altered as to be denatured, including many designed by major early American architects. 245 plates. xvii + 248pp. 7⅞ x 10¾.

21143-6 Paperbound $3.00

DOMESTIC ARCHITECTURE OF THE AMERICAN COLONIES AND OF THE EARLY REPUBLIC, Fiske Kimball. Foremost architect and restorer of Williamsburg and Monticello covers nearly 200 homes between 1620-1825. Architectural details, construction, style features, special fixtures, floor plans, etc. Generally considered finest work in its area. 219 illustrations of houses, doorways, windows, capital mantels. xx + 314pp. 7⅞ x 10¾.

21743-4 Paperbound $3.50

EARLY AMERICAN ROOMS: 1650-1858, edited by Russell Hawes Kettell. Tour of 12 rooms, each representative of a different era in American history and each furnished, decorated, designed and occupied in the style of the era. 72 plans and elevations, 8-page color section, etc., show fabrics, wall papers, arrangements, etc. Full descriptive text. xvii + 200pp. of text. 8⅜ x 11¼.

21633-0 Paperbound $4.00

THE FITZWILLIAM VIRGINAL BOOK, edited by J. Fuller Maitland and W. B. Squire. Full modern printing of famous early 17th-century ms. volume of 300 works by Morley, Byrd, Bull, Gibbons, etc. For piano or other modern keyboard instrument; easy to read format. xxxvi + 938pp. 8⅜ x 11.

21068-5, 21069-3 Two volumes, Paperbound $8.00

HARPSICHORD MUSIC, Johann Sebastian Bach. Bach Gesellschaft edition. A rich selection of Bach's masterpieces for the harpsichord: the six English Suites, six French Suites, the six Partitas (Clavierübung part I), the Goldberg Variations (Clavierübung part IV), the fifteen Two-Part Inventions and the fifteen Three-Part Sinfonias. Clearly reproduced on large sheets with ample margins; eminently playable. vi + 312pp. 8⅛ x 11.

22360-4 Paperbound $5.00

THE MUSIC OF BACH: AN INTRODUCTION, Charles Sanford Terry. A fine, nontechnical introduction to Bach's music, both instrumental and vocal. Covers organ music, chamber music, passion music, other types. Analyzes themes, developments, innovations. x + 114pp.

21075-8 Paperbound $1.25

BEETHOVEN AND HIS NINE SYMPHONIES, Sir George Grove. Noted British musicologist provides best history, analysis, commentary on symphonies. Very thorough, rigorously accurate; necessary to both advanced student and amateur music lover. 436 musical passages. vii + 407 pp.

20334-4 Paperbound $2.25

JOHANN SEBASTIAN BACH, Philipp Spitta. One of the great classics of musicology, this definitive analysis of Bach's music (and life) has never been surpassed. Lucid, nontechnical analyses of hundreds of pieces (30 pages devoted to St. Matthew Passion, 26 to B Minor Mass). Also includes major analysis of 18th-century music. 450 musical examples. 40-page musical supplement. Total of xx + 1799pp.
(EUK) 22278-0, 22279-9 Two volumes, Clothbound $15.00

MOZART AND HIS PIANO CONCERTOS, Cuthbert Girdlestone. The only full-length study of an important area of Mozart's creativity. Provides detailed analyses of all 23 concertos, traces inspirational sources. 417 musical examples. Second edition. 509pp.
(USO) 21271-8 Paperbound $2.50

THE PERFECT WAGNERITE: A COMMENTARY ON THE NIBLUNG'S RING, George Bernard Shaw. Brilliant and still relevant criticism in remarkable essays on Wagner's Ring cycle, Shaw's ideas on political and social ideology behind the plots, role of Leitmotifs, vocal requisites, etc. Prefaces. xxi + 136pp.
21707-8 Paperbound $1.50

DON GIOVANNI, W. A. Mozart. Complete libretto, modern English translation; biographies of composer and librettist; accounts of early performances and critical reaction. Lavishly illustrated. All the material you need to understand and appreciate this great work. Dover Opera Guide and Libretto Series; translated and introduced by Ellen Bleiler. 92 illustrations. 209pp.
21134-7 Paperbound $1.50

HIGH FIDELITY SYSTEMS: A LAYMAN'S GUIDE, Roy F. Allison. All the basic information you need for setting up your own audio system: high fidelity and stereo record players, tape records, F.M. Connections, adjusting tone arm, cartridge, checking needle alignment, positioning speakers, phasing speakers, adjusting hums, trouble-shooting, maintenance, and similar topics. Enlarged 1965 edition. More than 50 charts, diagrams, photos. iv + 91pp. 21514-8 Paperbound $1.25

REPRODUCTION OF SOUND, Edgar Villchur. Thorough coverage for laymen of high fidelity systems, reproducing systems in general, needles, amplifiers, preamps, loudspeakers, feedback, explaining physical background. "A rare talent for making technicalities vividly comprehensible," R. Darrell, High Fidelity. 69 figures. iv + 92pp.
21515-6 Paperbound $1.00

HEAR ME TALKIN' TO YA: THE STORY OF JAZZ AS TOLD BY THE MEN WHO MADE IT, Nat Shapiro and Nat Hentoff. Louis Armstrong, Fats Waller, Jo Jones, Clarence Williams, Billy Holiday, Duke Ellington, Jelly Roll Morton and dozens of other jazz greats tell how it was in Chicago's South Side, New Orleans, depression Harlem and the modern West Coast as jazz was born and grew. xvi + 429pp.
21726-4 Paperbound $2.00

FABLES OF AESOP, translated by Sir Roger L'Estrange. A reproduction of the very rare 1931 Paris edition; a selection of the most interesting fables, together with 50 imaginative drawings by Alexander Calder. v + 128pp. 6½x9¼.
21780-9 Paperbound $1.25

AGAINST THE GRAIN (A REBOURS), Joris K. Huysmans. Filled with weird images, evidences of a bizarre imagination, exotic experiments with hallucinatory drugs, rich tastes and smells and the diversions of its sybarite hero Duc Jean des Esseintes, this classic novel pushed 19th-century literary decadence to its limits. Full unabridged edition. Do not confuse this with abridged editions generally sold. Introduction by Havelock Ellis. xlix + 206pp.   22190-3 Paperbound $2.00

VARIORUM SHAKESPEARE: HAMLET. Edited by Horace H. Furness; a landmark of American scholarship. Exhaustive footnotes and appendices treat all doubtful words and phrases, as well as suggested critical emendations throughout the play's history. First volume contains editor's own text, collated with all Quartos and Folios. Second volume contains full first Quarto, translations of Shakespeare's sources (Belleforest, and Saxo Grammaticus), Der Bestrafte Brudermord, and many essays on critical and historical points of interest by major authorities of past and present. Includes details of staging and costuming over the years. By far the best edition available for serious students of Shakespeare. Total of xx + 905pp.
21004-9, 21005-7, 2 volumes, Paperbound $5.25

A LIFE OF WILLIAM SHAKESPEARE, Sir Sidney Lee. This is the standard life of Shakespeare, summarizing everything known about Shakespeare and his plays. Incredibly rich in material, broad in coverage, clear and judicious, it has served thousands as the best introduction to Shakespeare. 1931 edition. 9 plates. xxix + 792pp.   (USO) 21967-4 Paperbound $3.75

MASTERS OF THE DRAMA, John Gassner. Most comprehensive history of the drama in print, covering every tradition from Greeks to modern Europe and America, including India, Far East, etc. Covers more than 800 dramatists, 2000 plays, with biographical material, plot summaries, theatre history, criticism, etc. "Best of its kind in English," *New Republic*. 77 illustrations. xxii + 890pp.
20100-7 Clothbound $7.50

THE EVOLUTION OF THE ENGLISH LANGUAGE, George McKnight. The growth of English, from the 14th century to the present. Unusual, non-technical account presents basic information in very interesting form: sound shifts, change in grammar and syntax, vocabulary growth, similar topics. Abundantly illustrated with quotations. Formerly *Modern English in the Making*. xii + 590pp.
21932-1 Paperbound $3.50

AN ETYMOLOGICAL DICTIONARY OF MODERN ENGLISH, Ernest Weekley. Fullest, richest work of its sort, by foremost British lexicographer. Detailed word histories, including many colloquial and archaic words; extensive quotations. Do not confuse this with the Concise Etymological Dictionary, which is much abridged. Total of xxvii + 830pp. 6½ x 9¼.
21873-2, 21874-0 Two volumes, Paperbound $5.50

FLATLAND: A ROMANCE OF MANY DIMENSIONS, E. A. Abbott. Classic of science-fiction explores ramifications of life in a two-dimensional world, and what happens when a three-dimensional being intrudes. Amusing reading, but also useful as introduction to thought about hyperspace. Introduction by Banesh Hoffmann. 16 illustrations. xx + 103pp.   20001-9 Paperbound $1.00

CATALOGUE OF DOVER BOOKS

POEMS OF ANNE BRADSTREET, edited with an introduction by Robert Hutchinson. A new selection of poems by America's first poet and perhaps the first significant woman poet in the English language. 48 poems display her development in works of considerable variety—love poems, domestic poems, religious meditations, formal elegies, "quaternions," etc. Notes, bibliography. viii + 222pp.
22160-1 Paperbound $2.00

THREE GOTHIC NOVELS: THE CASTLE OF OTRANTO BY HORACE WALPOLE; VATHEK BY WILLIAM BECKFORD; THE VAMPYRE BY JOHN POLIDORI, WITH FRAGMENT OF A NOVEL BY LORD BYRON, edited by E. F. Bleiler. The first Gothic novel, by Walpole; the finest Oriental tale in English, by Beckford; powerful Romantic supernatural story in versions by Polidori and Byron. All extremely important in history of literature; all still exciting, packed with supernatural thrills, ghosts, haunted castles, magic, etc. xl + 291pp.
21232-7 Paperbound $2.00

THE BEST TALES OF HOFFMANN, E. T. A. Hoffmann. 10 of Hoffmann's most important stories, in modern re-editings of standard translations: Nutcracker and the King of Mice, Signor Formica, Automata, The Sandman, Rath Krespel, The Golden Flowerpot, Master Martin the Cooper, The Mines of Falun, The King's Betrothed, A New Year's Eve Adventure. 7 illustrations by Hoffmann. Edited by E. F. Bleiler. xxxix + 419pp.
21793-0 Paperbound $2.25

GHOST AND HORROR STORIES OF AMBROSE BIERCE, Ambrose Bierce. 23 strikingly modern stories of the horrors latent in the human mind: The Eyes of the Panther, The Damned Thing, An Occurrence at Owl Creek Bridge, An Inhabitant of Carcosa, etc., plus the dream-essay, Visions of the Night. Edited by E. F. Bleiler. xxii + 199pp.
20767-6 Paperbound $1.50

BEST GHOST STORIES OF J. S. LeFANU, J. Sheridan LeFanu. Finest stories by Victorian master often considered greatest supernatural writer of all. Carmilla, Green Tea, The Haunted Baronet, The Familiar, and 12 others. Most never before available in the U. S. A. Edited by E. F. Bleiler. 8 illustrations from Victorian publications. xvii + 467pp.
20415-4 Paperbound $2.50

THE TIME STREAM, THE GREATEST ADVENTURE, AND THE PURPLE SAPPHIRE— THREE SCIENCE FICTION NOVELS, John Taine (Eric Temple Bell). Great American mathematician was also foremost science fiction novelist of the 1920's. *The Time Stream,* one of all-time classics, uses concepts of circular time; *The Greatest Adventure,* incredibly ancient biological experiments from Antarctica threaten to escape; The *Purple Sapphire,* superscience, lost races in Central Tibet, survivors of the Great Race. 4 illustrations by Frank R. Paul. v + 532pp.
21180-0 Paperbound $2.50

SEVEN SCIENCE FICTION NOVELS, H. G. Wells. The standard collection of the great novels. Complete, unabridged. *First Men in the Moon, Island of Dr. Moreau, War of the Worlds, Food of the Gods, Invisible Man, Time Machine, In the Days of the Comet.* Not only science fiction fans, but every educated person owes it to himself to read these novels. 1015pp.
20264-X Clothbound $5.00

LAST AND FIRST MEN AND STAR MAKER, TWO SCIENCE FICTION NOVELS, Olaf Stapledon. Greatest future histories in science fiction. In the first, human intelligence is the "hero," through strange paths of evolution, interplanetary invasions, incredible technologies, near extinctions and reemergences. Star Maker describes the quest of a band of star rovers for intelligence itself, through time and space: weird inhuman civilizations, crustacean minds, symbiotic worlds, etc. Complete, unabridged. v + 438pp. 21962-3 Paperbound $2.00

THREE PROPHETIC NOVELS, H. G. WELLS. Stages of a consistently planned future for mankind. *When the Sleeper Wakes,* and *A Story of the Days to Come,* anticipate *Brave New World* and *1984,* in the 21st Century; *The Time Machine,* only complete version in print, shows farther future and the end of mankind. All show Wells's greatest gifts as storyteller and novelist. Edited by E. F. Bleiler. x + 335pp. (USO) 20605-X Paperbound $2.00

THE DEVIL'S DICTIONARY, Ambrose Bierce. America's own Oscar Wilde— Ambrose Bierce—offers his barbed iconoclastic wisdom in over 1,000 definitions hailed by H. L. Mencken as "some of the most gorgeous witticisms in the English language." 145pp. 20487-1 Paperbound $1.25

MAX AND MORITZ, Wilhelm Busch. Great children's classic, father of comic strip, of two bad boys, Max and Moritz. Also Ker and Plunk (Plisch und Plumm), Cat and Mouse, Deceitful Henry, Ice-Peter, The Boy and the Pipe, and five other pieces. Original German, with English translation. Edited by H. Arthur Klein; translations by various hands and H. Arthur Klein. vi + 216pp. 20181-3 Paperbound $1.50

PIGS IS PIGS AND OTHER FAVORITES, Ellis Parker Butler. The title story is one of the best humor short stories, as Mike Flannery obfuscates biology and English. Also included, That Pup of Murchison's, The Great American Pie Company, and Perkins of Portland. 14 illustrations. v + 109pp. 21532-6 Paperbound $1.00

THE PETERKIN PAPERS, Lucretia P. Hale. It takes genius to be as stupidly mad as the Peterkins, as they decide to become wise, celebrate the "Fourth," keep a cow, and otherwise strain the resources of the Lady from Philadelphia. Basic book of American humor. 153 illustrations. 219pp. 20794-3 Paperbound $1.25

PERRAULT'S FAIRY TALES, translated by A. E. Johnson and S. R. Littlewood, with 34 full-page illustrations by Gustave Doré. All the original Perrault stories— Cinderella, Sleeping Beauty, Bluebeard, Little Red Riding Hood, Puss in Boots, Tom Thumb, etc.—with their witty verse morals and the magnificent illustrations of Doré. One of the five or six great books of European fairy tales. viii + 117pp. 8⅛ x 11. 22311-6 Paperbound $2.00

OLD HUNGARIAN FAIRY TALES, Baroness Orczy. Favorites translated and adapted by author of the *Scarlet Pimpernel.* Eight fairy tales include "The Suitors of Princess Fire-Fly," "The Twin Hunchbacks," "Mr. Cuttlefish's Love Story," and "The Enchanted Cat." This little volume of magic and adventure will captivate children as it has for generations. 90 drawings by Montagu Barstow. 96pp. (USO) 22293-4 Paperbound $1.95

THE RED FAIRY BOOK, Andrew Lang. Lang's color fairy books have long been children's favorites. This volume includes Rapunzel, Jack and the Bean-stalk and 35 other stories, familiar and unfamiliar. 4 plates, 93 illustrations x + 367pp.
21673-X Paperbound $1.95

THE BLUE FAIRY BOOK, Andrew Lang. Lang's tales come from all countries and all times. Here are 37 tales from Grimm, the Arabian Nights, Greek Mythology, and other fascinating sources. 8 plates, 130 illustrations. xi + 390pp.
21437-0 Paperbound $1.95

HOUSEHOLD STORIES BY THE BROTHERS GRIMM. Classic English-language edition of the well-known tales — Rumpelstiltskin, Snow White, Hansel and Gretel, The Twelve Brothers, Faithful John, Rapunzel, Tom Thumb (52 stories in all). Translated into simple, straightforward English by Lucy Crane. Ornamented with head-pieces, vignettes, elaborate decorative initials and a dozen full-page illustrations by Walter Crane. x + 269pp.
21080-4 Paperbound $1.75

THE MERRY ADVENTURES OF ROBIN HOOD, Howard Pyle. The finest modern versions of the traditional ballads and tales about the great English outlaw. Howard Pyle's complete prose version, with every word, every illustration of the first edition. Do not confuse this facsimile of the original (1883) with modern editions that change text or illustrations. 23 plates plus many page decorations. xxii + 296pp.
22043-5 Paperbound $2.00

THE STORY OF KING ARTHUR AND HIS KNIGHTS, Howard Pyle. The finest children's version of the life of King Arthur; brilliantly retold by Pyle, with 48 of his most imaginative illustrations. xviii + 313pp. 6⅛ x 9¼.
21445-1 Paperbound $2.00

THE WONDERFUL WIZARD OF OZ, L. Frank Baum. America's finest children's book in facsimile of first edition with all Denslow illustrations in full color. The edition a child should have. Introduction by Martin Gardner. 23 color plates, scores of drawings. iv + 267pp.
20691-2 Paperbound $1.95

THE MARVELOUS LAND OF OZ, L. Frank Baum. The second Oz book, every bit as imaginative as the Wizard. The hero is a boy named Tip, but the Scarecrow and the Tin Woodman are back, as is the Oz magic. 16 color plates, 120 drawings by John R. Neill. 287pp.
20692-0 Paperbound $1.75

THE MAGICAL MONARCH OF MO, L. Frank Baum. Remarkable adventures in a land even stranger than Oz. The best of Baum's books not in the Oz series. 15 color plates and dozens of drawings by Frank Verbeck. xviii + 237pp.
21892-9 Paperbound $2.00

THE BAD CHILD'S BOOK OF BEASTS, MORE BEASTS FOR WORSE CHILDREN, A MORAL ALPHABET, Hilaire Belloc. Three complete humor classics in one volume. Be kind to the frog, and do not call him names . . . and 28 other whimsical animals. Familiar favorites and some not so well known. Illustrated by Basil Blackwell. 156pp.
(USO) 20749-8 Paperbound $1.25

MATHEMATICAL PUZZLES FOR BEGINNERS AND ENTHUSIASTS, Geoffrey Mott-Smith. 189 puzzles from easy to difficult—involving arithmetic, logic, algebra, properties of digits, probability, etc.—for enjoyment and mental stimulus. Explanation of mathematical principles behind the puzzles. 135 illustrations. viii + 248pp.
20198-8 Paperbound $1.25

PAPER FOLDING FOR BEGINNERS, William D. Murray and Francis J. Rigney. Easiest book on the market, clearest instructions on making interesting, beautiful origami. Sail boats, cups, roosters, frogs that move legs, bonbon boxes, standing birds, etc. 40 projects; more than 275 diagrams and photographs. 94pp.
20713-7 Paperbound $1.00

TRICKS AND GAMES ON THE POOL TABLE, Fred Herrmann. 79 tricks and games— some solitaires, some for two or more players, some competitive games—to entertain you between formal games. Mystifying shots and throws, unusual caroms, tricks involving such props as cork, coins, a hat, etc. Formerly *Fun on the Pool Table*. 77 figures. 95pp.
21814-7 Paperbound $1.00

HAND SHADOWS TO BE THROWN UPON THE WALL: A SERIES OF NOVEL AND AMUSING FIGURES FORMED BY THE HAND, Henry Bursill. Delightful picturebook from great-grandfather's day shows how to make 18 different hand shadows: a bird that flies, duck that quacks, dog that wags his tail, camel, goose, deer, boy, turtle, etc. Only book of its sort. vi + 33pp. 6½ x 9¼. 21779-5 Paperbound $1.00

WHITTLING AND WOODCARVING, E. J. Tangerman. 18th printing of best book on market. "If you can cut a potato you can carve" toys and puzzles, chains, chessmen, caricatures, masks, frames, woodcut blocks, surface patterns, much more. Information on tools, woods, techniques. Also goes into serious wood sculpture from Middle Ages to present, East and West. 464 photos, figures. x + 293pp.
20965-2 Paperbound $2.00

HISTORY OF PHILOSOPHY, Julián Marias. Possibly the clearest, most easily followed, best planned, most useful one-volume history of philosophy on the market; neither skimpy nor overfull. Full details on system of every major philosopher and dozens of less important thinkers from pre-Socratics up to Existentialism and later. Strong on many European figures usually omitted. Has gone through dozens of editions in Europe. 1966 edition, translated by Stanley Appelbaum and Clarence Strowbridge. xviii + 505pp.
21739-6 Paperbound $2.75

YOGA: A SCIENTIFIC EVALUATION, Kovoor T. Behanan. Scientific but non-technical study of physiological results of yoga exercises; done under auspices of Yale U. Relations to Indian thought, to psychoanalysis, etc. 16 photos. xxiii + 270pp.
20505-3 Paperbound $2.50

Prices subject to change without notice.
Available at your book dealer or write for free catalogue to Dept. GI, Dover Publications, Inc., 180 Varick St., N. Y., N. Y. 10014. Dover publishes more than 150 books each year on science, elementary and advanced mathematics, biology, music, art, literary history, social sciences and other areas.